AMBER WAVES

a cookbook

Theme and Cover Design
by
Phyllis Nyberg Chapin

The Junior League of Omaha
Omaha, Nebraska
1983

The purpose of the Junior League is exclusively educational and charitable and is to promote voluntarism; to develop the potential of its members for voluntary participation in community affairs; and to demonstrate the effectiveness of trained volunteers.

Proceeds realized from the sale of **Amber Waves** will be returned to the community through the projects of the Junior League of Omaha.

Additional copies may be obtained by addressing:

AMBER WAVES

Junior League of Omaha, Inc.
7400 Court Building, Suite 102
808 South 74th Plaza
Omaha, Nebraska 68114

For your convenience, order blanks are included in the
back of the book.

First Printing: 10,000 copies   March, 1983

Printed by

Omaha Printing Company
Omaha, Nebraska

International Standard Book Number: 0-96091-16-0-9

All recipes have been tested and represent favorite recipes of Junior League members, their relatives and friends. Brand names of ingredients have been used only when necessary.

Waving, golden grain is a symbol of harvest and hospitality in the heartland of America. This is an easy, open hospitality. A friendly welcome, that's a part of the cooking and dining customs in homes throughout Nebraska.

Amber Waves began with more than 2,500 recipes submitted to the Junior League of Omaha Cookbook Committee. After 18 months of cooking and testing, only the most outstanding recipes were selected.

The 660 recipes in **Amber Waves** represent the finest of both new and old customs. Traditional favorites handed down from our pioneer heritage, and brand new delights created by today's Nebraskans.

As you sample the recipes in **Amber Waves,** you'll find that they bring the same warmth to your home. A practical and delicious adventure in cooking from the heart of America.

COOKBOOK I COMMITTEE
Development and Production

CHAIRMAN
Julie Jacobsen

ASSISTANT CHAIRMAN
Nancy Hornstein

EDITOR
Pam Scott

ARTIST
Phyllis Chapin

PUBLIC RELATIONS
Kathy Allen

TESTING COORDINATORS

Sunny Lundgren

Marjorie Jones

Cheryl Anderson

TESTERS

Jan Buresh	Anne Kelly	Mary Patterson
Chris Chilian	Susie Knox	Judy Sartin
Jan Connor	Lynda Madden	Linda Shearer
Janet Darst	Judy Manuel	Julie Sherrets
Carol Dvorak	Patti McClellen	Denise Stalnaker
Jodeen Fletcher	Ruth Muchemore	Janie Stratton
Linda Grubb	Kay Owen	Patti Wiederholt
Sheryn Joffe	Ann Pape	

TYPISTS	INDEXER	PROOFREADERS
Janice Bock	Sarah Watson	Judy Duffy
Linda Ewasiuk		Jane Funk
Nancy Ford		

COOKBOOK II
Promotion and Marketing

CHAIRMAN
Vicki Walker

ASSISTANT CHAIRMAN
Mary Wurdeman

COVER DESIGN AND THEME
Phyllis Chapin

ILLUSTRATIONS, NEBRASKA HERITAGE SECTION
Sue Olson-Mandler

TABLE OF CONTENTS

The Nebraska Heritage Collection

Illustrations by Sue Olson-Mandler

JOSLYN EXHIBITION GALA

Pitcher Champagne Punch	Rhubarb-Citrus Cooler
Marinated Broccoli with Curry Dip	
Sour Cream Dip for Fruit	
Ribbon Paté	Caviar Pie Romanoff
Greek Turnovers	Oriental Fillet of Beef
Chocolate Truffles	

Joslyn Art Museum opened in Omaha in 1931. It was a gift to the city from Mrs. Sarah A. Joslyn in memory of her late husband. The galleries hold a fine collection of art from all periods, including a large collection of Western Art. Opening night parties for major exhibitions are usually held in the Fountain Court with it's graceful "Sunburst" sculpture by Henry Bertoia.

PITCHER CHAMPAGNE PUNCH · 8 servings

1   **6-ounce can frozen concentrated lemonade**
2½ **cups water**
½   **cup orange flavored liqueur (Triple Sec)**
⅘   **quart champagne, chilled**
    Fresh whole strawberries
    Pineapple chunks

Mix ½ of the frozen lemonade concentrate with 1½ cups water. Pour into ice cube trays and freeze. This may be done the day before. In a serving pitcher, combine the rest of the lemonade, orange flavored liqueur, 1 cup water, lemonade ice cubes and the chilled bottle of champagne. Stir gently and serve. Thread a toothpick with a fresh pineapple chunk and a whole fresh strawberry and place one in each glass after filling.

RHUBARB-CITRUS COOLER   12 servings

1   **pound fresh rhubarb, cut up (approximately 4 cups)**
¾   **cup sugar**
4   **cups water**
⅔   **cup orange juice**
3   **tablespoons lemon juice**
2   **16-ounce bottles chilled ginger ale**

In a large saucepan, cook rhubarb, sugar and water until fruit is very soft, about 15 minutes. Press juice through sieve or food mill. Add orange and lemon juice to rhubarb syrup. Cover and chill. To serve, pour ½ cup rhubarb liquid over ice cubes in tall glass. Fill glasses with ginger ale. Stir gently and serve. NOTE: Can be "spiked" with 1 jigger vodka per serving.

MARINATED BROCCOLI WITH CURRY DIP

1   **bunch fresh broccoli**
⅓   **cup vinegar**
½   **cup light salad oil**
1   **tablespoon dried dill weed**
½   **cup sugar**
    Salt
    Crushed pepper
1   **cup mayonnaise**
1   **tablespoon curry**
1   **tablespoon catsup**

Wash broccoli, remove most of stem and cut into pieces. Mix together vinegar, oil, dill, sugar, salt and pepper. Pour over broccoli and toss to coat. Marinate at least 6 hours, stirring once or twice. Drain and arrange on a platter. Mix mayonnaise, curry and catsup. Serve in bowl as a dip for the broccoli.

SOUR CREAM FRUIT DIP

⅛ **teaspoon cinnamon**
⅛ **teaspoon mace**
⅛ **teaspoon ground clove**
   Dash salt
2 **tablespoons sugar**
1 **cup sour cream**
½ **teaspoon vanilla**
⅛ **teaspoon rum extract**
   Pineapple shell, fruit removed

Combine sour cream with spices and flavorings. Chill two hours. Serve in hollowed out pineapple. Any combination of fresh fruit can be served with this dip.

ORIENTAL FILLET OF BEEF

1 **3 to 4 pound fillet of**
   beef, trimmed
½ **cup olive oil**
½ **cup soy sauce**
½ **cup Madeira or sherry**
1 **tablespoon grated fresh**
   ginger
1 **teaspoon ground ginger**
1 **tablespoon grated**
   orange rind
1 **teaspoon coarsely**
   ground pepper

Combine all ingredients, except beef, to make marinade. Roll fillet in marinade and turn frequently for 8 to 12 hours. Remove meat from marinade and dry with paper towels. Place in shallow roasting pan. Roast meat in a preheated 500 degree oven for 10 minutes. Remove meat from oven and brush with marinade. Reduce heat to 400 degrees and roast for 10 more minutes. Remove from oven, brush with marinade; reduce oven to 350 degrees and roast 10 more minutes. Insert meat thermometer. When internal temperature reaches 130 degrees (medium rare) or desired degree of doneness; remove from oven to a carving board and let rest for 10 minutes before carving. Serve thinly sliced with cocktail buns or party rye bread as an appetizer.

RIBBON PATÉ

ASPIC

1	envelope unflavored gelatin
2	beef bouillon cubes
1	cup water
1	tablespoon lemon juice
3	ripe olives, pitted and sliced

Combine gelatin, bouillon cubes and water in small saucepan. Heat, stirring constantly, just until gelatin dissolves. Measure ¼ cup of mixture into a 6-cup mold. Stir lemon juice into remaining aspic. It will be used in ham and liver mixtures.

CHEESE LAYER

2	8-ounce packages cream cheese, softened
½	cup sour cream
1	teaspoon grated onion
1	4½-ounce can cocktail shrimp, drained
1	tablespoon finely chopped green pepper
5	ripe olives, finely chopped

In medium-size bowl, cream the cream cheese. Add other ingredients, blending until smooth.

HAM LAYER

2	4½-ounce cans deviled ham
¼	cup prepared sweet mustard relish

In small bowl, blend deviled ham and mustard with ¼ cup aspic.

LIVER LAYER

1	9-ounce can liver paté
¼	cup salad dressing
2	tablespoons chopped parsley
1	teaspoon grated onion

Blend liver pate, salad dressing, parsley and onion into remaining ¼ cup aspic.

Keep 3 mixtures at room temperature while molding. Set mold with aspic in a pan of ice water to speed setting. When aspic layer is just beginning to be sticky-firm, arrange a ring of olive slices on top. Let set until firm. Spoon half of the cheese mixture on top; let set until firm. Cover with all of ham mixture, remaining cheese mixture, and all of the liver mixture. Wait each time until layer on top is sticky-firm. Chill several hours, or until firm. Unmold. and serve with a combination of crackers.

GREEK TURNOVERS

5 dozen

1 pound Greek Phyllo dough, thawed
1 cup unsalted butter, melted

Lay out 1 pastry sheet on board; keep the remainder covered with a damp cloth. Working quickly so the dough will not dry out, brush the sheet with melted butter and cut into long strips 4-inches wide. Fold strips in ½, lengthwise, so that width is now 2-inches. Place 1 teaspoon of cheese or spinach mixture on the narrow strip and fold corner of strip over spinach. Continue folding triangular shape up the length of the strip as if folding a flag. Finished pastry will be a triangular shape with the filling completely enclosed. Repeat with remaining strips. Place all triangles on a greased baking sheet and brush tops with melted butter. Bake at 350 degrees for about 45 minutes or until golden. Serve warm. Turnovers freeze beautifully.

CHEESE FILLING:
½ pound Feta cheese
⅛ cup grated Parmesan cheese
1 egg
  Dash of oregano
  Pepper
1 teaspoon olive oil

Crumble the Feta cheese and combine with the Parmesan cheese, egg, oregano, pepper to taste and oil. Mix well.

SPINACH FILLING:
1 10-ounce package frozen spinach, chopped
1 small onion, chopped
4 tablespoons butter, melted
½ pound Feta cheese, crumbled
2 eggs, beaten
½ cup milk
¼ teaspoon pepper
¼ cup bread crumbs

Sauté onion in 2 tablespoons butter until transparent. Add thawed, drained spinach and simmer a few minutes. Combine crumbled cheese, eggs, milk and pepper; add to spinach. Mix well and stir in bread crumbs and 2 tablespoons melted butter.

CAVIAR PIE ROMANOFF

6 hard-boiled eggs, chopped
3 tablespoons mayonnaise
1 cup chopped white onion
1 8-ounce package cream
   cheese, softened
⅔ cup sour cream
1 4-ounce jar caviar
   Party rye slices

Combine eggs and mayonnaise. Spread on bottom of well greased 8-inch springform pan. Sprinkle onions on top of mixture. Blend cream cheese and sour cream until smooth. Using a wet spatula, spread over onions. Cover and chill overnight. Top with caviar. Run knife around edges and remove pan sides to serve. Garnish with parsley and lemon wedges. Serve with party rye bread.

CHOCOLATE TRUFFLES

60 pieces

¼ cup cocoa
1 teaspoon cinnamon
1½ pounds semisweet chocolate,
   melted
¼ cup heavy cream
¼ cup half-and-half
2 tablespoons rum
1 teaspoon rum flavoring

Mix cocoa and cinnamon together and set aside. Mix remaining ingredients until well blended. Beat until fluffy. Chill until firm, about 30 minutes. Shape into balls and roll in cocoa mixture. Chill until ready to serve.

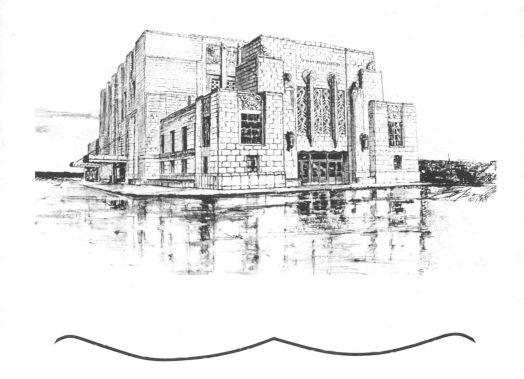

LUNCH AT UNION STATION

Tomato-Pineapple Stacks

Swiss Toast   **Gabby Crabby**

Fruit Slush

Frozen Chocolate Pie   **Pumpkin-Cream Cheese Roll**

The growth of Nebraska as a state can be linked to the construction of the Union Pacific Railroad west to California. Union Station was built in 1931 as the passenger terminal for the U.P. The Art Deco building is on The National Register of Historic Places and now houses the Western Heritage Museum.

TOMATO PINEAPPLE STACKS

4 servings

2	3-ounce packages cream cheese, softened
1	tablespoon chopped onion
½	cucumber, peeled, chopped and squeezed dry
	Dash white pepper
8	½-inch thick tomato slices
4	slices canned pineapple
½	cup French dressing

Combine cream cheese, onion, cucumber and white pepper. To assemble individual servings, spread half the cream cheese mixture on 4 tomato slices. Place a pineapple slice on each. Spread remaining cream cheese mixture on pineapple and top with remaining tomato slices. Pour some French dressing on each salad. NOTE: Cream cheese mixture can be made ahead. Do not assemble too far in advance.

SWISS TOAST

12 servings

2	pounds mushrooms, sliced
½	cup chopped onion
1	cup butter
½	cup dry white wine
¾	cup flour
2	cups half-and-half
1	teaspoon lemon juice
	Pepper
12	slices French bread, buttered
12	slices ham, cut in ½
12	slices Swiss cheese
	Paprika

Cook onions in ½ cup of butter until tender. Add mushrooms and white wine. Cook covered for 10 minutes. Remove mushrooms from pan and reduce juices; blend in ½ cup butter and flour. Slowly add cream, stirring constantly until thickened. Stir in mushrooms and lemon juice and season with pepper. This can be made a day ahead and refrigerated. Toast buttered bread in oven on jelly roll pan. Assemble 12 sandwiches by layering as follows: toast, ham, mushroom mixture, ham, cheese. Sprinkle with paprika and bake for 7 minutes in 375 degree oven or until cheese melts.

GABBY CRABBY

12 servings

1¼ pounds King crabmeat, cut
    into large pieces
1¼ cups mayonnaise
3 green onions, chopped
½ head iceberg lettuce, chopped
1 tablespoon seasoning salt
½ tablespoon fresh lemon juice
12 tomato slices
6 English muffins, split, toasted
    and buttered
12 slices Mozzarella cheese

Mix together crab, mayonnaise, onion, lettuce, salt and lemon juice. Place tomato slice on each toasted muffin half. Arange crab salad on top of tomato, dividing equally among sandwiches. Top each with a slice of Mozzarella. Transfer to baking sheet and bake 15 to 20 minutes at 350 degrees or until cheese is lightly browned.

FRUIT SLUSH

12 servings

1 6-ounce can frozen concen-
    trated orange juice
1 6-ounce can frozen concen-
    trated pink lemonade
1 large can crushed pineapple
    including juice
3 large bananas, sliced and
    cubed
2 10-ounce packages frozen
    raspberries
1 cup sugar
14 ounces 7 UP

Thaw juices. Combine all ingredients. Stir until sugar is dissolved. Spoon into plastic glasses or foil cupcake cups, cover and freeze. Thaw 45 to 60 minutes before serving. Should be cold and slushy.

FROZEN CHOCOLATE PIE

9-inch pie

1 9-inch baked pie crust, pastry
    or graham cracker
1 cup confectioners' sugar
½ cup butter, softened
1 6-ounce package semisweet
    chocolate chips, melted
1 teaspoon vanilla
4 eggs
1 cup heavy cream, chilled
2 tablespoons confectioners'
    sugar
1 teaspoon vanilla
    Shaved chocolate

In small bowl, blend 1 cup confectioners' sugar with butter until fluffy. Blend in melted chocolate and vanilla. On high speed, beat in eggs, one at a time. Beat thoroughly after each addition. Pour into baked pie shell and cover with plastic wrap. Freeze several hours or until firm. In chilled bowl, beat cream, sugar and vanilla until stiff. Spread on frozen pie and garnish with shaved chocoalate.

PUMPKIN-CREAM CHEESE ROLL   10 servings

3	eggs
1	cup sugar
⅔	cup pumpkin
1	teaspoon baking soda
1	teaspoon ginger
½	teaspoon salt
1	teaspoon lemon juice
¾	cup flour
2	teaspoons cinnamon
1	teaspoon nutmeg
1	teaspoon ground cloves
1	cup chopped walnuts
1	cup confectioners' sugar
1	8-ounce package cream cheese
4	tablespoons butter
½	teaspoon vanilla

Beat eggs on high for 5 minutes. Add sugar, pumpkin, soda, ginger, salt, lemon juice, flour, cinnamon, nutmeg and cloves. Spread into greased and floured jelly roll pan; sprinkle with chopped nuts. Bake at 375 degrees for 15 minutes. Turn cake onto a towel sprinkled with confectioners' sugar. Roll up cake with towel; cool. Beat until smooth; confectioners' sugar, cream cheese, butter and vanilla. Unroll cake and remove towel. Spread cream on unrolled cake; roll back up. Place in refrigerator until set. Slice and serve. Freezes well up to 2 months.

ARBOR DAY CELEBRATION DINNER

Cream of Morel Soup

Crown Roast of Lamb with Wild Rice

Orange Sauced Broccoli

Salad of Fresh Greens with Creamy Vinaigrette

Popovers

Nebraska City Cake   **Marlborough Pie**

Arbor Day, celebrated internationally on April 22, began in Nebraska through the efforts of J. Sterling Morton. A journalist by profession, he had a consuming passion for agriculture, especially tree-planting. The grounds of his home, Arbor Lodge, feature over 200 varieties of trees and shrubs. The 52 room Lodge is open to the public.

CREAM OF MOREL SOUP

6 servings

1   **pound morels (wild mushrooms)**
4   **tablespoons butter**
2   **cups chicken broth**
½   **cup chopped celery**
¼   **cup sliced onion**
⅛   **cup parsley**
2   **tablespoons flour**
1   **cup milk**
4   **whole cloves**
1   **bay leaf**
   Salt and pepper to taste
⅛   **teaspoon paprika**
⅛   **teaspoon nutmeg**
3   **tablespoons white wine or sherry**
   Whipped cream
   Mushroom slices

Soak mushrooms in salt water; pick over and chop. Sauté in 2 tablespoons butter. Add chicken broth, celery, sliced onion and parsley. Cover and simmer for 20 minutes. Drain; reserve stock. Prepare cream sauce. Make a roux of 2 tablespoons butter and 2 tablespoons flour. Cook and stir until bubbly; cool. Slowly add 1 cup milk, 4 cloves and 1 bay leaf. Cook sauce, stirring, until smooth and thickened. Place pan with sauce in a 350 degree oven for 20 minutes. Strain. Add broth to sauce. Season with salt, pepper, paprika, nutmeg and white wine or sherry. Add cooked vegetables. Heat until hot and serve with a dollop of whipped cream and 1 mushroom slice. NOTE: Morels can be found during April in wooded areas. Gourmet stores often have them available in cans.

CROWN ROAST OF LAMB WITH WILD RICE

10 servings

1   **crown roast of lamb, 20 ribs**
1   **cut garlic clove**
   Thyme or oregano
   Salt and pepper
   Empty coffee can, top and bottom removed
   Tin foil lamb chop ruffles
½   **cup dry white wine**
½   **cup water**
½   **stick butter, softened**

Rub lamb with cut garlic clove, sprinkle with thyme or oregano, salt and pepper. Fit empty can into the hollow center. This helps brown the inner part of the roast and keep the shape. Cover bone ends of chops with the foil. Place lamb in a pan just large enough to hold it; roast at 400 degrees for 20 minutes. (During this time the rice can be made.) Reduce heat to 325 degrees and roast, basting several times with pan juices, 40 minutes more. Increase heat to 375 degrees for another 15 to 20 minutes. Transfer roast to platter. Remove tin can. Fill cavity with mounded wild rice. Keep lamb hot. Pour off fat from roasting pan, add ½ cup each dry white wine and water, stir in brown bits clinging to bottom of pan. Reduce liquid by ½ over high heat, season with salt and pepper and remove pan from heat.

Swirl in ½ stick butter, cut in slices. Strain juices, pour around the roast and garnish with parsley.

WILD RICE WITH MUSHROOMS

4	tablespoons butter
2	tablespoons finely chopped carrots and celery
2	tablespoons finely chopped onion
1	cup wild rice
1	teaspoon salt
2	cups chicken stock
½	pound mushrooms, sliced
2	tablespoons chopped parsley
¼	cup chopped pecans

In a 2-quart saucepan, melt 2 tablespoons butter over moderate heat. Add carrots, celery and onions, cook 10 to 15 minutes, or until soft. Stir in rice and salt. Cook 2 to 3 minutes uncovered, stirring to coat rice with butter. In small saucepan, bring stock to a boil and pour over rice. Bring to a boil again, cover tightly, reduce heat to simmer. Cook 30 to 45 minutes until stock is absorbed. Over moderate heat, melt remaining 2 tablespoons butter. Add mushrooms and parsley. Cook and stir 5 minutes, add pecans and cook 2 to 3 minutes. Add to rice. Season to taste.

CREAMY VINAIGRETTE

1	egg
¼	teaspoon Worcestershire
5	drops Tabasco
½	tablespoon Dijon mustard
1	teaspoon salt
¼	teaspoon white pepper
½	cup cider vinegar
2	cups oil
½	tablespoon chopped parsley
1	tablespoon chopped onion
½	teaspoon chopped tarragon (fresh or in wine vinegar)

Combine in blender egg, Worcestershire, Tabasco, mustard, salt, pepper and vinegar. Run at high speed for 30 seconds; switch to low speed. On low, slowly pour in oil. Add parsley, onions and tarragon leaves. Continue to blend for 10 seconds. Refrigerate until needed.

ORANGE SAUCED BROCCOLI

6 servings

1   bunch fresh broccoli
2   tablespoons butter
2   tablespoons flour
½   cup orange juice
½   cup mandarin orange sections
¼   teaspoon dried tarragon
¼   teaspoon salt
½   cup plain yogurt

Wash and trim broccoli. Split into spears. Steam on a rack over a small amount of boiling water for 10 minutes until tender but still crisp. Drain well and arrange on serving dish; keep warm. Melt butter in a heavy saucepan over low heat; add flour and cook 1 minute stirring constantly. Gradually add orange juice. Stir in orange sections, tarragon and salt. Cook until thickened and bubbly. Stir in yogurt. Serve sauce over broccoli spears.

POPOVERS

8 servings

1½   cups flour
½   teaspoon salt
4   eggs
1½   cups milk
1   tablespoon unsalted butter, melted
4   teaspoons unsalted butter

Oil popover tins or custard cups. Preheat oven to 450 degrees and set pans in lower ⅓ of the oven while preparing batter. Combine flour, salt, eggs, and 1 tablespoon butter in food processor or blender and mix until consistency of whipping cream. Batter can be prepared ahead to this point, covered and refrigerated. Remove hot pans from oven and place ½ teaspoon butter in each; return to oven until butter is bubbling. Fill each tin ½ full. Bake 20 minutes in 450 degree oven. Reduce oven temperature to 350 degrees and bake 15 to 20 minutes more. Serve immediately.

NEBRASKA CITY CAKE

CAKE

2	cups sugar
2	eggs
½	cup shortening
2	cups flour
2	teaspoons baking soda
1	teaspoon salt
1	teaspoon nutmeg
2	teaspoons cinnamon
4	cups raw diced apples (6 apples)
1	cup nuts

Cream together sugar and shortening. Add eggs. Mix well. Add flour, soda, salt, cinnamon and nutmeg; mix. Stir in apples and nuts. Mixture will be dry. Pour into 9x13-inch greased pan and bake at 350 degrees for 50 to 60 minutes.

SAUCE

½	cup margarine
2	tablespoons flour
1	cup sugar
½	cup brown sugar
½	cup half-and-half

Over low heat, melt margarine. Add flour and sugars. Stir in cream; cook, stirring constantly, until thickened. Serve warm over cake.

MARLBOROUGH PIE

8 servings

3	cups apples, peeled and grated or chopped fine
1	tablespoon lemon juice
2	eggs, beaten
1	cup heavy cream
¾	cup sugar
3	tablespoons butter, melted
1	9-inch unbaked pie shell

Sprinkle apples with lemon juice. Combine with eggs, heavy cream, sugar and melted butter. Pour into pie shell. Bake at 450 degrees for 15 minutes. Reduce heat to 325 degrees and bake 30 minutes longer. Serve warm.

FAIRVIEW BENEFIT BRUNCH

Aunt Tess' Brunch Drink

Mushrooms Claudius Crêpes   **Salmon Broccoli Crêpes**

Oriental Ginger Fruit

Walnut Graham Torte

Nebraska's William Jennings Bryan, known as the "Great Commoner", was nominated three times for President. A leading spokesman for the Free Silver Movement, he served as Secretary of State from 1913-1915. In 1903, he built Fairview in Lincoln, Nebraska as a midwestern oasis for friends and visitors. His home is now open to the public and maintained by a non-profit organization. The house is on the National Register of Historic Places.

AUNT TESS' BRUNCH DRINK

4 servings

1 6-ounce can frozen concentrated lemonade
1 6-ounce can milk
1 6-ounce can vodka or gin
  Dash orange flower water
  Ice

Combine all ingredients in blender. Blend until ice is crushed.

BASIC CRÊPES

12 crepes

3 eggs, beaten
1¾ cups milk
1¼ cups flour
¼ cup butter, melted
½ teaspoon salt

Add milk, flour, butter and salt to beaten eggs. Prepare in crêpe pan or 10-inch skillet, pouring in just enough batter to lightly coat. Turn over quickly when lightly browned. Use immediately or stack between waxed paper and freeze.

MUSHROOMS CLAUDIUS

3 cups

1 cup chicken stock, heated
1½ tablespoons flour
¼ pound ham, julienned
3 tablespoons butter
1 shallot, minced
2 ounces dry sherry
  Juice of ½ lemon
¼ pound mushrooms, sliced
½ ounce brandy
  Salt and pepper
  Hollandaise Sauce
  Chopped chives

Melt 1 tablespoon butter in saucepan. Add flour; stir and cook for 2 minutes. Whisk in hot stock gradually, stirring until smooth and thickened; set aside. In large skillet, sauté ham in 2 tablespoons butter with shallot. Add wine and lemon juice and simmer for 5 minutes. Stir in mushrooms and cream sauce; simmer 15 minutes. Add brandy. Correct seasoning with salt and pepper. Fill and roll crêpes; top with hollandaise and garnish with chopped chives.

SALMON BROCCOLI CRÊPES

6 servings

SAUCE
4 tablespoons butter
¼ cup chopped onion
¼ cup flour
¼ teaspoon salt
2¼ cups milk
8 ounces mild Cheddar cheese,
   shredded

Melt butter, add onion and cook until soft. Stir in flour and salt. Slowly add milk; cook, stirring until thick and bubbly. Add cheese and stir until melted.

FILLING
1 10-ounce package frozen
   chopped broccoli
1 8-ounce can salmon, drained,
   boned and flaked
12 crêpes

Cook broccoli as package directs. Drain and dice. Fold in salmon and ¾ cup sauce. Spoon 3 tablespoons filling on each crêpe. Roll and place, seam side down, in baking pan. Cover with remaining sauce. Cover pan and bake at 375 degrees for 20 to 25 minutes.

ORIENTAL GINGER FRUIT

8 servings

1 cup blueberries
1 cup green seedless grapes
1 cup cantaloupe balls
1 cup watermelon balls
1 cup honeydew balls
2 bananas
1 jar Spice Island crystallized
   ginger, diced into small
   pieces

Wash and drain blueberries, grapes and melon balls. Put them into separate containers to chill in the refrigerator before using. When ready to eat, slice banana into a bowl and add refrigerated fruit. Serve immediately in individual salad bowls sprinkled with the diced crystallized ginger. NOTE: This can also be served as a dessert with an oriental meal. Serve in a watermelon shell.

WALNUT GRAHAM TORTE

TORTES

5   eggs, separated
1½ cups sugar
1½ cups graham cracker crumbs
1   teaspoon baking powder
½   teaspoon salt
⅔   cup walnuts
1   teaspoon vanilla

Beat egg yolks well. Add sugar, cracker crumbs, baking powder, salt, walnuts and vanilla. Beat egg whites until stiff. Fold into cracker mixture. Pour into 3 greased 8 or 9-inch round cake pans. Bake at 350 degrees for 35 minutes.

FILLING

1   cup milk
1   cup sugar
1   egg
1   tablespoon cornstarch, stirred
    in a little water
½   teaspoon vanilla
    Heavy cream, whipped and
      sweetened with
      confectioners' sugar
    Finely crushed walnuts

In a double boiler over hot water, boil together milk, sugar, egg, cornstarch and vanilla. Cook, stirring, until thick. Cool. Stack torte layers; filling between each layer with custard. Frost with whipped sweetened heavy cream. Dust top with finely crushed walnuts.

BAND CONCERT PICNIC

Sangria Blanca

Zucchini Bisque

Cold Lemon Chicken

Vegetable Bouquet

Herb Bread Sticks

Almond Sandwich Cookies

The town square with a bandstand is a familiar sight in many small towns throughout Nebraska. In Broken Bow, the bandstand is still the focal point for townspeople, farmers, and ranchers to gather around for summertime entertainment.

ZUCCHINI BISQUE

6 servings

4 tablespoons butter
1 cup unpeeled, thinly sliced
  potatoes
1 cup chopped green onions
3 cups chicken broth
1 teaspoon salt
  Pepper
2 medium zucchini, unpeeled
  and sliced
1 cup sour cream or yogurt

In large saucepan, melt butter. Sauté potatoes and onions for five minutes. Stir in chicken broth, salt, dash of pepper and zucchini. Heat to boiling; reduce heat and simmer for 15 minutes. Remove from heat; cool. Stir in sour cream or yogurt. Blend mixture, half at a time, in blender until smooth. May be served chilled or warm.

SANGRIA BLANCA

5 cups

1 fifth bottle dry white wine,
  chilled (3½ cups)
½ cup Cointreau or Triple Sec
¼ cup sugar
1 orange, thinly sliced
1 lemon, sliced
2 limes, sliced
4 fresh pineapple sticks
  (optional)
1 unpeeled green apple, sliced
1 small bunch green grapes
  Ice cubes
10 ounces club soda, chilled

Combine wine, Cointreau and sugar until well blended. Add fruit; marinate for 1 hour or more in the refrigerator. When ready to serve, stir in ice cubes and add club soda. Garnish clear pitcher and glasses with fruit.

COLD LEMON CHICKEN

6 servings

4 tablespoons butter
6 whole chicken breasts,
  skinned, split and boned
½ cup dry white vermouth
¾ cup fresh lemon juice
½ teaspoon salt
¼ teaspoon white pepper
1½ cups mayonnaise
  Pitted black olives, sliced
  Fresh parsley, chopped

Melt butter in skillet and sauté chicken. Remove to heavy casserole. Add vermouth to skillet and reduce over medium heat to approximately ⅓ cup. Remove from heat. Add ⅓ cup lemon juice, salt and pepper. Pour over chicken in casserole. Bake covered at 350 degrees for 30 minutes. Remove chicken to platter. Cook sauce to reduce by ½. Pour over the chicken. Cool to room temperature. Cover tightly and refrigerate overnight. To serve, slowly add remaining lemon juice to mayonnaise. Pour over chicken and garnish with slices of black olives and chopped fresh parsley. Serve cool or at room temperature.

VEGETABLE BOUQUET

6-8 servings

1   15-ounce can cut green
     beans, drained
1   15-ounce can red kidney
     beans
1   7-ounce can pitted whole ripe
     olives
1   15-ounce can artichoke
     hearts
1½ cups celery, diagonally sliced
1   medium onion, sliced
¼   cup tarragon vinegar
1½ teaspoons MSG (monosodium
     glutamate)
1   8-ounce can whole
     mushrooms
1   4-ounce jar pimiento, sliced
1¼ teaspoons salt
1   tablespoon fine herbs
1   teaspoon sugar
¼   teaspoon Tabasco
½   cup salad oil
2   tablespoons capers
¼   cup chopped parsley

Combine all ingredients except capers and parsley. Marinate overnight. Sprinkle with capers and parsley before serving.

HERB BREADSTICKS

24 breadsticks

1   package active dry yeast
1¼ cups warm water (105-115
     degrees)
3   tablespoons sugar
1½ teaspoons salt
1   tablespoon butter
3   teaspoons caraway seeds
1   teaspoon ground sage
3½ cups flour, sifted

Sprinkle dry yeast over water in large mixing bowl. Let stand for a few minutes; stir until dissolved. Add sugar, salt, butter, 2 teaspoons caraway seeds, sage and flour. Mix well. Turn out on lightly floured board and knead until smooth and elastic, about 10 minutes. Put dough in a greased bowl, turn once, cover and let rise until double. Punch down; turn out onto floured board and divide in ½. Roll each ½ of dough into a 12x8-inch rectangle. Cut into 12 pieces. Roll each piece to form a rope ½-inch thick and 12-inches long. Put on greased cookie sheets and sprinkle with remainder of caraway seeds. Cover and let rise until double in bulk. Bake at 400 degrees for 15 to 20 minutes.

ALMOND SANDWICH COOKIES

¾ cup almonds, blanched
1¼ cups flour
½ cup butter, softened
⅓ cup sugar
¼ teaspoon salt
Apricot preserves
½ cup semisweet chocolate
  chips
1 tablespoon butter
1 tablespoon milk
1½ teaspoons light corn syrup

Finely grind almonds in blender or food processor. In a large bowl mix together flour, butter, sugar, salt and ground almonds. Knead until well blended, dough will be dry. Dough may be made in advance. Between two long sheets of waxed paper, roll ½ of the dough to ⅛-inch thick. Cut into 1½ inch rounds with a cookie cutter and bake on a greased baking sheet at 350 degrees for 8 minutes. Remove to cake rack and cool. In a double boiler, over hot water, melt chocolate chips and butter. Remove from heat; add milk and corn syrup. Blend well. Spread ½ teaspoon of the preserves on half of the cookies and top with another cookie. Spread each with the chocolate glaze.

FORT ROBINSON RECEPTION

Summertime Spiced Coffee   **Mint Tea**

Spiced Peanuts

Chutney-Ham and Cucumber-Shrimp Tea Sandwiches

Florentines   **Sugar Plums**

Criss Cross Bars

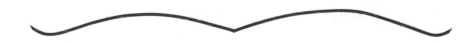

Fort Robinson was begun in 1874 as a military encampment to guard the Red Cloud Indian Agency. It played a leading role in the tragic drama of the Cheyenne and Sioux nations. Later, the fort served as an army remount depot, the training site for the 1935 U.S. Army Equestrian Team, a training center for World War II K-9 Corps dogs and as a German Prisoner of War camp. The restored fort is now a state park, open to visitors who wish to sample the life of a frontier fort and tour the unique Pine Ridge country of northwestern Nebraska.

SUMMERTIME SPICED COFFEE

4 servings

4 **cups strong coffee**
¼ **cup sugar**
10 **whole allspice**
10 **whole cloves**
4 **small cinnamon sticks**
½ **cup coffee flavored liqueur**
Ice cubes

Mix hot coffee, sugar and spices in large mixing bowl. Stir to blend coffee and sugar, then cover with plastic wrap and let stand at room temperature for one hour. Strain coffee into a 1-quart pitcher, add 6 to 8 ice cubes and liqueur. If preparing ahead, strain coffee mix into pitcher and add liqueur. Store covered in refrigerator. Before serving, add ice and stir. NOTE: Serve in a wine glass over ice cream for a good summer dessert.

MINT TEA

1 gallon

2 **cups water**
3 **regular-size tea bags**
10 **sprigs mint**
1¾ **cups sugar**
4 **lemons, juiced**
1 **orange, juiced**

Bring water to a boil. Add tea bags and boil 1 minute. Add mint and boil 2 minutes. Remove from heat and stir in sugar until dissolved. Add lemon juice and orange juice. Strain tea and pour into a 1-gallon container. Fill jar with cold water. Chill. NOTE: The mint tea syrup can be divided in half and poured into two 2-quart containers then filled with water. Syrup can also be stored in refrigerator without the water until needed.

CUCUMBER SHRIMP TEA SANDWICHES

1 **medium cucumber, peeled**
 and chopped
2 **tablespoons diced onion**
1 **4½-ounce can of shrimp,**
 drained
1 **8-ounce package cream**
 cheese, softened
1 **tablespoon sour cream**
 Rye bread rounds

Mix all ingredients together. Chill before serving. Serve on rye bread rounds. Garnish with fresh fruit, if desired.

CHUTNEY HAM SPREAD

1½ cups

1 4½-ounce can deviled ham
1 cup sour cream
⅓ cup finely chopped chutney
Parsley

Combine ingredients thoroughly. Freeze in sealed container if using later. Serve on bread rounds or crackers. Garnish with small piece of parsley.

SPICED PEANUTS

2 cups

1 egg white
1 teaspoon water
1½ cups salted peanuts
½ cup sugar
1 teaspoon cinnamon
½ teaspoon nutmeg
¼ teaspoon ginger

Beat egg white and water until frothy; add nuts. Stir to coat well. Blend sugar and spices. Add to nuts and mix well. Spread nuts on oiled shallow pan. Bake at 250 degrees for 1 hour, turning nuts every 15 minutes. Cool completely. Store in covered container.

FLORENTINES

3 dozen

1 cup mixed candied fruits
and peels
¼ cup white raisins, finely
chopped
⅓ cup almonds, finely chopped
¼ cup sugar
¼ cup butter
1 tablespoon light corn syrup
1 teaspoon lemon juice
½ cup flour
1 6-ounce package semisweet
chocolate chips

Chop mixed fruits and combine with raisins and almonds. Melt butter, sugar, corn syrup and lemon juice in saucepan. Toss fruit in flour and stir into butter mixture. Pinch off a walnut-sized piece and roll into a ball. Flatten until thin on cookie sheet using wet fingers or bottom of a wet glass. Bake at 350 degrees for 12 minutes or until edges are lacey. Let stand a few minutes; remove to cake rack to cool. Melt chocolate and frost undersides of cooled cookies. Store in a cool place for 2 weeks or freeze.

CRISS CROSS BARS

40 bars

3 cups flour
1 cup margarine, softened
1 cup sugar
2 egg yolks
2 tablespoons Marsala or
   dry sherry
   Grated rind of 1 lemon or
   orange
1 10-ounce jar apricot or
   strawberry preserves
   Confectioners' sugar

Mix together flour, margarine, sugar, yolks, wine and rind to make a soft dough. Wrap and chill for one hour. Spread ⅔ of dough in 9x11-inch pan or round pizza pan. Spread dough with preserves. Roll remaining dough and cut into strips. Place in criss cross design on top of preserves. Bake at 350 degrees for 20 to 25 minutes. When cool, sprinkle with confectioners' sugar and cut into pieces.

SUGAR PLUMS

36 pieces

½ cup dried apricots
½ cup chopped pecans
¼ cup plus 1 tablespoon grated
   sweet coconut
¼ cup golden raisins
¼ cup dried apples
2 tablespoons Kirsh (apricot
   brandy may be substituted)
3 tablespoons sugar

Chop finely in food processor: apricots, pecans, coconut, raisins and apples. Add Kirsh while motor is running and blend 5 seconds. Form into ¾-inch balls, pressing firmly into shape. Roll in sugar to coat evenly. Keep in airtight container for up to two weeks at room temperature. May be frozen for several months.

OREGON TRAIL COOKOUT

Beef Ragout

Picnic Asparagus   **Country-Fried Biscuits**

Strawberry Patch Jam   **Dutch Honey**

Chocolate Peanut Swirl Ice Cream

Fudge Sauce

Scotts Bluff National Monument is located in northwestern Nebraska. It took 90 to 120 days to travel by oxen from Independence, Mo. to Oregon or California. To the 150,000 men, women and children traveling the Oregon Trail, Scotts Bluff and nearby Chimney Rock were landmarks that stood out for miles across the plains. The ruts left by the passing of their heavily loaded wagons are still evident along the trail.

BEEF RAGOUT

6 servings

2 pounds stewing beef, or
   round steak cut in
   bite-sized pieces
3 tablespoons butter, melted
12 small white onions, peeled
6 carrots, peeled and cut
1 pound mushrooms, sliced
1 clove garlic, crushed
1 6-ounce can tomato paste
¼ cup fresh parsley, cut
2 tablespoons flour
   Salt and pepper to taste
1 bay leaf, crushed
   Dash each of rosemary,
      basil, oregano
2 cups red wine
   Sour cream for garnish

In a skillet, brown meat in butter. Remove to baking dish or Dutch oven. Brown onions, carrots and mushrooms in same skillet. Add garlic, tomato paste, parsley and flour, blending until smooth. Add all seasonings. Combine with meat. Add wine to within 1 inch of top of meat mixture. Cover and bake 1½ to 2 hours in 350 degree oven. Add dollop of sour cream for garnish when serving.

PICNIC ASPARAGUS

8 servings

2 pounds fresh asparagus
1 medium onion, finely chopped
1 tomato, chopped
1 cup mayonnaise
   Salt

Cut asparagus stalks into 1-inch pieces and cook in boiling salted water 5 to 7 minutes. Add tips, cover and cook 5 to 8 minutes longer. Drain and cool. In a large bowl, toss asparagus with finely chopped onion and tomato. Stir in mayonnaise. Add salt to taste. Chill well.

COUNTRY FRIED BISCUITS

2 dozen

2 cups creamed cottage
   cheese
2 teaspoons salt
¼ cup sugar
½ teaspoon baking soda
2 eggs, slightly beaten
½ cup warm water
2 packages dry yeast
2 tablespoons caraway
   seed
4⅔ cups flour

Heat cottage cheese in a saucepan until bubbly. Stir in salt, sugar, baking soda and eggs. Remove from heat. Dissolve yeast in warm water. Add caraway seeds and flour. Combine flour and cheese mixtures. Knead 5 minutes. Put into greased bowl and cover. Let rise until doubled in bulk. Grease hands and pinch off dough to make walnut-sized balls. Set aside to rise 1 hour. Deep-fat fry in 375 degree oil until golden brown. Serve piping hot with butter and jam or apple butter. NOTE: Can also serve as cocktail buns with slices of beef or ham and seasoned mustard.

DUTCH HONEY

2 cups

1 cup sugar
1 cup light corn syrup
1 cup heavy cream,
   whipped

Mix all ingredients and bring to a boil. Boil exactly 3 minutes. Turn into bowl and serve hot with waffles, pancakes or rolls.

STRAWBERRY PATCH JAM

8 pints

12 cups strawberries,
   hulled
3 tablespoons minced
   fresh orange peel
3 tablespoons minced
   fresh lime peel
½ cup fresh lime juice
12½ cups sugar

Mash strawberries to desired consistency to yield 9 cups. In a large heavy pot, combine strawberries, orange and lime peel and lime juice. Cook over high heat to boiling point. Add sugar and boil until jam reaches proper consistency or 221 degrees on a candy thermometer. Remove from heat; skim off foam. Pour into sterilized jars and seal.

CHOCOLATE-PEANUT SWIRL ICE CREAM   3 quarts

2   cups sugar
¼   cup flour
¼   teaspoon salt
1   quart milk
4   eggs, beaten
1   tablespoon vanilla extract
1   quart heavy cream
1½   cups dry-roasted peanuts
1   cup chocolate fudge sauce

In saucepan, combine sugar, flour and salt. Gradually add milk. Cook over medium heat, stirring constantly, until thickened, about 20 minutes. Blend small amount of hot mixture into eggs before adding to pan. Cook 1 minute without boiling. Transfer to large bowl and chill. Blend in vanilla and cream. Churn and freeze in ice cream maker. After churning, add 1½ cups peanuts and layer in container with chocolate sauce. Put 1 layer ice cream and peanut mixture in bottom of container. Drizzle chocolate sauce over top and swirl with knife for marble effect. Repeat layers ending with sauce. Freeze for 3 to 4 hours. Serve with Hot Fudge Sauce.

HOT FUDGE SAUCE   1 cup

2   1-ounce squares
       unsweetened chocolate
1   tablespoon butter
⅓   cup boiling water
1   cup sugar
2   tablespoons corn syrup
1   teaspoon vanilla

Melt chocolate in top of double boiler over hot water. Add and melt butter; stir to blend well. Add boiling water. Stir while adding sugar and corn syrup. Boil slowly for 5 minutes. Add vanilla.

Appetizers & Beverages

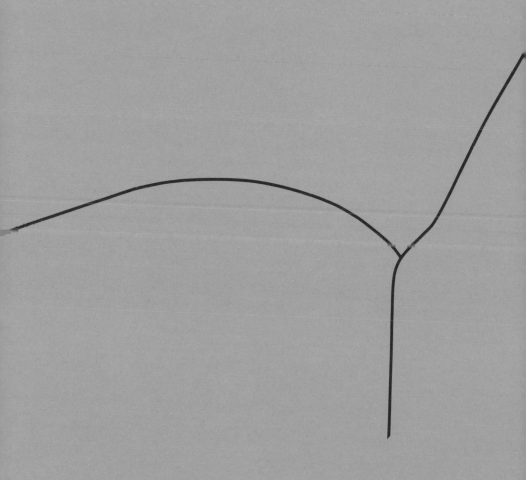

PARTY WEDGES

30 appetizers

½ cup chopped pecans
¼ teaspoon salt
2 tablespoons butter
1 8-ounce package cream
    cheese, softened
2 teaspoons milk
1 tablespoon grated onion
½ teaspoon garlic salt
¼ teaspoon pepper
½ cup sour cream
1 2½-ounce jar dried chipped
    beef
¼ cup finely chopped
    green pepper
10 crêpes

In small skillet, combine pecans with salt and butter. Cook until golden, stirring several times. Set aside. Mix cream cheese with milk; add onion, garlic salt, pepper and sour cream. Chop beef and add to cheese. Add green pepper. Spread 2 to 3 tablespoons mixture on a crêpe, making two stacks of five crêpes each. Reserve a small amount of mixture to spread on top. Sprinkle top with pecans. Refrigerate at least one hour. Cut into wedges.

BEEF TURNOVERS

25 tarts

PASTRY
1 cup crushed onion crackers
1 cup flour
¼ cup Parmesan cheese
6 tablespoons butter
1 3-ounce package cream
    cheese
5 tablespoons cold water
1 egg, beaten

FILLING
½ pound ground beef
½ cup frozen chopped spinach,
    cooked and drained
1 3-ounce can chopped
    mushrooms, drained
½ cup bottled spaghetti sauce
¼ teaspoon basil
¼ teaspoon thyme
¼ teaspoon garlic salt
1 egg, beaten

Combine cracker crumbs, flour and Parmesan cheese. Cut in cream cheese and butter to form fine crumbs. Sprinkle 4 to 5 tablespoons cold water over mixture one at a time and mix with a fork. Form a ball, cover and chill for at least 30 minutes. Dough can be made a day in advance. To make filling, brown ground beef and drain. Add spinach, mushrooms, spaghetti sauce, basil, thyme and garlic salt. Set aside until ready to put into tarts. On floured board, roll chilled dough ⅛ inch thick. Cut 3-inch circles, rerolling scrapes. On ½ of circle put about 1 tablespoon filling. Brush edges with beaten egg and fold over to form tart. Seal edges with tines of fork. Place on greased cookie sheet, brush with beaten egg and bake 18 to 20 minutes at 400 degrees. Tarts can be frozen after baking. Cool, wrap in foil and freeze. To serve, place unwrapped frozen turnovers on baking sheet and bake 15 minutes at 375 degrees.

PETITE QUICHE
24 servings

SHELLS
½ cup butter
1 3-ounce package cream cheese
1 cup flour
¼ teaspoon salt

FILLING
2 eggs
½ cup half-and-half
¼ teaspoon salt
¼ teaspoon pepper
⅛ teaspoon nutmeg
Pinch cayenne
¼ pound Gruyere cheese, grated
3 tablespoons minced onion
¾ teaspoon tarragon

Blend butter, cream cheese, flour and salt; chill for at least 1 hour. Form into balls and push into bottom and sides of 2-inch muffin tins to form shells. Beat together eggs, cream and seasonings. Mix cheese, onion and tarragon in separate bowl. Put cheese-onion mixture in shells and fill ¾ full. Pour egg mixture on top, dividing it between all shells. Bake on cookie sheet at 350 degrees for 30 to 35 minutes, until golden and bubbly. Let sit in pan for 10 minutes before removing from tins with tip of knife. NOTE: These can be made ahead and frozen; reheat for 15 minutes.

HOT CHEESE BREAD SQUARES

1 10-ounce package sharp
  Cheddar cheese, grated
1 stick butter or margarine
1 egg white
  Garlic salt
  Paprika
1 loaf white sandwich bread

Mix together cheese and butter. Beat egg white until stiff and fold into cheese mixture. Add garlic salt and paprika. Mix until light and spreadable. Trim crusts off bread; spread each slice with cheese. Stack into stacks of three slices each. Cut each stack into four equal squares. Frost sides of each little stack with more of the cheese mixture. Put onto cookie sheet, do not touch together. Chill for several hours. Bake about 10 minutes at 400 degrees, or until lightly brown. Serve hot.

WRAPPED CHEESE

1 package refrigerated crescent
  dough
1 Gouda or Bondel cheese
  round

Spread out crescent dough to make 1 large piece with no holes. Wrap the piece of dough around the cheese. Check for holes. Put the cheese in a small baking dish and bake for 45 minutes at 350 degrees.

LITTLE CHEESE GOODIES

36 slices

½ cup mayonnaise
2 cups grated Swiss cheese
¼ cup chopped ripe olives
⅓ cup bacon bits
2 tablespoons chopped chives
1 loaf party rye bread

Mix mayonnaise, cheese, olives, bacon and chives; spread on slices of party rye. Place on cookie sheet. Bake in 400 degree oven until cheese is hot and bubbly, about 10 minutes.

MUSHROOM SWIRLS

1 can refrigerated crescent rolls
1 can chopped mushrooms, drained well
1 3-ounce package cream cheese, softened
Poppy seeds
1 egg white

Form 2 rectangles from perforated pieces of crescent roll dough. Spread with softened cream cheese. Sprinkle mushrooms on top of cheese. Roll into logs and slice. Place on cookie sheet, brush with egg white and sprinkle with poppy seeds. Bake 10 to 13 minutes at 375 degrees

MEATBALLS WITH CRANBERRY WINE SAUCE

1½ pounds ground beef
½ pound ham, shredded
2½ cups soft bread crumbs, well-packed
2 tablespoons minced onion
¾ cup milk
2 eggs, slightly beaten
½ cup dry red table wine
½ cup brown sugar
1 1-pound can whole cranberry sauce
¼ teaspoon ground cloves
1 tablespoon cornstarch

Mix together ground beef, ham, bread crumbs, onion, milk and eggs. Shape into meatballs and place in 400 degree oven on broiler pan so drippings drain off. Bake 30 minutes or until done, turning once during cooking. Mix together wine and brown sugar. Stir in cranberry sauce, cloves and cornstarch. Heat to warm. Place cooked meatballs and warm sauce in a chaffing dish. Keep warm while serving.

SUMMER SAUSAGE

2 rolls

2 pounds lean ground beef
1 cup water
¼ teaspoon onion powder
¼ teaspoon garlic powder
¼ teaspoon dry mustard
½ teaspoon pepper
2 tablespoons liquid smoke
3 tablespoons Morton's Tender Quick Salt

Mix all ingredients and form into 2 rolls, 2-inches thick. Wrap in aluminum foil, shiny side in. Refrigerate 24 hours. After 24 hours, punch holes in foil with fork. Place on rack in covered baking pan with 3 or 4 tablespoons water. Bake at 325 degrees for 90 minutes. Refrigerate until served.

41

SUPER NACHO DIP

1	16-ounce can refried beans
½	pound ground beef
½	pound chorizo sausage
1	onion, chopped
1	3-ounce can chopped green chilies
9	ounces grated Monterey Jack cheese
9	ounces grated Cheddar cheese
	Bottled taco sauce
8	ounces sour cream
2	avocados
	Chopped green onions
	Sliced black olives

Place refried beans in the bottom of a round dish with a 2-inch lip. Brown beef, chorizo sausage and onion. Drain. Layer on top of beans as follows: beef mixture, green chilies, cheese and taco sauce. Bake at 350 degrees for 30 minutes. Spread center with sour cream. Place mashed avocados around edges. Sprinkle with chopped green onions and sliced black olives. Serve with tortilla chips.

ALMOST-A-MEAL DIP

1	16-ounce can refried beans
1	pound lean ground beef
2	4-ounce cans chopped green chilies
1	pound Monterey Jack cheese, grated
1	large bottle mild taco sauce
6	scallions, chopped
2	cans frozen guacamole dip, thawed
1	8-ounce carton sour cream

Grease a 9x13-inch casserole dish. Brown the ground beef; drain. Add refried beans. Mix well. Spread this mixture in the bottom of the pan. Top with the following layers: chopped chilies, grated Monterey Jack cheese and taco sauce. Bake at 400 degrees for 20 to 25 minutes until the cheese melts. Remove from oven. Cool 10 minutes to set. Top with layers of the following: chopped scallions, guacamole dip and sour cream. Serve warm with tortilla chips.

BACON SURPRISE

24 appetizers

1	5-ounce can smoked oysters, drained and chopped
½	cup herb stuffing mix
¼	cup water
8	slices bacon, cut in thirds

Combine oysters, stuffing and water. Mix well. Using a spoon, shape into pecan-size pieces. Wrap with bacon slices and secure with toothpick. Place on rack in a shallow pan. Bake at 350 degrees for 25 to 30 minutes. Turn once during cooking. Can be frozen before baking.

BUFFET HAM VOLCANO

10	pounds ham, shaved
1	16-ounce package fillo dough
½	cup butter

In a spring-form pan, heap ham into shape of mountain. Bake at 350 degrees for 45 minutes to an hour, until steaming. Remove from oven and take sides off spring-form pan. Start applying sheets of fillo, one at a time, buttering each sheet as you go. Cover all sides and top of mountain with at least six sheets of fillo, the more the better. Bake at 350 degrees until fillo is deep golden brown, approximately 30 minutes. To serve, cut off the very top of mountain. As the ham is pulled out, the mountain should be cut down. Serve with cocktail buns and spicy mustard.

EASY SUGARED BACON

1	pound bacon slices
1	cup brown sugar

Rub or pat brown sugar into both sides of bacon slices. If you wish you may cut each bacon slice into 3 pieces to make bite-sized pieces. Arrange bacon slices in teflon coated jelly roll pan and bake at 325 degrees for 25 to 30 minutes, or until crisp. Serve as an appetizer or as an accompaniment for brunch.

SPICED TONGUE

1	beef tongue or heart
2	tablespoons salt
3	ribs of celery
12	whole cloves
2	bay leaves
12	whole peppercorns
2	cups sugar
2	cups water
2	cups vinegar
6	small onions, thinly sliced

Wash tongue. Cover with water; add celery and spices. Cook slowly until tender, about 1 hour per pound. Drain. Cool until warm; skin and slice. Cook sugar, water and vinegar together for 10 minutes. Pour over tongue and onions. Put in covered container and refrigerate. Can be kept for several weeks.

THREE-WAY EGG ROLLS

12 servings

1 **package egg roll skins or wrappers**
Egg white
Oil for frying

Open the egg roll wrapper package. Keep them moist by covering with a damp towel. To assemble an egg roll; place a square wrapper on the counter with a corner pointing toward you. Put 2 to 3 tablespoons of filling on the wrapper. Pat the filling with the edge of a knife to make a tight filling. Brush the edges of the wrapper with egg white for a good seal. Fold the corner farthest from you, up and over the filling. Fold the left-hand corner over, then the right hand corner. Roll toward the remaining corner to form a cylinder. Repeat with rest of squares. Cover with a damp towel until ready to use. You may dip the egg rolls in the batter mixture before frying. Heat 2-inches of oil to 375 degrees in a deep, heavy pan or skillet. Cook rolls, 3 to 4 at a time, until crisp and golden. Drain. Serve with choice of dipping sauces.

BATTER:

1 **egg**
½ **tablespoon cornstarch**
½ **cup flour**
1 **teaspoon baking powder**
1 **teaspoon salt**
1 **teaspoon sugar**
½ **teaspoon MSG**
½ **cup milk**
½ **cup water**

Combine all ingredients and blend well. Dip filled egg rolls in batter before frying.

FILLING I:

1½ **cups cooked, finely chopped pork**
1 **4-ounce can shrimp, finely chopped**
1½ **cups bean sprouts**
1 **8-ounce can water chestnuts, finely chopped**
1 **cup chopped celery**
2 **tablespoons butter, melted**
1 **teaspoon salt**

Combine pork, shrimp, bean sprouts, water chestnuts, celery, butter and salt.

FILLING II:

2 cups ham
5 dried Chinese mushrooms
½ pound fresh bean sprouts
3 stalks celery
2 stalks green onion
2 tablespoons oyster sauce
1 teaspoon salt
1 teaspoon sugar

Soak mushrooms for 2 hours. Discard stems. Slice ham, mushrooms, celery and onions into very small diagonal pieces. Rinse bean sprouts in water and drain. Heat wok or fry pan. Add 1 tablespoon oil. Cook vegetables and set aside as follows; bean sprouts for 1 minute, celery for 2 minutes, mushrooms seasoned with sugar for 2 minutes and ham for 2 minutes. Add more oil as needed. Pour oyster sauce over ham and mix. Put all vegetables and green onions in wok. Season to taste. Cool. Add ham to vegetables.

FILLING III:

1 bunch green onions, finely
   chopped
1 cup chopped fresh mushrooms
1 cup finely chopped parsley
4 cups fresh beans sprouts,
   chopped
1 8-ounce can water chestnuts,
   chopped
1 8-ounce can bamboo shoots,
   chopped
2 cups cooked chopped shrimp,
   chicken or pork
4 tablespoons soy sauce, or
   more to taste

All ingredients should be finely chopped. Do not shred into a pastey consistency. A food processor can be used. Lightly sauté onions in oil, add mushrooms and sauté until moisture is nearly gone. Add other ingredients and toss with soy sauce. Meat can be any cooked meat or a combination.

CHINESE MUSTARD:

½ cup boiling water
¼ cup dry English mustard
½ teaspoon salt
2 teaspoons oil

Stir water into mustard. Add salt and oil.

PINEAPPLE SAUCE:

½ cup brown sugar
1 teaspoon salt
½ cup vinegar
1½ tablespoons cornstarch
1 tablespoon catsup
¾ cup pineapple juice
1 cup crushed pineapple

Stir cornstarch into pineapple juice. Add the remaining ingredients and heat until thick and bubbly.

DEEP-FRIED WONTONS

4 dozen

1 pound ready-made egg roll wrappers, or ½ pound ready-made wonton wrappers

Cut wonton or egg roll wrappers into 3½-inch squares. To assemble; place 1½ teaspoons of chosen filling in the center of each wrapper. With a finger dipped in water, moisten edges of wrapper. Bring one corner up over the filling to the opposite corner, fold wrapper at an angle so that two overlapping triangles are formed, with their points side by side. Pull bottom corners of the folded triangle forward and below the folded edge so they meet one another and slightly overlap. Moisten one end with a finger dipped in water and pinch the two ends firmly together. If wontons are prepared longer than 30 minutes before frying, cover and refrigerate. Heat oil in a wok or deep fat fryer to 375 degrees. Deep-fry wontons, 8 to 10 at a time for about 2 minutes. Drain on paper towels. Serve hot. Can be kept warm for up to an hour in a 250 degree oven, or reheated for 5 minutes in a 450 degree oven. Serve with Chinese mustard (see Three-Way Egg Rolls) and sweet and sour sauce.

FILLING I:
1 pound raw shrimp
2 tablespoons peanut oil
½ pound lean boneless pork, freshly ground
2 tablespoons soy sauce
1 tablespoon Chinese rice wine or pale, dry sherry
5 water chestnuts, finely chopped
1 scallion, finely chopped
1 teaspoon cornstarch dissolved in 1 tablespoon cold water
3 cups peanut oil

Shell and devein shrimp. Chop fine. Set wok over high heat for 30 seconds. Pour in peanut oil and heat. Add pork and stir-fry for 1 minute, or until the meat is no longer pink. Add shrimp, soy sauce, wine, salt, water chestnuts and scallions. Stir-fry another minute. Pour cornstarch mixture into pan. Stir constantly until liquid thickens. Transfer contents of pan to a bowl and cool.

FILLING II:
1 pound ground pork
¼ teaspoon salt
1 teaspoon MSG

Mix together all ingredients.

FILLING III:

8   ounces crab, drained
8   ounces cream cheese
2   tablespoons soft bread crumbs

Mix together all ingredients.

SWEET AND SOUR SAUCE:

1   cup sugar
½   teaspoon salt
3   tablespoons catsup
½   cup vinegar
1   cup water
1   tablespoon cornstarch

Cook together sugar, salt, catsup and vinegar until thickened like syrup. Mix cornstarch and water. Add to sauce and cook until thick. Keep warm. Dip wontons in sauce.

SWEET AND SOUR APRICOT SAUCE:

¼   cup apricot preserves
½   cup brown sugar
2   tablespoons cider vinegar
2   tablespoons soy sauce
½   teaspoon dry mustard

Combine all ingredients in small saucepan. Cook, stirring, over medium-low heat until sugar dissolves. Serve warm or at room temperature.

KOREAN APPETIZERS

½   cup soy sauce
3   cloves garlic, sliced
2   teaspoons crushed dried
     red pepper
2   teaspoons sugar
2   green onion tops, sliced
2   teaspoons ginger
1½ pounds top round or sirloin
¼   cup toasted sesame seeds
2   tablespoons peanut oil

Mix soy sauce, garlic, red pepper, sugar, onion and ginger. Cut meat into ½-inch cubes. Marinate beef in sauce mixture for one hour before serving. Drain meat. Fry in peanut oil in hot skillet for 2 minutes. Serve on skewers. Sprinkle with toasted sesame seeds.

ORIENTAL MEATBALLS

48 meatballs

1   cup fresh bread crumbs
½   cup milk
½   pound ground beef
½   pound ground pork
1   teaspoon soy sauce
1   teaspoon garlic salt
1   8-ounce can water chestnuts,
     drained

Soak bread crumbs in milk 5 minutes. Add remaining ingredients except chestnuts; mix well. Cut water chestnuts in half. Roll meat mixture around each chestnut half to form ½-inch balls. (This works better if you keep your hands wet.) Bake on ungreased cookie sheet at 325 degrees for 15 to 20 minutes. Turn once or twice while baking to maintain round shape. Sprinkle with soy sauce while baking for stronger soy flavor.

SANGANAKI HORS D'OEUVRE

4 servings

4 ½-inch thick pieces Kasseri or Kesalotyri cheese, cut in half to make triangles or rectangles 2 to 3-inches long
1 egg, slightly beaten with fork
Flour
1 tablespoon butter
3 ounces Metaxa or other brandy
1 lemon, rolled to soften and cut in half

Dip cheese in egg then flour. Fry at medium-low setting until brown. Turn and brown other side. When thoroughly heated; pour brandy over the cheese and ignite with a match. Extinguish flame by squeezing lemon over the flame. Serve immediately. NOTE: This is a Greek appetizer. Cheese may be purchased in some grocery stores and most specialty or gourmet shops. Have cheese cut when purchased to avoid crumbling.

ORIENTAL CHICKEN WINGS

8 servings

3 pounds chicken wings
½ cup soy sauce
2 tablespoons salad oil
2 tablespoons chili sauce
¼ cup honey
1 teaspoon salt
½ teaspoon ginger
½ teaspoon garlic powder
¼ teaspoon cayenne

Halve wings, remove and discard tips. Wash and pat dry. Mix soy sauce, salad oil, chili sauce, honey, salt, ginger, garlic powder and cayenne. Pour over wings. Cover and refrigerate for 1 hour or overnight. Turn occasionally for even color. Place wings on a foil-covered cookie sheet. Bake 15 minutes at 350 degrees. Brush with marinade and turn wings over. Bake another 15 minutes. Brush with remaining marinade.

CHICKEN PICK-UP STICKS

1½ pounds chicken wings
1 egg whipped with 1 tablespoon water
⅔ cup finely chopped toasted almonds or peanuts
2 tablespoons flour
½ teaspoon salt
¼ teaspoon ginger
¼ cup butter or margarine
½ cup soy sauce

Cut tips off wings; dip in egg and water mixture. Mix nuts, flour, salt and ginger together. Roll each chicken piece in this mixture. Place in a 9x13-inch baking pan. Mix butter and soy sauce together and drizzle over chicken wings. Bake at 250 degrees for 5 to 6 hours.

COCKTAIL TURKEY BREAST

1   **5 pound turkey breast**
1   **tablespoon fines herbs**
1   **tablespoon salt**
½   **teaspoon pepper**
1   **tablespoon curry powder**
1   **teaspoon paprika**
1   **onion**
1   **carrot**
1   **stalk of celery**
½   **orange, sliced**
1   **cup gin**
1   **cup water**

Rub both sides of the turkey breast with a mixture of fines herbs, salt, pepper, curry and paprika. Place the turkey in a pan with the onion, carrot, celery and orange slices. Roast, uncovered, at 350 degrees until tender, about 2½ to 3 hours. Baste frequently with gin and water mixture. Cool in juices. Remove from pan and wrap in foil. Refrigerate. To serve, carefully remove meat in one piece from the side of the bone. Slice paper-thin across the grain of the meat. Form slices into original shape. Return to the breast bone. Serve with mayonnaise, thin bread slices, crackers and mustard. May be frozen.

CLAM SOUFFLÉ CANAPÉ

8 servings

1   **8-ounce package cream cheese, softened**
2   **tablespoons mayonnaise**
2   **tablespoons Vermouth**
1   **6½-ounce can minced clams, drained**
½   **teaspoon curry**
½   **teaspoon sugar**
¼   **teaspoon garlic salt**
¼   **teaspoon salt**
1   **tablespoon minced onion**
¼   **teaspoon slivered almonds**

Combine cream cheese, mayonnaise and Vermouth. Stir in clams, curry, sugar, garlic salt, salt and onion. Spoon into greased 1-quart casserole dish. Sprinkle with almonds. Bake at 325 degrees for 20 minutes. Serve with crackers.

CRAB DIP

1   **8-ounce package cream cheese**
1   **10-ounce can cream of mushroom soup**
1   **cup mayonnaise**
2   **stalks celery, finely chopped**
5   **green onions, finely chopped**
2   **tablespoons water**
½   **envelope unflavored gelatin**
5   **drops lemon juice**
1   **pound crab meat**

Melt the cream cheese and mushroom soup over low heat; add mayonnaise, celery and onions. Dissolve gelatin in water and add to the cheese-soup mixture. Mix well and remove from heat. Add crab meat and mix again. Pour into oiled fish mold and refrigerate overnight. Unmold and serve with crackers.

SALMON AND SOUR CREAM PICNIC
4 servings

1 14-ounce can salmon, chilled
and drained
½ pint sour cream
1 teaspoon dillweed
½ cucumber, thinly sliced
2 teaspoons capers
2 green onions or scallions,
chopped
Seasoned salt
Pepper
Chopped lettuce
1 lemon, cut into wedges

Bone salmon and mound it on plate. Cover with sour cream mixed with dill. Arrange cucumber slices overlapping across top. Sprinkle capers and chopped onions on top. Season with salt and pepper. Surround with chopped lettuce. Place lemon wedges around edge. Serve at once with melba toast.

SHRIMP DIP

11 ounces cream cheese,
softened
2 tablespoons mayonnaise
2 tablespoons lemon juice
1 tablespoon Worcestershire
2 tablespoons minced onion
flakes
½ teaspoon garlic powder
1 12-ounce bottle chili sauce
2 4½-ounce cans small shrimp,
drained
2 cups shredded Mozzarella
cheese
Parsley flakes
Oregano

Layer dip on a 10-inch serving platter. For the first layer, mix cream cheese, mayonnaise, lemon juice, Worcestershire, onion flakes and garlic powder until smooth. Spread on serving platter. Cover with chili sauce. Sprinkle shrimp on top. Scatter cheese over shrimp. Sprinkle parsley and oregano over all. Refrigerate until ready to serve. Serve with onion crackers.

SHRIMP BUTTER

½ cup butter
1 8-ounce package cream
cheese, softened
1 4½-ounce can shrimp pieces
Garlic salt
Salt and pepper to taste
1 tablespoon lemon juice
½ small onion, finely
chopped
4 teaspoons mayonnaise

Combine all ingredients and refrigerate overnight. Serve with crackers or fill snowpea pods with mixture.

CURRIED SHRIMP CRACKER SPREAD

1   8-ounce package cream cheese
2   teaspoons mayonnaise
¼   teaspoon curry powder
    Salt and pepper
1   4½-ounce can shrimp pieces
¼   cup chopped green onions
1   hard-boiled egg, chopped

Soften cream cheese and break up with a fork. Add other ingredients and stir slightly. Let flavors combine for 2 hours. Serve with crackers.

MOM'S SHRIMP COCKTAIL

8 servings

1   quart whole tomatoes,
       drained and chopped
1   cup V-8 juice
⅓   cup diced green pepper
½   cup diced celery
½   cup diced onion
1   tablespoon horseradish
2   tablespoons sugar
¼   cup vinegar
1   4½-ounce can small shrimp
    Salt

Mix all ingredients together, except salt. Chill. Just before serving taste for amount of salt needed. Serve as an appetizer over cream cheese with crackers, or on a bed of shredded lettuce as a first course.

OYSTER ROLL

1   8-ounce package cream
       cheese, softened
1   tin smoked oysters, chopped
1   lemon rind, grated
    Lemon pepper
    Minced fresh parsley

Roll out cream cheese on a piece of foil and refrigerate. If needed, cheese may be softened by adding a little sour cream or lemon juice. Spread cream cheese rectangle with chopped oysters. Sprinkle with grated lemon rind and lemon pepper. Roll up like a jellyroll and roll in grated parsley. Cover with Saran wrap and refrigerate. This may be made a day ahead if wrapped very tightly. Serve on a small tray with crackers of your choice.

ESCABECHE

6 servings

2 pounds halibut steaks,
   cut ¾ inch thick
⅓ cup plus ¾ cup olive oil
2 large onions, peeled and
   sliced into rings
4 medium carrots, scraped and
   coarsely grated
1 cup white wine vinegar
2 large bay leaves, crumbled
2 teaspoons finely chopped garlic
2 teaspoons salt
¼ teaspoon crushed dried hot
   red pepper
¼ teaspoon freshly ground
   pepper

In a heavy 12-inch skillet, heat ⅓ cup olive oil over moderate heat. Add the fish steaks and cook them 4 to 5 minutes on each side. When they are golden brown, transfer to paper towels to drain. In a clean 12-inch skillet, heat ¾ cup of oil. Add onions and cook for 5 minutes until soft and transparent, but not brown. Stir in carrots, vinegar, bay leaf, garlic, salt, crushed red pepper and black pepper. Cook for 5 minutes longer, stirring occasionally. Taste for seasoning. Remove skin and any bones from fish. Spread a cup or so of the hot marinade evenly in glass or enamel dish, about 6-inches in diameter and 4-inches deep. Arrange half the fish on top and cover it with a cup of marinade. Add the remaining fish and spread the remaining marinade over it. Cover tightly with foil or plastic wrap and marinate in refrigerator for at least 2 days. Serve this from the dish in which it has been marinated.

CAPONATA

2 medium eggplants
2 large onions
½ cup olive oil
1½ cups sliced celery
2 green peppers, chopped
2 cloves garlic, minced
1 28-ounce can Italian plum
   tomatoes, undrained and
   chopped
⅓ cup red wine vinegar
2 tablespoons salt
2 tablespoons sugar
¼ cup fresh basil, chopped, or
2 tablespoons dried basil

Sauté eggplants and onions in olive oil for 5 minutes. Add all other ingredients and simmer 20 minutes, covered, and 15 minutes, uncovered, until consistency of thick relish. Serve with French bread.

3 tablespoons tomato paste
½ cup parsley
1 teaspoon pepper
¾ cup sliced stuffed green olives
4 tablespoons capers (optional)
½ cup pine nuts, lightly
   browned in olive oil
   (optional)

MEDITERRANEAN EGGPLANT DIP

2 pounds eggplant
2 small cloves garlic, pressed
¼ cup tahini (Middle Eastern
   sesame paste)
¼ cup lemon juice
1 cup peeled and chopped
   tomatoes
1 green or red pepper, diced
1 cup sliced scallions
¼ cup chopped parsley
2 teaspoons salt

Pierce eggplant several times and bake at 400 degrees for 25 to 35 minutes until a knife will go into it with no resistance. Slice eggplant in half. Using a spoon, remove eggplant flesh from skin. This is easiest while eggplant is still hot. Purée eggplant. When eggplant has cooled, add all remaining ingredients, reserving a little parsley and diced peppers for garnish. Taste for salt. Serve with crackers or pita bread wedges.

MARINATED ARTICHOKES AND MUSHROOMS

1 16 ounce can jumbo black
   olives, pitted
1 14-ounce can artichoke
   hearts
2 pounds fresh medium
   mushrooms
1½ cups water
1 cup cider vinegar
1 cup vegetable oil
1 clove garlic (on toothpick)
1½ tablespoons salt
½ teaspoon pepper
½ teaspoon thyme
½ teaspoon oregano

Combine all ingredients and refrigerate overnight, stirring often. Remove garlic clove before serving.

CHAMPIGNONS À LA BOURGUIGNONNE
3 dozen

3 dozen medium mushrooms
¾ cup butter, melted
9 garlic cloves, peeled
¼ medium white onion, cut in
   pieces
4 teaspoons white wine
2 teaspoons fresh lemon juice
1 teaspoon nutmeg
   Salt and pepper to taste

Clean mushrooms and remove stems. Preheat oven to 375 degrees. Set mushrooms in escargot plates or shallow baking dish. Place remaining ingredients in blender or food processor. Blend at high speed for 10 seconds. Spoon sauce into mushroom caps. Bake until butter sauce begins to bubble, about 10 minutes. Place under broiler 1 minute until sauce turns golden brown.

STUFFED MUSHROOMS
20 appetizers

20 mushrooms, cleaned
¼ cup minced onion
¼ cup finely minced ham
2 tablespoons oil
2 tablespoons chopped parsley
1 egg, lightly beaten
1 cup fine bread crumbs
½ cup beef broth

Remove stems from mushrooms and mince enough of stems to measure ½ cup; reserve the rest for another use. Cook onion and ham in oil for 2 minutes; add minced stems and parsley. Cook over low heat until liquid has evaporated. Let mixture cool. Add egg, bread crumbs, broth and cheese; combine and divide among caps. Arrange in buttered baking dish and bake at 450 degrees for 15 minutes, or until lightly browned. These can be prepared a day ahead and baked just before serving.

BACON CHEESE MUSHROOMS
25 mushrooms

25 mushrooms
¾ cup mayonnaise
1 small onion, chopped
5 strips bacon, cooked and
   crumbled
   Grated Cheddar cheese

Remove stems. Wash and clean mushroom caps, pat dry. Mix mayonnaise, onion and bacon. Put a teaspoon of mixture in each mushroom cap. Put mushrooms in buttered pan and cover with grated cheese. Bake at 350 degrees for 15 minutes.

MUSHROOM SPREAD

4 slices bacon, chopped
½ pound fresh mushrooms,
   chopped
½ cup chopped onion

Cook bacon until crisp; reserve 2 tablespoons drippings. Sauté mushrooms, onion and garlic in drippings until tender and most of the liquid is

54

1 clove garlic, minced
1 tablespoon flour
¼ teaspoon salt
⅛ teaspoon pepper
2 teaspoons Worcestershire
1 teaspoon soy sauce
1 8-ounce package cream
   cheese, cubed
½ cup sour cream

absorbed. Add flour, salt, pepper, Worcestershire and soy sauce; mix well. Add cubed cream cheese. Stir over medium heat until cream cheese is melted. Add sour cream and bacon. Do not boil. Serve with cocktail rounds or crackers.

MEXICALI RELISH

1 4-ounce can green chilies,
   chopped
1 4½-ounce can black olives,
   chopped
2 tomatoes, peeled and chopped
5 green onions, chopped
1 tablespoon olive oil
2 tablespoons salad oil
1½ tablespoons wine vinegar
   Garlic salt to taste

Combine all ingredients and refrigerate. Drain well and correct seasonings before serving. Serve with tortilla chips.

VEGETABLE TEMPURA

1 cup flour
2 tablespoons cornstarch
½ teaspoon salt
1 cup ice water
1 egg yolk
2 egg whites, whipped
   Vegetable pieces

Combine flour, cornstarch and salt. Make a well in the center of dry ingredients. Beat together ice water and egg yolk; pour all at once into well in dry ingredients. Stir until just moistened. The batter will be slightly lumpy. Fold in egg whites. Place the bowl in a larger bowl of ice water. Pour oil into wok to a 3-inch depth. Heat to 400 degrees. Dip raw vegetable pieces; asparagus, broccoli, cauliflower, okra, eggplant, cucumbers, green pepper, mushrooms or green beans in tempura batter. Fry, a few at a time, until golden brown. Drain well. Keep warm in a 250 degree oven until all are fried. Serve with Chinese mustard or Sweet and Sour sauce for a dip.
(see Three-Way Egg Rolls)

STUFFED TOMATOES

2   3-ounce packages cream
      cheese, cut into pieces
¼   cup butter
2   cloves garlic, minced
½   teaspoon salt
1   pint cherry tomatoes

Scoop out tomatoes. Rinse and drain. Process cream cheese, butter, garlic and salt in a food processor or blender until smooth. Fill cherry tomatoes. Chill.

SPINACH POM-POMS

Makes 65 balls

FILLING
2   10-ounce packages frozen
      chopped spinach, thawed
2   cups crushed herb seasoned
      stuffing mix
1   cup grated Parmesan cheese
      Dash nutmeg
6   eggs, beaten
¾   cup softened butter

Drain spinach and squeeze out all excess moisture. Place in medium bowl and blend in remaining ingredients. Shape into balls the size of walnuts; refrigerate or freeze. Preheat oven to 350 degrees. Lightly grease baking sheets; bake spinach balls 10 to 15 minutes or until hot. Drain on paper towels. Serve with toothpicks and mustard sauce.

SAUCE
½   cup dry mustard
½   cup white vinegar
½   cup sugar
1   egg yolk

Combine mustard and vinegar in small bowl. Cover and let stand at room temperature overnight. In small saucepan, combine mustard-vinegar mixture, sugar and egg yolk. Simmer over low heat until slightly thickened. Cover and store in refrigerator up to one month. Serve at room temperature.

ASPARAGUS ROLL-UPS

1   10-ounce package frozen
      asparagus spears
20 slices white bread
1   2½-ounce jar Roka cheese
1   8-ounce package cream
      cheese, softened
1   egg
⅔   cup melted butter

Remove crust from bread and flatten with rolling pin. Combine cheeses and egg. Spread cheese mixture on each bread slice. Place 1 asparagus spear on each slice and roll up. Dip in melted butter. Place rolls in freezer for 20 minutes; remove and cut each roll into thirds. Put in baggie or container and freeze. Remove as desired and bake at 400 degrees for 15 minutes. Watch closely while baking.

FROSTED CAULIFLOWER

6 servings

1 head cauliflower
1 cup mayonnaise
  Juice of ½ lemon
1 teaspoon curry powder

Mix mayonnaise, lemon juice and curry powder in small bowl. Cook cauliflower in boiling, salted water 10 minutes until fork tender; drain and place on serving plate. While hot, frost with mayonnaise mixture. Place in refrigerator to cool. It will turn a bright yellow. Serve with large crackers.

SAUERKRAUT APPETIZER

1 1-pound 11-ounce can
   sauerkraut, squeezed
   dry and chopped
2 cups grated Cheddar cheese
2 tablespoons chopped onion
3 tablespoons chopped green
   pepper
1 hard-boiled egg, grated
⅓ cup bread crumbs
¼ cup mayonnaise
1 teaspoon salt
1 tablespoon sugar

Combine all ingredients. Additional mayonnaise may be added if it appears dry. Form into a ball. Sprinkle with paprika. Refrigerate at least 2 hours before serving with crackers. Easy to make in a food processor; no need to chop the sauerkraut.

BLUE CHEESE CABBAGE SPREAD

2 cups chopped cabbage
8 ounces Blue cheese, softened
¼ cup chopped green olives
¼ cup chopped black olives
  Dash salt and pepper
¼ cup mayonnaise
  Dash garlic salt

Mix all ingredients together. Toss with mayonnaise until mixture is of spreading consistency. Serve with assorted crackers. NOTE: Strong Blue cheese flavor—for Blue cheese lovers only!

CHEESE-STUFFED PEPPERS

2 servings

1 green pepper
1 3-ounce package cream
   cheese, softened
½ cup finely diced Longhorn
   Cheddar cheese
2 small scallions, finely diced
  Salt
  Tabasco
  Onion juice

Cut off top of pepper and clean out seeds. Combine cream cheese, Cheddar cheese and scallions. Add salt, Tabasco and onion juice to taste. Fill pepper with mixture. Refrigerate for several hours. Slice into wedges when ready to serve.

PIQUANT CREAM CHEESE

½   **cup chopped onion**
2   **cloves garlic, minced**
1½ **cups ketchup**
2   **tablespoons vinegar**
½   **teaspoon salt**
1   **tablespoon prepared mustard**
½   **teaspoon pepper**
2   **tablespoons steak sauce**
¼   **cup lemon juice**
1   **cup honey**
1   **8-ounce package cream
     cheese**

Combine all ingredients except cream cheese in a saucepan. Cook over low heat for 10 minutes. Chill. To serve, pour part of the sauce over cream cheese block and serve with crackers. Remaining sauce keeps well in refrigerator for weeks.

CHEESE WITH CHUTNEY APPETIZER

2   **3-ounce packages cream
     cheese, softened**
1   **cup shredded sharp Cheddar
     cheese**
4   **teaspoons sherry or dry
     white wine**
½   **teaspoon curry powder**
¼   **teaspoon salt**
1   **jar chutney**

Mix the cream cheese, Cheddar cheese, wine, curry and salt together. Mold into a rounded, flat shape. Chill. When ready to serve, pour chutney over the top. Serve with crackers.

CHUTNEY LOG

2   **8-ounce packages cream
     cheese, softened**
½   **cup chutney, cut up**
2   **teaspoons curry powder**
¼   **teaspoon dry mustard**
3½ **tablespoons mayonnaise**
⅓   **cup golden raisins**
1   **cup slivered almonds**
1   **cup chopped pecans**

Combine all ingredients except the pecans. Form into a ball or log and roll in the pecans. Refrigerate until ready to serve.

CHILI-PECAN ROLL

1	cup pecans
1	clove garlic
2	3-ounce packages cream cheese, softened
1½	tablespoons chili powder
1	tablespoon A1 sauce

Grind pecans and garlic. Blend in cream cheese and A1 sauce. Chill. Shape into a long 1-inch thick roll. Roll in chili powder. Wrap and chill. Serve with crackers.

APPLES AND CHEESE   1⅔ cups

1	8-ounce package cream cheese, softened
½	cup mayonnaise
½	cup shredded Cheddar cheese
½	cup finely chopped apple
¼	cup chopped walnuts (optional)
	Apple wedges

Combine cream cheese and mayonnaise. Stir in cheese and apple. Chill. Serve with apple wedges or crackers.

SESAME-HERB CHEESE BALL   serves 8

2	8-ounce packages cream cheese, softened
½	cup creamy Italian dressing
1	teaspoon onion powder
1	teaspoon garlic powder
1	tablespoon minced onion
1	tablespoon bacon bits
1	tablespoon chives
1	teaspoon herb seasoning
½	cup crushed potato chips
½	cup crushed herb seasoned stuffing
1	cup Parmesan cheese
1½	cups chopped slivered almonds
1	cup toasted sesame seeds

Combine all ingredients, except sesame seeds. Shape into a ball. Roll ball in sesame seeds. Wrap and chill. Serve with assorted crackers. If this is prepared in a food processor, the chips and stuffing can be put in whole.

CHIVE-ROQUEFORT DIP

1 cup sour cream
1 cup mayonnaise
1 1¼-ounce package Roquefort,
      grated
   Dash lemon juice
   Dash Worcestershire
   Dash salt
1 teaspoon onion juice
1 package frozen chives,
      thawed and squeezed dry

Mix all ingredients until well blended. Serve with chips or Ritz crackers. This is very good on baked potatoes or as a salad dressing.

MOTHER MILDRED'S MARVELOUS MIX

2 8-ounce packages cream
      cheese, softened
1 8-ounce package whipped
      butter, softened
2 cloves garlic, minced
¼ teaspoon salt
¼ teaspoon pepper
¼ teaspoon marjoram
¼ teaspoon basil
¼ teaspoon dill weed
¼ teaspoon thyme

In food processor, finely chop the garlic. Add everything else and mix well. You can also press garlic and mix all ingredients well with an electric mixer. Chill at least 24 hours. Remove from refrigerator 1 hour before serving. Serve with crackers, french bread or on top of baked potatoes.

BEV'S GREAT VEGETABLE DIP

2 cups mayonnaise
4 tablespoons minced onion
4 teaspoons soy sauce
1 tablespoon milk
1 teaspoon ginger
1 teaspoon vinegar
   Pinch garlic powder

Mix all ingredients together. Chill. Serve with assorted raw vegetables.

HERB CHEESE ON RYE

36 slices

1   8-ounce package cream
      cheese, softened
1   package dry Italian
      dressing mix
1   loaf party rye bread
1   cucumber, sliced
      Dill weed

Mix together cream cheese and package of dressing mix. Spread generously on slices of rye. Top with cucumber slice and sprinkle with dill weed. Chill until ready to serve.

SAUCIE SUSANS

1½ cups shredded sharp
      Cheddar cheese
1   cup sliced ripe black
      olives
½   cup sliced green
      onions
½   cup mayonnaise
1   loaf party rye bread

Mix together all ingredients, except bread. Spread on party rye. Broil until browned.

SWISS-CHEDDAR FONDUE

1   garlic clove, halved
1½ cups dry white wine
      or sauterne
½   pound grated Swiss cheese
½   pound grated Cheddar cheese
½   teaspoon baking soda
2   tablespoons flour
⅛   teaspoon cayenne pepper
      Dash garlic salt

Rub inside of fondue pot with garlic clove. Pour wine into pot and heat until wine bubbles, about 4 to 5 minutes. Do not boil wine. In bowl, toss cheese with baking soda and flour. Add cheese mixture to wine, ¼ cup at a time. Stir until evenly blended and melted. (Stir cheese in figure eight motion to prevent it from becoming stringy.) Add cayenne pepper and garlic salt. Stir until blended. Heat 5 minutes to develop flavors. Serve with any of the following for dipping: french bread, apples, pineapple, ham or brussel sprouts.

CHEESE RING

1	**pound grated sharp Cheddar cheese**
½	**small onion, grated**
1	**cup chopped pecans**
¼	**teaspoon Tabasco**
½	**teaspoon garlic salt**
	Mayonnaise
1	**6-ounce jar strawberry jam**

Combine all ingredients, except jam, using just enough mayonnaise to moisten to the consistency of a thick cocktail spread. Chill several hours or overnight. Spoon mixture onto plate in a ring. Spoon jam into center and serve with crackers.

CRAZY CRUNCH

2 quarts

2	**quarts popped large kernel popcorn**
1½	**cups pecans, toasted and salted**
⅔	**cup almonds, toasted and salted**
1½	**cups sugar**
1	**cup margarine**
1	**teaspoon vanilla**
½	**cup light corn syrup**

Mix popcorn and nuts. Combine sugar, margarine and syrup in ½-quart pan. Bring to a boil over medium heat; stir constantly. Continue boiling until mixture is light brown, 10 to 15 minutes, or to 300 degrees on candy thermometer. Remove from heat; add vanilla. Pour syrup over popcorn and nuts. Mix to coat. Spread out on cookie sheets to dry. Break apart. Store in covered container.

HOLIDAY FRUIT TREE

Styrofoam cone
Egg whites, beaten slightly
Parsley, snipped
Toothpicks
Green seedless grapes
Apple slices, unpeeled
Pear slices, unpeeled
Bananas, sliced thick
Strawberries
Orange slices
Orange juice

Secure parsley pieces to cover cone, using egg whites as glue. Cut fruit slices into thirds. Soak apples, pears and bananas in orange juice. Arrange grapes in a circle at top, attach with toothpicks. Then attach with toothpicks, apples, pears and bananas. Add orange sections at bottom of cone. Decorate with strawberries. As fruit is removed from cone, dip in sauce. Combine strawberry yogurt and cream cheese. Mix well with beater. Fold in Cool Whip and chill.

SAUCE

1	**cup strawberry yogurt**
1	**3-ounce package cream cheese**
¾	**8-ounce container Cool Whip**

OREO COOKIE DRINK

3 Oreo cookies
2 scoops French vanilla ice
cream
1 jigger dark Crème de Cacao
1 jigger whipping cream

Place cookies in blender to crush; add other ingredients and blend until thick and smooth. Serve in chilled glass immediately. To serve to children, leave out the Crème de Cacao.

RAZZAMATAZZ

2½ cups French vanilla ice
cream
2½ ounces raspberry liqueur
1½ ounces brandy
6-8 fresh raspberries

Blend very briefly in blender. Serve in champagne glasses after dinner. Garnish with fresh raspberries.

COFFEE CANTATA

2 ounces Kahlúa
2 large scoops of coffee or
vanilla ice cream
1 ounce half-and-half
½ ounce vodka

Mix all ingredients in a blender until smooth. You may need to add additional ice cream for desired thickness. Pour into short glasses and top with a dash of nutmeg.

LATE NIGHT BODY WARMERS

1 cup coffee (approximately
6-ounces)
1 teaspoon Kahlúa
1 teaspoon rum
1 teaspoon Crème de Cacao
2 teaspoons Galliano
Whipped sweetened cream

Combine all ingredients in the hot cup of coffee. Stir in some of the cream and garnish top with a dollop of whipped cream. NOTE: For six mugs, use one jigger to each teaspoon.

PLAYHOUSE PUNCH

24 servings

2 cups pineapple juice
2 10-ounce packages frozen
strawberries
½ cup sugar
1 6-ounce can frozen concentrated lemonade
2 4/5 bottles rosé wine
1 quart club soda
Ice ring

Blend all ingredients, except club soda, in large mixing bowl or punch bowl at least 1 hour ahead. Add ice ring and club soda at serving time.

FROZEN CRANBERRY PUNCH

3 quarts

2 quarts Cranberry Juice
Cocktail
⅔ cup sugar
1 quart 7-UP
1 cup bourbon

Combine ingredients and freeze. Remove from freezer 1 hour before serving. Serve slushy. NOTE: Double or triple the ingredients for a holiday punch bowl.

WAKE UP PUNCH

12 servings

3 cups water
1 cup sugar
3 very ripe bananas
1 24-ounce can pineapple juice
1 6-ounce can frozen concentrated orange juice
2 tablespoons lemon juice
2½ cups vodka or rum
7-UP or ginger ale

Purée bananas and thaw orange juice. Mix the water, sugar, bananas, pineapple juice, orange juice, lemon juice and vodka or rum. Stir well. Freeze in a 9x13-inch pan or plastic ice cream container. To serve, put 2 scoops of frozen punch in a blender and add 4 ounces of 7-UP or ginger ale. Blend just until slushy. NOTE: You may omit the vodka or rum and add 2½ cups water.

HOT WINE PUNCH

4 cups water
1½ cups sugar
4 cinnamon sticks
12 whole cloves
6 whole allspice
½ teaspoon ginger
2 cups apple cider
1 6-ounce can frozen concentrated orange juice
1 6-ounce can frozen concentrated lemonade
4 cups burgundy wine

Combine water, sugar and spices in saucepan and heat to boiling. Reduce heat and simmer 10 minutes. Strain the orange juice and lemonade into the sugar water. Stir in the cider and wine. Heat through, but do not boil. Serve warm. If not using immediately; you may want to remove the cinnamon sticks, cloves and allspice. NOTE: The sugar may be decreased to ½ cup without changing the flavor. This drink is also good served cold in a tall glass filled with ice.

HAP'S DRINK

2 ounces dry gin, vodka or white rum
2 ounces orange juice
1 ounce apricot brandy
1 ounce pineapple juice
1 ounce grapefruit juice
  Grenadine syrup (a few drops)
  Orange slices
  Maraschino cherries

Combine all ingredients and serve over ice. Garnish with orange slice and cherry.

FANCY FRUIT SLUSH

4 cups water
4 cups sugar
4 cups cold water
¾ cup lemon juice
2 10-ounce packages frozen raspberries, thawed
1 15-ounce can pineapple chunks
20 ounces fresh or frozen blueberries
6 bananas, sliced

Bring first 4 cups of water and sugar to a boil. Boil for 5 minutes. Add cold water, lemon juice, raspberries, pineapple with juice and blueberries. Freeze. To serve, place in punch bowl and let thaw for 1½ hours. Add sliced bananas and serve. You can add rum or vodka.

PEACHIES

4 servings

1 6-ounce can frozen concentrated pink lemonade
1 10-ounce package frozen
   peaches
6 ounces vodka
10 ice cubes

Mix all ingredients in blender until frothy. Keep in freezer until ready to serve.

RASPBERRY COCKTAIL

4 servings

1 10-ounce package frozen
   raspberries, thawed
¼ cup sugar
3 tablespoons lemon juice
2 ounces vodka
   Club soda
   Crushed ice

Mash berries with juice as fine as possible. Place in a cheesecloth bag; set in strainer. Let drain into bowl for several hours. Press bag to remove any remaining juice. Discard bag and pulp. Mix juice with sugar in a saucepan and heat gently for 10 minutes. Remove from heat and stir in lemon juice and vodka. Cool; refrigerate for 1 week. Just before serving, shake well. Pour over crushed ice in 4 glasses and add club soda to taste.

SOUTH SEAS BANANA COOLER

30 servings

3 6-ounce cans frozen concentrated lemonade
3 6-ounce cans frozen concentrated orange juice
14 cans cold water
1 16-ounce package frozen
   strawberries, thawed
10- 12 ripe bananas, mashed
2-3 bottles of dry white
     champagne
   Strawberries
   Pineapple cubes

Combine all ingredients except champagne. Can be done in a blender. Freeze overnight. Take out several hours before serving. Add champagne and stir unil "slush" forms. Serve immediately in stemmed glasses garnished with fresh strawberries and pineapple cubes on picks.

AMARETTO

1½ quarts

2 cups sugar
2 cups water
1 pint brandy
1 pint vodka
4½ teaspoons almond extract

Boil water and sugar together until clear. Cool. Add brandy, vodka and almond extract.

CHERRY LIQUEUR

1½ quarts

3 pounds sour cherries, unpitted
2 pounds sugar
1 quart vodka

Wash cherries and mix with sugar and vodka in a large jug. Stir once daily for 6 weeks. Drain through a cheesecloth and serve as an after-dinner liqueur. NOTE: Save the cherries and use to garnish the drink.

EVER-READY BUTTERED RUM

2 quarts

1 pound brown sugar
1 pound confectioners' sugar
1 pound butter, softened
1 teaspoon cinnamon
1 teaspoon nutmeg
1 quart French vanilla ice cream, softened

Cream sugars and butter. Mix in spices. Mix in softened ice cream and beat on high until blended into a thick batter. To serve, place 2-4 tablespoons of mix in a mug. Add a jigger of dark rum. Fill with boiling water. Stir and serve. Batter can be stored in freezer 8 weeks or in refrigerator 3 weeks. Ready when needed, especially over the holidays.

LUNCHEON SHERRY

8 servings

1 bottle cream sherry
1 6-ounce can frozen concentrated lemonade

In a pitcher, mix cream sherry with lemonade until the lemonade is evenly mixed. Return the mixture to the empty bottle, plus additional container. Serve over crushed ice.

TOM AND JERRY MIX

8 servings

12 eggs, separated
4 cups confectioners' sugar
1 teaspoon vanilla
½ teaspoon nutmeg
½ teaspoon cream of tartar
2 envelopes gelatin

Beat the 12 egg whites until stiff. Add 2 cups of confectioners' sugar, vanilla, ¼ teaspoon nutmeg and ¼ teaspoon cream of tartar. Beat about 5 minutes. Set aside. Beat the egg yolks for 1 minute and add remaining 2 cups confectioners' sugar, ¼ teaspoon nutmeg and ¼ teaspoon cream of tartar. Add the gelatin and beat 5 minutes more. Combine both mixtures and beat another 5 minutes. If not using immediately, refrigerate and rebeat for 5 minutes just before serving. To make a Tom and Jerry drink, add 1 ounce of brandy to 2 ounces of boiling water in a cup. Add 1 large tablespoon of the mix and stir. Add another tablespoon of the mix to float on top. More of the mix may be used if desired. Sprinkle nutmeg on top.

EGGNOG

8 servings

6 eggs, separated
½ cup sugar
1 pint whipping cream
2 cups whole milk
½ cup confectioners' sugar
½ cup brandy
¼ cup Amaretto
1¼ cups rum

Beat egg yolks. Add sugar, cream and milk; set aside. Beat egg whites until stiff. Gradually add confectioners' sugar until stiff peaks form. Set aside. Add liquor to the egg yolk mixture. Fold in ½ of the egg whites until blended. Spread the remaining egg whites over the top and refrigerate for 24 hours.

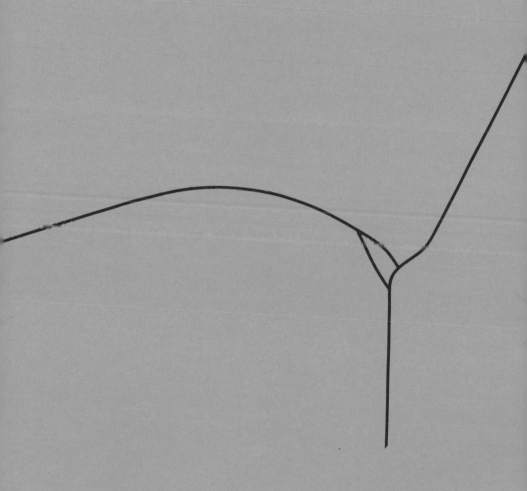

Soups & Sandwiches

SAUSAGE ZUCCHINI SOUP

3½ quarts

1 pound hot Italian sausage
2 cups ½-inch celery pieces
2 pounds zucchini, ½-inch pieces
1 cup chopped onion
2 25-ounce cans tomatoes
2 teaspoons salt
1 teaspoon Italian seasonings
1 teaspoon oregano
1 teaspoon sugar
½ teaspoon basil
¼ teaspoon garlic powder
2 green peppers, ½-inch pieces

Brown sausage and drain fat. Add celery and cook 10 minutes, stirring. Mix in remaining ingredients except green pepper; simmer 20 minutes. Add green peppers and cook covered 20 minutes. NOTE: Best made a day ahead. A hearty meal soup.

CASSOULET

8 servings

6 strips bacon, cut into pieces
1 large green pepper, diced
1 large onion, chopped
2 cups sliced and cooked carrots
2 16-ounce cans whole tomatoes, drained
½ teaspoon salt
½ teaspoon pepper
¼ teaspoon tarragon
¼ teaspoon fennel seeds
½ teaspoon crushed bay leaves
1 cooked chicken, boned
1½ pounds sweet Italian sausage
½ pound cooked ham, cut in chunks
5 cups Navy beans, cooked
½ cup dry sherry

In a large pot or Dutch oven, cook bacon until just crisp. Add pepper and onion. Cook until limp. Add carrots, drained tomatoes and seasonings. Stir well. Add chicken, sausages and ham. Cook for 30 minutes, stirring occasionally. Drain beans and add to pot. Adjust seasoning. Stir well. Bake in 350 degree oven, covered for 1 hour. Add sherry, stir and cook 15 minutes. Can be served now, but is better if reheated the next day. NOTE: May be reheated over a grill or on hot coals. Also, pot may be wrapped in foil and newspapers to keep warm for later use at a picnic. This is an excellent way to use leftover chicken.

SPICY CHILI

6 servings

3 pounds boneless
    chuck, cubed
3 tablespoons flour
2 tablespoons oil
2 garlic cloves, chopped
4 tablespoons chili powder
2 tablespoons cumin
1 tablespoon crumbed leaf
    oregano
2 13¾-ounce cans beef broth
1 teaspoon salt
¼ teaspoon pepper
1 can pinto or kidney beans

Dredge beef in flour and brown in oil. Add remaining ingredients except beans. Bake, covered, in 350 degree oven until tender, about 1 hour. Bake an additional ½ hour uncovered to thicken. Add beans and cook until heated. Serve with dollops of sour cream or with a thin slice of lime. Can also be served on bed of rice.

HAM AND PEA SOUP

8 servings

Ham bone or ham hocks
2 small potatoes, diced
4 carrots, diced
3 onions, diced
1½ pounds split peas
2 cups diced ham
    Salt and pepper

Combine all ingredients except diced ham in a large pot. Add water to cover. Simmer gently, taking care not to scorch, for 2½ to 3 hours. Remove ham bone. Strain through coarse strainer or mash with a potato masher depending on texture desired. Remove meat from ham bone or hock and return to soup. Add the diced ham; salt and pepper to taste. Cook an additional 10 to 15 minutes and serve. If the soup becomes too thick in preparation or reheating, water may be added.

MICROWAVE ORIENTAL SOUP

6 servings

4 cups chicken broth
1 cup roast pork or cooked
    chicken, sliced into very
    thin strips
½ package frozen Chinese pea
    pods
5 waterchestnuts, sliced
5 large mushrooms, sliced
1 teaspoon soy sauce

In a 2-quart casserole, microwave chicken broth on high for 10 minutes or until broth boils. Add sliced meat, pea pods, waterchestnuts, mushrooms, soy sauce and spinach. Microwave on high for 3 to 5 minutes until soup boils again. Stir in lettuce; microwave on 50% power for 2 minutes. Season to taste. Serve immediately with crisp Chinese noodles.

1   **cup finely chopped fresh spinach**
1   **cup shredded lettuce**
    Salt and pepper
    Chinese Noodles

SUPER SUPPER SOUP

6 servings

½ **pound sliced fresh mushrooms**
¼ **pound butter**
4 **tablespoons flour**
¼ **teaspoon white pepper**
3 **teaspoons salt**
1 **quart chicken broth**
2 **cups heavy cream**
2 **cups milk**
2 **cups finely chopped fresh spinach**
3 **cups diced cooked chicken**

Sauté mushrooms in butter until tender. Stir in flour, pepper and salt. Mix well. Add chicken broth, cream and milk. Stir until well-mixed, smooth and hot; do not boil. Remove from heat and add uncooked spinach and chicken. Cover pan and let sit for 45 minutes. Reheat and serve. NOTE: This soup may be made a day ahead up to the point of adding the spinach. When serving the soup, heat it again and add the raw spinach, following the rest of the recipe. Serve with fresh fruit and bread.

RED SNAPPER SOUP

6 servings

1 **1½-pound red snapper**
2½ **cups water**
1 **tablespoon whole pickling spice**
2 **teaspoons salt**
2 **tablespoons butter**
¼ **cup diced onion**
½ **cup diced celery**
½ **cup diced green pepper**
1 **10½-ounce can condensed beef broth**
1 **10½-ounce can condensed tomato soup**
½ **cup sherry**
    Fresh dill

Place whole fish in a large skillet. Add water, pickling spice and salt. Cover and simmer for 10 to 15 minutes or until fish is easily flaked. Strain broth; reserve 2 cups. Melt butter in a large kettle; brown onion, celery and green pepper. Add fish stock and simmer gently until vegetables are tender. Stir in beef broth and tomato soup. Bone and skin fish and break into large chunks. Add fish to soup. Stir in sherry and simmer for 5 minutes. Serve hot, sprinkled with finely chopped fresh dill.

BOUILLABAISSE

10 servings

4 large garlic cloves, peeled and chopped
6 sprigs parsley, chopped
2 teaspoons crushed thyme
2 small bay leaves, crumbled
1 teaspoon allspice
1 tablespoon salt
10 tablespoons vegetable oil
7 large red snapper fillets, skinned
2 cups finely chopped onions
3 14-ounce cans tomatoes plus juice, chopped
5 cups clam juice
½ teaspoon saffron
½ teaspoon cayenne
15 very large scallops, cut Into quarters
20 large shrimp, shelled and deveined
1 bag steamer clams
30 crab legs, enough for 20 4-inch lengths

With mortar and pestle or back of spoon in a bowl, crush garlic cloves, parsley, thyme, bay leaves, allspice and salt; stir in 4 tablespoons oil to make a paste. Cut red snapper fillets in half and spread with garlic paste; reserve. Thaw and thoroughly rinse the other fish and store covered in refrigerator on bed of ice. In heavy 12-inch skillet, heat remaining oil. Add onions and cook for 5 minutes until soft and translucent. Place snapper on top of onions, cover skillet and cook for 5 minutes until fish is firm and opaque. Transfer fillets to plate. Add tomatoes, clam juice, saffron and cayenne to the onion mixture and bring to a high boil. Add 1 fillet, cut in small pieces. Cook until liquid is reduced and thickened. At this point, the stock may be stored for a day in the refrigerator. Add snapper fillets to stock, heat through. Eight minutes before serving, bring stock to a boil. Add scallops, crab legs, clams and shrimp. This version of bouillabaisse is creole and, therefore, quite spicy. For a milder version, cut down on cayenne and garlic. NOTE: This should be served with fluffy white rice. Traditionally, it is spooned directly into the soup. Serve with French bread and salad.

CRAB MUSHROOM BISQUE

4 servings

6   tablespoons butter
4   tablespoons finely chopped
    onion
4   tablespoons finely chopped
    green pepper
1   finely chopped scallion with
    top
2   tablespoons finely chopped
    parsley
1   cup sliced fresh mushrooms
    Dash Tabasco
2   tablespoons butter
2   tablespoons flour
1½ cups milk
1   teaspoon salt
⅛   teaspoon pepper
¼   teaspoon ground mace
1   cup half-and-half
1½ cups cooked crab, drained
3   tablespoons dry sherry

In a medium skillet, melt 4 tablespoons butter; sauté onion, green pepper, scallion, parsley and mushrooms until soft. Set aside. In a large saucepan, heat 2 tablespoons butter. Remove from heat and stir in flour; gradually add milk. Cook until thick and smooth; stirring constantly. Add salt, pepper, mace and Tabasco. Add sautéed vegetables plus half-and-half. Bring to a boil. Stir. Reduce heat and add crab. Simmer uncovered 5 minutes. Before serving, stir in sherry. Serve warm.

OLD FASHIONED BEAN SOUP

6 servings

1   pound Great Northern beans,
    rinsed and picked over
8   cups water
2   tablespoons butter
1   large onion, chopped
2   stalks celery, chopped
1   clove garlic, minced
3   ham hocks
¼   teaspoon pepper

In a kettle, bring beans and water to a boil. Boil 2 minutes; cover, turn off heat and let stand 1 hour. In a skillet, melt 2 tablespoons butter and sauté onion, celery and garlic until lightly browned. Add vegetables and ham hocks to beans. Cover and simmer 2 hours until beans are very tender. Remove ham hocks from pan and cut off meat. Slightly mash some of beans with a potato masher. Add ham and reheat.

FRENCH MUSHROOM AND LENTIL SOUP — 8 servings

1   cup dry lentils
3   cups water
12 ounces fresh mushrooms
2   tablespoons butter or
     margarine
4   cups chicken broth
1¼ teaspoons salt
½ teaspoon crushed marjoram
¼ teaspoon crushed thyme
1   cup thinly sliced carrots
2   cups half-and-half
¼ cup flour
2   tablespoons dry sherry
1   teaspoon Worcestershire

Place lentils in large saucepan; cover with about 3 cups of water. Bring to a boil; remove from heat, cover and let stand for 1 hour, adding more water if needed. Rinse, pat dry and slice mushrooms. Melt butter in a large skillet. Add mushrooms and sauté until tender, about 5 minutes. Set aside. Drain lentils and return to saucepan. Add chicken broth, salt, marjoram and thyme. Bring to a boil; reduce heat and simmer, covered, until lentils are almost tender, about 10 minutes. Add carrots and reserved mushrooms. Simmer, covered, until vegetables are tender, about 5 minutes. Mix a small amount of cream with the flour; blend in the rest of the cream, sherry and Worcestershire sauce. Add cream mixture to soup, mixing well. Cook, stirring until thickened, about 3 minutes.

BLACK BEAN SOUP — 8 servings

2   cups black beans, washed
8   cups hot water
2   tablespoons salt
1   large onion, minced
1   cup minced green pepper
¾ cup minced celery
¾ cup minced carrots
6   tablespoons olive oil
5   garlic cloves, minced
½ tablespoon cumin
1   tablespoon white vinegar
1   large onion, minced
3   hard-boiled eggs, sieved

Simmer beans in water with 2 tablespoons salt until soft. Sauté onion, green pepper, celery and carrots in oil until onions are brown. Add garlic, cumin and vinegar. Cook and stir 3 minutes. Drain a little water from beans and add to vegetables. Cover and cook slowly for 30 minutes. Combine vegetable mixture with beans, adding more water if needed. Adjust seasonings with salt and pepper. Serve with bowls of onion and egg for garnish. Can be served over rice.

MINESTRONE

3 tablespoons olive oil
2 onions, chopped
4 quarts meat stock or
   bouillion
3 celery stalks with leaves,
   diced
¼ pound spinach, chopped,
   cooked and drained
1 tablespoon minced parsley
3 fresh carrots, sliced
¼ boiled cabbage, drained
   and chopped
1 can garbanzos (chick peas)
1 potato, diced
1 green pepper, chopped
1 cup frozen peas
1 6-ounce can tomato paste
   Salt and pepper to taste
   Oregano, garlic powder, basil
   and crushed red pepper to
   taste
½ pound ditali or other small
   Italian pasta

Sauté onions in oil until light yellow and soft. Add soup stock and bring to boil. Add celery, spinach, parsley, carrots, cabbage, garbanzos, potato, peas, green pepper, tomato paste and seasonings. Cover pot and simmer 20 minutes. Add more stock if soup gets too thick. Add pasta and continue cooking until vegetables and pasta are cooked (30 to 60 minutes). Stir occasionally. Serve hot with garnish.

Garnish
1 teaspoon dried basil
1 tablespoon finely chopped
   fresh parsley
½ teaspoon finely chopped
   garlic
½ cup Parmesan cheese

Combine all ingredients and serve with hot soup.

CREAMY MUSHROOM-TOMATO BISQUE   10 servings

1	pound fresh mushrooms, cleaned and sliced
8	tablespoons butter or margarine
1	10¾-ounce can chicken broth
2½	pounds fresh tomatoes, skinned and sliced
1	medium yellow onion, minced
2½	tablespoons sugar
1	clove garlic, crushed
½	teaspoon white pepper
1	teaspoon thyme
1	teaspoon tarragon
1	teaspoon oregano
4	tablespoons flour
2	cups heavy cream
3	teaspoons salt
	Pinch baking soda
1	cup milk

Sauté mushrooms in 4 tablespoons butter or margarine in a large pot for 5 to 6 minutes until golden brown. Add broth, cover and simmer for 15 to 20 minutes. Cool. Put in blender or food processor and purée; set aside. Put tomatoes, onion, sugar, garlic, pepper, thyme, tarragon and oregano in same pot; cover and simmer for ½ to ¾ hour. Purée half the tomato mixture. If desired, strain through a fine sieve. Set aside with mushroom mixture. Melt remaining butter in pot, blend in flour; add cream and cook over medium heat until smooth and thickened. Add mushroom and tomato purées, tomatoes, salt, soda and milk. Heat, stirring, until soup is heated through, about 5 to 10 minutes.

CREAM OF CAULIFLOWER SOUP   8 servings

2	tablespoons shortening
½	cup chopped onion
1	peeled and grated carrot
1	cup chopped celery
1	pound cauliflower, cut in florets
2	tablespoons parsley
8	cups chicken stock
	Bouquet garni of 1 bay leaf, ½ teaspoon peppercorns and 1 teaspoon tarragon, tied in bag
4	tablespoons butter
¾	cup flour
1	tablespoon salt
2	cups milk
1	cup half-and-half
1	cup sour cream

Heat shortening in 8 quart pot. Sauté onion until transparent. Add carrots and celery and cook 2 minutes, stirring frequently. Add cauliflower and 1 tablespoon parsley. Cover and simmer 15 minutes, stirring occasionally. Add chicken stock and Bouquet garni. Cover and simmer 5 minutes. In a saucepan, melt butter; stir in flour and salt. Blend in milk and cook until thickened. Stir in half-and-half. Pour cream sauce into vegetable mixture. Simmer uncovered for 20 minutes. Before serving remove Bouquet garni. Stir in sour cream and remaining tablespoon parsley. Heat and serve.

SWISS BROCCOLI CHOWDER
4 servings

2 tablespoons minced onion
3 tablespoons butter
3 tablespoons flour
1½ teaspoons salt
2 cups milk
3 cups chicken stock
1 10-ounce package frozen
   chopped broccoli
2 cups thinly sliced carrots
   Pepper
1 cup sour cream, room
   temperature
6 ounces Swiss cheese, diced

In a large saucepan, sauté onion in butter until tender. Stir in flour and salt. Gradually add milk, stirring until it boils. Warm chicken stock and add to mixture along with broccoli and carrots. Cook over very low heat, stirring occasionally until carrots are tender, about 40 minutes. Add pepper. Stir in sour cream and cheese. Heat until cheese melts; do not boil. Makes about two quarts. This soup freezes well.

BLENDER CREAM SOUP
2 servings

2 cups milk
2 tablespoons flour
2 tablespoons butter
1 teaspoon salt
⅛ teaspoon pepper
1 thin slice of onion
1 tablespoon chopped parsley
¼ cup chopped celery
   Raw, canned or cooked
   vegetables, cut into small
   pieces

Mix all ingredients in blender container and blend until smooth. Heat over low heat, stirring occasionally until mixture boils. If cooked leftover food is used, season after blending. Frozen vegetables do not have to be defrosted before blending. Delicious way to use leftover vegetables.

POTATO SOUP
4 servings

2 cups peeled and diced
   potatoes
¼ cup chopped celery
1 cup chopped onion
1 chicken bouillon cube
1½ cups boiling water
2 cups sour cream with chives
   Salt and pepper to taste
1½ tablespoons minced parsley

Combine potatoes, celery and onion in a saucepan. Dissolve chicken bouillon cube in boiling water. Add bouillon to vegetables. Simmer for 20 minutes or until vegetables are tender. Add sour cream with chives, salt, pepper and parsley. Simmer 5 minutes.

CHEESE SOUP

10 servings

3 green onions, chopped
3 stalks of celery, chopped
2 carrots, grated
3 tablespoons butter, melted
2 10¾-ounce cans chicken
   broth
3 10¾-ounce cans cream of
   potato soup
8 ounces Colby cheese, grated
6 ounces sour cream
   Tabasco
3 tablespoons dry sherry

Sauté green onions, celery and carrots in melted butter. Add the chicken broth and simmer, covered, for 30 minutes. Add potato soup, Colby cheese and a few drops of Tabasco. Mix well and simmer over low heat. Add sour cream and simmer for 15 minutes. Just before serving, stir in sherry.

LEMON SOUP

8 servings

⅓ cup uncooked rice
6 cups chicken broth
2 eggs
½ cup fresh lemon juice
   Salt and pepper to taste

Boil rice in broth for 15 minutes. Beat eggs until lemon colored. Add the lemon juice to ½ cup of the boiling broth. Add the lemon broth slowly to eggs, beating constantly. Stir this mixture into the hot rice broth. Serve hot or cold. Refreshing served cold in the summertime as an appetizer.

CURRY CONSOMMÉ

6 servings

2 10½-ounce cans beef consommé,
   with gelatin added
1 8-ounce package cream
   cheese
1 teaspoon curry powder
   Chives or shallots, chopped
   for garnish

Have all ingredients at room temperature. Blend 1 can consomme with the cream cheese and curry powder in a food processor or blender. Pour into serving cups. Refrigerate. When firm, spoon second can of consommé on top of mixture in cups. Refrigerate several hours. Top with chopped chives or shallots. Serve with rye wafers as an appetizer or as a first course with dinner.

GAZPACHO

6 servings

2 tomatoes, peeled and chopped
1 cucumber, seeded and chopped
½ cup diced celery
¼ cup diced onion
½ cup chopped green pepper
2 teaspoons snipped chives
1 teaspoon chopped parsley
1 small garlic clove, minced
3 tablespoons red wine vinegar
2 tablespoons olive oil
1 teaspoon Worcestershire
1 teaspoon salt
¼ teaspoon pepper
Dash Tabasco (optional)
2 cups tomato juice
Sour Cream
Croutons

Process vegetables as indicated. Combine all ingredients. Cover and chill thoroughly. Serve with a dollop of sour cream and croutons.

CHILLED CUCUMBER SOUP

8 servings

¼ medium onion, chopped
1 medium cucumber, peeled and cubed
¾ cup chicken broth
1 10¾-ounce can cream of chicken soup
1 cup sour cream
6 dashes Tabasco
6 dashes Worcestershire
¼ teaspoon celery salt
¼ teaspoon curry powder

Combine all ingredients in order given. Purée in blender or food processor until liquid. Refrigerate until serving time.

COLD SOUR CHERRY SOUP

8 servings

3 cups cold water
1 cup sugar
1 cinnamon stick
4 cups drained canned sour
    cherries or fresh cherries,
    pitted
1 tablespoon arrowroot
¼ cup heavy cream, chilled
¾ cup dry red wine, chilled

In large 2-quart saucepan, combine water, sugar and cinnamon stick. Bring to a boil and add the cherries. Partially cover and simmer over low heat. Fresh cherries take 35-40 minutes. Canned cherries take only about 10 minutes. Remove cinnamon stick. Mix arrowroot and 2 tablespoons cold water into a paste. Beat mixture into cherry soup. Stirring constantly, bring soup almost to a boil. Reduce heat and simmer 2 minutes until clear and slightly thickened. Chill. Before serving, stir in the cream and wine. Serve in cantaloupe or honeydew melon halves.

VAL'S PIZZA

6 servings

DOUGH
7 ounces warm water
1 package active dry yeast
1½ teaspoons sugar
3 tablespoons olive oil
1½ teaspoons salt
3 cups flour

SAUCE
1 8-ounce can tomato sauce
1 6-ounce can tomato paste
1 garlic clove, crushed
1 bay leaf
¼ teaspoon each oregano,
    rosemary, caraway seed and
    thyme

TOPPING
½ pound Mozzarella cheese,
    grated
½ pound Monterey Jack
    cheese, grated
    Hamburger, pepperoni,
    sausage or any other meat

Mix ingredients for dough. Knead; let rise 1 to 2 hours in an oiled bowl until doubled in bulk. Divide dough in ½ and roll out 2 12-inch rounds. Place on greased cookie sheets or pizza pans. Combine ingredients for sauce in a saucepan and mix. Simmer 30 minutes. Mix the grated cheeses together. Divide sauce and place on dough rounds. Put choice of meat on top and cover with cheese. Bake at 450 degrees for 12 to 15 minutes.

CANADIAN BACON SANDWICHES

4 servings

4 bagels, halved horizontally
2 tablespoons butter or margarine, softened
1½ cups sliced fresh mushrooms
2 tablespoons chopped onion
1 tablespoon butter or margarine
12 slices Canadian bacon, ⅛-inch thick
4 slices American cheese
4 thin green pepper rings (optional)

Spread cut surfaces of bagels with softened butter. In a skillet, sauté mushrooms and onions in the remaining 1 tablespoon butter until tender but not brown. Slash edges of bacon. Place 3 slices of bacon on each of 4 bagel halves. Top each with ¼ of the mushroom mixture. Place on broiler pan. Broil 5 inches from heat, 3 to 4 minutes, until bacon is crisp around the edges. Place a cheese slice and pepper ring atop the remaining bagel halves. Sprinkle with paprika if desired. Broil 2 minutes or until cheese melts. Serve as open-face sandwiches.

LEBANESE MEAT PIES

8 servings

2 loaves frozen bread dough
2 10-ounce packages frozen, chopped spinach
1 pound ground lamb or beef
1½ teaspoons salt
⅓ cup diced onion
Pinch cinnamon
Pinch pepper
4 tablespoons chopped parsley
5 tablespoons lemon juice
Nutmeg
Butter

Thaw dough overnight in the refrigerator. Cook spinach and squeeze out all liquid. Mix spinach with meat, onions, lemon juice and spices. Cut each loaf of dough into 8 pieces and roll pieces into triangles with 4-inch sides. Spoon 2 tablespoons filling into center of each. Fold corners to center and pinch together. Place on cookie sheet; cover and let rise 45 minutes in a warm place. Bake 25 minutes at 350 degrees. Brush with butter while still warm. Serve hot. NOTE: May be made ahead and chilled on cookie sheets until ready to rise. Remove from refrigerator 1½ hours before baking.

SPECIALTY BURGERS

8 servings

2 pounds ground beef chuck
3 pounds ground round steak
2 tablespoons Accent
2 teaspoons seasoned salt
½ teaspoon pepper
¾ cup herb stuffing mix
⅓ cup half-and-half (or milk)
⅓ cup finely cut celery
½ cup sour cream
1 10½-ounce can onion soup
Barbecue sauce
Sandwich buns

Mix meat with seasonings. Add stuffing mix, half-and-half, celery, sour cream and soup. Grill, basting with favorite barbecue sauce. Serve on buns. This can also be formed into a meat loaf, covered with barbecue sauce and baked at 350 degrees for 1 hour.

SLOPPY JOE PITAS

8 servings

1 pound ground beef
½ cup chopped onion
½ cup chopped celery
1 cup tomato sauce
½ cup ketchup
1 tablespoon brown sugar
1 tablespoon vinegar
1 tablespoon Worcestershire
1 teaspoon dry mustard
¼ teaspoon salt
⅛ teaspoon pepper
4 6-inch Pita (pocket) bread
   rounds
Grated Monterey Jack
   cheese
Lettuce, shredded
Pickle slices
Tomato slices

Combine ground beef, onion and celery in a skillet. Cook until meat is brown. Drain well. Add the rest of the ingredients except bread. Bring to a boil and cover. Reduce heat and simmer 15 to 20 minutes. Stir occasionally. Cut pita bread rounds in half. Fill pockets with meat mixture, grated cheese, lettuce, pickles and tomatoes.

MICROWAVE CHEESEBURGERS

12 servings

2 pounds ground beef
1½ pounds Velveeta cheese
1 large onion, chopped
1 cup black olives,
    chopped (optional)
  Seasonings to taste
  Hamburger buns

Brown meat and drain. Add cheese, onions and olives. Stir until the cheese melts. Add seasoning. Let cool slightly. Spread between hamburger buns. Wrap each burger in plastic wrap and freeze. Do not thaw to serve. Place directly in microwave and cook on high for 45 to 60 seconds. These will be very hot to handle. Toppings can be added after cooking.

POCKET SANDWICH

6 servings

4 Pita bread (pockets)
    sliced in half
8 ounces shredded ham
8 ounces shredded turkey
8 pieces bacon, fried
4 ounces fresh bean sprouts
8 ounces grated Cheddar
    cheese
1 avocado, thinly sliced
8 black olives, sliced
1 tomato, thinly sliced
  Thousand Island dressing

Slice the Pita bread in ½ and layer the filling ingredients into pockets. Divide amounts evenly to stuff all eight halves. Spoon Thousand Island dressing into each in desired amount; wrap in foil and heat at 350 degrees for 8 to 10 minutes or until cheese melts. Serve with fresh fruit.

SPICY CORN DOGS

10 servings

1 cup biscuit mix
2 tablespoons yellow cornmeal
⅛ teaspoon dry mustard
¼ teaspoon paprika
⅛ teaspoon cayenne pepper
¼ teaspoon seasoned salt
1 egg
⅓ cup milk
10 hot dogs
  Oil
  Wooden skewers (optional)

In medium bowl, combine biscuit mix, cornmeal, seasonings, egg and milk. Blend until smooth. Heat oil to 375 degrees in deep fat fryer. Dip hot dogs into batter. Let the excess drip off. Fry in oil until golden brown. Drain. Insert a wooden skewer into each corn dog for ease in handling. Serve hot. May be made ahead and refrigerated or frozen. Reheat in 300 degree oven until warmed through.

CHILI BEEF

12 servings

1 16-ounce can whole
   tomatoes
1 large onion, chopped
1 cup chopped celery
1 tablespoon hot salsa
1 4-ounce can green
   chilies
1 teaspoon ground pepper
¾ teaspoon garlic salt
½ teaspoon salt
1 5-pound boneless beef
   chuck roast
   Onion rolls

Combine all ingredients and use to marinate roast in refrigerator overnight. Bake covered at 275 degrees 8 to 12 hours. When finished, shred and serve on onion rolls. Serves 25 on cocktail buns as an appetizer.

SAVORY CHICKEN PINWHEELS

4 sandwiches

1 3-ounce package cream
   cheese, softened
3 tablespoons margarine,
   melted
⅓ cup cream of chicken soup
2 cups cooked cubed chicken or
   1 5-ounce can boned
   chicken
¼ teaspoon salt
⅛ teaspoon pepper
2 tablespoons milk
1 tablespoon chopped chives or
   onion
1 tablespoon chopped pimiento
1 8-ounce can refrigerated
   crescent dinner rolls
¾ cup seasoned croutons,
   crushed

In medium bowl, blend cream cheese, 2 tablespoons margarine (reserve 1 tablespoon) and soup until smooth. Add chicken soup, milk, chives, pimiento and seasonings; mix well. Separate dough into 4 rectangles; firmly press perforations to seal. Spoon ½ cup meat mixture onto center of each rectangle. Gently pull four corners of the dough to top center of chicken mixture; twist slightly and seal edges well. Brush tops with reserved tablespoon of margarine and dip in crouton crumbs. Place on ungreased cookie sheet. Bake at 350 degrees for 20 to 25 minutes.

CHICKEN SUPPER SANDWICHES
4 servings

2 chicken breasts, boned
Salt and pepper
Flour
1 tablespoon butter
1 tablespoon oil
1 onion, sliced
½ cup chopped green pepper
4 tablespoons butter
1 teaspoon Italian seasoning
4 Italian sandwich rolls, split
Sliced tomato
4 slices Mozzarella cheese

Pound chicken breasts until ¼-inch thick. Cut each breast in half. Season with salt and pepper and dust with flour. Sauté quickly in a mixture of butter and oil. Remove chicken from pan when browned and cooked through. Add onion and green pepper; cook until heated. Spread rolls with butter mixed with Italian seasoning. Top with chicken; add a layer of sautéed vegetables. Add tomato slices and top with slice of cheese. Run under a preheated broiler until cheese melts. Serve hot.

CRABBY BUNS
8 servings

1 6½-ounce can crab, flaked
1 cup ripe olives, chopped
1¼ cups diced Swiss cheese
1 tablespoon sliced green olives
¼ cup mayonnaise
1 tablespoon lemon juice
Salt and pepper to taste
8 English muffins, rusks,
or hamburger buns

Combine crab, olives, cheese and onion. Add mayonnaise, lemon juice and seasonings. Pile on muffins or buns. Bake in a preheated 400 degree oven 15 to 20 minutes, until lightly browned.

CUCUMBER-SHRIMP SPREAD
4 servings

1 medium cucumber, skinned,
seeded and chopped
2 tablespoons chopped onion
1 4¼-ounce can small shrimp or
8-ounces small frozen
shrimp
1 8-ounce package cream
cheese, softened
1 tablespoon sour cream

Mix cucumber, onion, shrimp, cream cheese and sour cream. Chill. Before serving, remove from refrigerator and let stand at room temperature for 10 minutes. Spread on slices of rye bread for an open-face sandwich.

VEGGIE MELT

1 serving

2 slices whole wheat bread
1 slice of cheese
     (American, Cheddar,
     Monterey Jack or
     your choice)
     Avocado slices
     Tomato slices
     Mushrooms, raw or sauteed
     Lettuce
     Alfalfa sprouts
     Horseradish

Toast bread. Grill cheese on one slice of the bread. Pile on slices of avocado, tomato and mushrooms. Top with lettuce and alfalfa sprouts. Spread the other piece of bread with horseradish. NOTE: For a heartier sandwich, you can add slices of turkey, chicken or ham.

BROILED CHEESE SANDWICH

10 servings

1 pound Cheddar cheese,
     grated
4 hard-boiled eggs, chopped
1 small can chopped black
     olives
1 4-ounce can chopped green
     chilies
1 8-ounce can tomato sauce
2 tablespoons vinegar
6 green onions, chopped
½ cup oil (optional)
10 English muffins, split

Mix together all ingredients except oil. Add enough oil to hold mixture together. Toast English muffins slightly under a broiler. Spread cheese mixture on muffins and broil until bubbly.

STUFFED FRENCH BREAD

10 servings

1 20-inch loaf crusty
     French bread, cut in
     4 pieces
½ cup mayonnaise
½ cup chopped parsley
2 8-ounce packages cream
     cheese, softened
1 ¾-ounce package
     Italian salad
     dressing mix
1 4-ounce jar pimiento,
     drained and chopped

Hollow out bread pieces, leaving ½-inch thick wall. Spread the interior with ¼ of the mayonnaise; sprinkle with ¼ of the parsley. Combine remaining ingredients. Pack mixture into bread. Wrap and chill several hours. Cut into ½-inch slices.

Breads

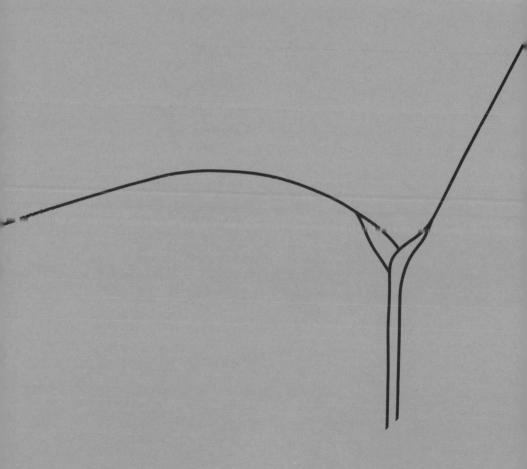

PROCESSOR ITALIAN BREAD

1 loaf

3¼ cups white flour
1 tablespoon sugar
1 teaspoon salt
1 tablespoon butter
1 package active dry yeast
1 cup plus 2 tablespoons very
    warm water (120 degrees)
    Cornmeal
    Vegetable oil
1 egg white, room temperature
1 tablespoon water

Using metal blade (or bread blade) add 2 cups flour, sugar, salt, butter and yeast to work bowl. Process until butter is cut into dry ingredients. Add ½ cup water and pulse 4 times. Add 1 cup flour and remaining water. Pulse 4 times; process until ball of dough forms. If dough is too sticky, add remaining flour 1 tablespoon at a time. When proper consistency, let processor run 40 to 60 seconds to knead dough. Cover bowl and let rest for 20 minutes. Roll dough into 10 x 15-inch oblong. Beginning at wide end, roll tightly. Place on greased baking sheet sprinkled with cornmeal. Rub with vegetable oil. Cover loosely with plastic wrap and refrigerate 2 to 24 hours. When ready to bake, remove plastic wrap and let stand at room temperature 10 minutes. Make 3 to 4 cuts on top of loaf. Bake at 425 degrees for 20 minutes. Remove bread from oven and brush with mixture of egg white and water. Bake 5 to 10 minutes longer or until golden brown.

FRENCH BREAD

1 loaf

1 package active dry yeast
1¼ cups warm water
1½ teaspoons salt
1 tablespoon sugar
1 tablespoon salad oil
3½ cups flour
1 egg white

Mix yeast in warm water until dissolved. Add salt, sugar, salad oil and flour; mix well. Knead for 1 minute and cover with a towel. Knead again for 1 minute every 10 minutes for the next hour. Roll out to ½-inch thickness. Roll dough into a log shape. Place on cookie sheet and let rise again for 30 minutes. Brush top with egg white. Bake 30 minutes at 350 degrees.

PUMPERNICKEL BREAD

3 large loaves

9 cups unsifted flour
3 cups unsifted rye flour
2 tablespoons salt
1 cup whole bran cereal
¾ cup yellow cornmeal
2 packages active dry yeast
3½ cups water
¼ cup molasses
2 ounces unsweetened
   chocolate
1 tablespoon butter or
   margarine
2 cups mashed potatoes
2 teaspoons caraway seeds

Combine white and rye flours. In a large bowl, thoroughly mix 2 cups flour mixture, salt, cereal, cornmeal and undissolved dry yeast. Combine water, molasses, chocolate and butter in saucepan. Heat over low heat until liquids are very warm, 120 to 130 degrees. Butter and chocolate do not need to melt. Gradually add to dry ingredients and beat 2 minutes at medium speed. Add potatoes and 1 cup flour mixture. Beat at high speed for 2 minutes. Stir in caraway and enough of the remaining flour mixture to make a soft dough. Turn out onto lightly floured board. Cover and let rest for 15 minutes. Knead until smooth and elastic, about 15 minutes. More flour may be added, if necessary. Place in greased bowl, turning once. Cover. Let rise in warm place until doubled in bulk, about 1 hour. Punch dough down; let rise again for 30 minutes. Punch dough down. Turn out onto lightly floured board. Divide into 3 equal parts. Shape into round balls. Place in 3 greased 9-inch round pans. Cover. Let rise in warm place until doubled in bulk. Bake at 350 degrees about 50 minutes. Remove from pan and cool on wire racks. NOTE: Food processor may be used to knead this dough. Some additional kneading by hand may still be necessary.

OATMEAL BREAD

3 small loaves

2 cups quick cooking oatmeal
¼ cup light brown sugar
1 tablespoon salt
½ cup evaporated milk
2 tablespoons shortening
1½ cups boiling water
1 package active dry yeast
1 teaspoon sugar
½ cup warm water (110 degrees)
5 cups flour

In a large bowl, combine the oatmeal, brown sugar, salt, milk and shortening. Pour boiling water over mixture and cool to lukewarm. Dissolve yeast and sugar in warm water and let rest to proof. Add yeast mixture to oatmeal mixture. Gradually add 4 to 5 cups flour. On a floured board, knead dough until smooth and elastic. Set in a greased bowl; cover and let rise

1 hour. Divide dough into 3 parts. Set each part in a greased 1-pound coffee can. Put lids on cans and allow dough to rise 45 minutes. Remove lids and bake at 350 degrees for 45 to 55 minutes. Cool and cut in slices. Great toasted.

SWEDISH RYE

3 loaves

1½ cups rye flour
½ cup sugar
1 teaspoon salt
2 cups boiling water
3 tablespoons margarine, softened
1 package active dry yeast
¼ cup lukewarm water
½ teaspoon sugar
½ cup molasses
1½ teaspoons anise seed
5 cups white flour
 Vegetable shortening
 Vegetable oil

Combine rye, sugar, salt and boiling water. Stir in margarine; set aside. In another bowl combine yeast, lukewarm water and sugar; set aside. To first mixture, add molasses and anise seed. Add yeast mixture. Stir in 4 to 5 cups white flour; knead in the last cup to make a stiff dough. Let rise for 2 hours until double in bulk. Grease 3 loaf pans with solid shortening. Punch and work dough; divide into thirds. Place in greased pans and let rise again, 30 to 45 minutes. Bake at 350 degrees for 35 to 40 minutes. Brush each loaf with oil after removing from oven.

THREE FLOUR BREAD

2 loaves

2 packages active dry yeast
1 cup flour
1½ cups whole wheat flour
½ cup rye flour
2 cups milk
½ cup brown sugar
3 tablespoons vegetable shortening
2 tablespoons sugar
1 teaspoon salt
2½ cups flour

Combine yeast with 1 cup white, whole wheat and rye flours. Heat together milk, brown sugar, shortening, sugar and salt. Add liquid to dry mixture. Beat at low speed ½ minute, then at high speed 3 minutes. Stir in 2¼ to 2½ cups white flour, just enough to make a moderately stiff dough. Turn onto floured surface and knead 8 to 10 minutes. Place in greased bowl, turning once. Cover and let rise until doubled, about 1½ hours. Punch down and let rest 10 minutes. Shape into 2 loaves and place in greased pans. Let rise 45 to 60 minutes. Bake at 375 degrees for 40 minutes.

BEST BREAD IN THE WORLD

2 loaves

2 cups boiling water
1 cup uncooked oatmeal
1 tablespoon salt
½ cup honey
2 tablespoons butter, melted
2 packages active dry yeast
⅓ cup warm water
2½ cups unbleached white flour
2½ cups whole wheat flour
1 egg yolk, slightly beaten
Sesame seeds

Pour boiling water over oats. Add salt, honey and butter. Cool to lukewarm. Add yeast to water and mix until dissolved. Add to oat mixture and mix well. Gradually add flours. Knead about 10 minutes. Cover and let rise 1 hour. Divide dough in half, knead briefly and shape into loaves. Let rise in greased loaf pans until dough is barely over top. Brush with egg yolk and sprinkle with sesame seeds. Bake at 350 degrees for 35 to 40 minutes.

HONEY WHOLE WHEAT

1 loaf

1 cup milk
¾ cup shortening
½ cup honey
2 teaspoons salt
¾ cup warm water
2 packages active dry yeast
3 eggs
4½ cups unsifted flour
1½ cups whole wheat flour
1 teaspoon butter, softened

Scald milk. Remove from heat and add shortening, honey and salt. Stir until melted; cool to lukewarm. Sprinkle yeast over warm water in large bowl; stir until dissolved. Stir in milk mixture and eggs. Combine flours and add ⅔ of flour mixture to yeast mixture; beat at low speed until blended. Beat at medium speed until smooth. With wooden spoon, beat in remaining flour. Mix with hands, squeezing dough between fingers to develop gluten. Cover with waxed paper and a towel. Let rise until double. Punch down; beat with a spoon until smooth. Turn into lightly greased 3-quart round casserole. Pat evenly and cover. Let rise until doubled. Cut a 4-inch cross in top of dough with a very sharp knife or razor blade. Bake at 375 degrees for 40 to 50 minutes. Butter top of bread while hot. Cut in wedges with a sharp knife to serve. This is a rough-textured bread.

ENGLISH MUFFIN LOAF

2 loaves

2 packages active dry yeast
6 cups unbleached white flour
1 tablespoon sugar
½ teaspoon baking soda
2 teaspoons salt
½ cup water
2 cups milk
  Cornmeal

Combine 3 cups flour, yeast, sugar, salt and soda. Heat water and milk until very warm, 120 to 130 degrees. Add to dry mixture. Beat well. Stir in remaining flour to make a stiff batter. Spoon into 2 loaf pans, greased and sprinkled with cornmeal. Sprinkle tops with cornmeal. Cover and let rise in warm place for 45 minutes. Bake at 400 degrees for 25 minutes. Remove from pans immediately and cool. NOTE: To prepare in a microwave, reduce flour by ½ cup in second step. Mix and let rise in glass loaf pans as directed. Microwave each loaf on high power for 6½ minutes. Surface of loaf will be flat and pale. Allow to rest for 5 minutes before removing from pans. Slice and toast.

ENGLISH MUFFINS

2 dozen

1 package active dry yeast
¼ cup warm water
1¼ cups milk, scalded
3 tablespoons sugar
1½ teaspoons salt
1 egg, slightly beaten
¾ cup cornmeal
3 tablespoons butter
4 cups flour

Soften yeast in water. Pour milk over sugar, salt and butter; cool to lukewarm. Beat in egg and 1 cup flour. Add softened yeast and cornmeal. Stir in enough remaining flour to make soft dough. Turn out on lightly floured board and knead until smooth, about 10 minutes. Gather dough into a ball; place in a greased bowl and cover with plastic wrap and a towel. Let rise in a warm place until double, about 1 hour. Punch down and roll to ¼-inch thickness on a board heavily sprinkled with cornmeal. Cut with 3-inch round cutter and place on waxed paper sprinkled with cornmeal. Cover and let rise about 45 minutes. Heat lightly greased griddle to 325 degrees. Place muffins, cornmeal-side down, on griddle and cook about 8 minutes until golden. Turn and cook the other side.

PRETZELS

1 **package active dry yeast**
1 **tablespoon sugar**
1½ **cups warm water**
   (115 degrees)
1 **teaspoon salt**
5 **cups flour**
4 **cups grated Cheddar cheese**
1 **egg**
   Coarse salt (optional)

Dissolve yeast and sugar in water. Combine salt, 4 cups flour and cheese. Stir in yeast mixture and add more flour, if necessary, to form a stiff dough. Knead 5 to 10 minutes until smooth. Break off small pieces of dough and shape. Traditional pretzel shapes are made by rolling the dough between hands and a floured table top to form a long rope. Loop rope, twist the middle a couple of turns, then spread the ends and press them against the looped part. Place pretzels on ungreased pans, leaving room between them for expansion. Brush each with beaten egg and sprinkle very lightly with coarse salt. Bake at 425 degrees for 15 to 18 minutes, or until golden brown.

APPLE-PRUNE BREAKFAST RING

10 servings

¾ **cup lukewarm milk**
¼ **cup sugar**
1 **teaspoon salt**
1 **package active dry yeast**
¼ **cup warm water (110 degrees)**
1 **egg, slightly beaten**
¼ **cup melted shortening**
3½ **cups sifted flour**
2 **tablespoons butter, melted**
¾ **cup dried, pitted, chopped**
   prunes, or whole raisins
1½ **cups Golden Delicious apples,**
   peeled and diced
½ **cup light brown sugar**
1 **teaspoon cinnamon**
1 **tablespoon lemon juice**
¾ **cup chopped walnuts**
   (optional)
   Confectioner's sugar icing

In a large bowl, combine milk, sugar and salt. Dissolve yeast in warm water; stir into milk mixture. Blend in egg and shortening. Stir in just enough flour to make a soft dough. Knead on floured surface about 5 minutes, until soft and elastic. Place dough in greased bowl. Cover and let rise in a warm place until double in bulk, 1½ to 2 hours. Punch down; let rise 30 to 45 minutes until doubled again. On a floured surface, roll out dough to 9x18-inch rectangle. Spread with melted butter. Combine prunes, apples, brown sugar, cinnamon, lemon juice and walnuts. Spread over dough. Roll up from long side and seal edges. Place on greased baking sheet, seam-side down, and form into a circle. Seal ends together. With sharp knife slash part way into the ring from the outer edge at 1 inch intervals. Turn each section slightly to the side. Cover and let rise until double, about 1 hour. Bake at 375 degrees for 25 to 35 minutes. Frost with confectioners' sugar icing.

KOLACHES

2½ dozen

½ cup sugar
½ cup butter
1 teaspoon salt
2 eggs
¾ cup warm water
2 packages active dry yeast
4 cups flour
1 12-ounce can filling (poppy apricot, almond, prune, etc.)

Cream together butter, sugar, salt and eggs. Dissolve yeast in water; add butter mixture and 1½ cups flour. Beat well. Stir in remaining flour; let rise until double in size, about 1½ hours. Roll ½ inch thick and cut into 4-inch squares. Place on greased cookie sheet. Make deep depression in center of each square and fill with 1 tablespoon filling. Bring 4 corners to center and pinch together. Cover and let rise about 30 minutes or until light. Bake at 375 degrees for 15 to 18 minutes. Brush with melted butter; dust with powdered sugar.

CINNAMON TWISTS

2 dozen

½ cup milk, scalded
½ cup butter
3 tablespoons sugar
1½ teaspoons salt
1 teaspoon vanilla
2 packages active dry yeast
½ cup very warm water
3 cups flour
3 eggs
¾ cup chopped pecans
¾ cup sugar
2 teaspoons cinnamon

Combine scalded milk, butter, sugar, salt and vanilla. Let cool slightly. Soften yeast in warm water. Add to milk mixture. Blend in 1½ cups flour; beat until smooth. Cover and allow to rest 15 minutes. Uncover and add eggs, one at a time, beating well after each addition. Blend in 1½ cups flour. Dough will be sticky. Cover and let rise in warm place until double. Mix pecans, sugar and cinnamon in a small bowl. Oil hands lightly to handle dough. To form rolls, drop dough from tablespoon into sugar mixture. Coat well. Twist and turn dough to form a log. Place rolls, touching, in a greased 9x13-inch pan. Cover and let rise 20 minutes. Bake at 350 degrees for 15 to 20 minutes.

PECAN ROLLS

2 dozen

DOUGH

2 cups milk
½ cup butter
½ cup sugar
3 packages active dry yeast
½ cup warm water
1 teaspoon sugar
2 eggs
Milk
2 scant teaspoons salt
6 cups flour
Cinnamon and sugar
Melted butter

Scald milk; add sugar and butter. Cool to lukewarm. Dissolve yeast in warm water and add 1 teaspoon of sugar. Let stand 3 to 4 minutes. In large bowl of electric mixer, add eggs mixed with a little milk; beat until well blended. Add salt, part of the flour and mix well. Alternately add remaining milk and flour, ending with flour. Dough will be light and quite sticky. Turn into well greased bowl; cover and let rise in a warm place until doubled. Punch down. Divide dough in half. Roll each half on a floured surface to form a rectangle about 1-inch thick. Brush each half with melted butter. Sprinkle with cinnamon and sugar and roll up as for jelly roll. Cut into 1-inch slices and place in baking pans with topping. Cover loosely with waxed paper, not plastic wrap or foil. Place in refrigerator overnight. Next morning carefully remove waxed paper. Place in cold oven and heat to 350 degrees. Rolls will rise while oven is heating. Bake 30 to 40 minutes.

TOPPING

1½ cups butter
½ cup corn syrup
2 cups brown sugar
2 cups chopped pecans

Melt butter in heavy skillet. Add brown sugar and corn syrup; stir with wooden spoon or wire whisk until sugar is dissolved. When thoroughly blended, add pecans. Do not boil mixture or sauce will harden. Divide mixture in half and spread in bottom of baking pans.

ORANGE SWEET ROLLS

DOUGH
1   recipe Pecan Roll
     Dough, prepared

FILLING
1   stick margarine
1   cup sugar
     Juice of 1 orange

Cook margarine and sugar in a skillet until the mixture just thickens. Add the juice of 1 orange (start with ⅛ cup and add more if necessary). Bring to a boil until mixture thickens slightly. Add 2 teaspoons grated orange rind. Cool before putting on dough. When dough has been rolled out, spread with orange filling and roll. Cut into 1-inch pieces and place in a buttered pan.

TOPPING
¾   cup sugar
½   cup cream
2   tablespoons orange juice
¼   cup butter
     Shredded coconut

Combine topping ingredients in a small saucepan. Bring to boil and cook, stirring, for 3 minutes. Spread over prepared rolls. Sprinkle with shredded coconut. Bake according to directions for Pecan Rolls.

DANISH CHRISTMAS TREES

3 dozen

1 **pound Imperial margarine,
   chilled**
3 **cakes compressed yeast**
¼ **cup sugar**
   Dash of salt
2 **eggs**
1 **cup milk**
2 **cups flour**
   Confectioners' sugar frosting
   Green food coloring
   Red sugar

Take margarine out of refrigerator 20 mintues before preparation. In large bowl, stir yeast, sugar and salt until a liquid forms. Add eggs to yeast mixture, stirring with a spoon. Stir in milk; add flour. Add enough additional flour to make a soft dough that will not spread out. Roll dough on a floured surface to a 14-inch square. Put margarine in center of dough and enclose by bringing 4 sides together; overlap. Roll out dough lengthwise and fold into thirds. Roll out dough in opposite direction and again fold into thirds. Repeat this process 2 more times, working quickly so margarine stays hard. Place dough on waxed paper and chill 15 minutes. Cut dough in half. Work 1 half at a time. Roll out thin and cut dough into 3 equal strips; cut each strip into triangle shapes. Slit twice from bottom to near top of triangle. Braid to form a tree. Arrange trees on jelly roll pans. Repeat process with remaining dough. Let sit for 15 minutes. Bake at 400 degrees for 10 to 15 minutes until lightly browned. Remove from pans and frost with confectioners' sugar and water frosting that has been tinted with green food coloring. Sprinkle with red sugar. Serve immediately. Dough can be formed into trees and refrigerated overnight. Remove from refrigerator and set in a warm place until they begin to get plump; bake as usual.

FRENCH PASTRY

40 rolls

½   pound margarine
2   cups flour
½   pint sour cream

FILLING
¾   cup chopped pecans
¾   cup sugar
2   teaspoons cinnamon

GLAZE
½   cup confectioners' sugar
1   teaspoon lemon juice
    Milk

Mix margarine, flour and sour cream; refrigerate at least four hours. Roll pastry into five pie-shaped rounds. Cut each round into eight wedges. Mix together pecans, sugar and cinnamon and put one scant tablespoon of mixture on each wedge; roll large end to small. Bake 20 to 30 minutes at 350 degrees. Mix confectioners' sugar and lemon juice; add milk until consistency of heavy cream. Pour glaze over each roll while warm. NOTE: Can be made ahead and frozen. These are nice to serve with coffee.

PECAN COFFEE CAKE

1   8-ounce package yellow cake mix
1   3-ounce package instant vanilla pudding
¾   cup vegetable oil
¾   cup water
4   eggs
1   teaspoon vanilla
1   teaspoon butter extract
¼   cup sugar
¼   cup chopped pecans
2   teaspoons cinnamon
½   cup butter, softened
⅓   cup chopped pecans

GLAZE
1   cup confectioners' sugar
3   tablespoons milk
½   teaspoon vanilla
½   teaspoon butter extract

Combine cake mix, pudding, vegetable oil and water. Add eggs. In a separate bowl mix sugar, cinnamon and ¼ cup pecans; set aside. Butter a bundt pan with ½ cup butter and sprinkle with ⅓ cup pecans. Pour in ½ of the batter, then sprinkle with cinnamon mixture. Layer again beginning and ending with batter. Bake 40 to 60 minutes. Set on rack to cool 8 minutes before removing from pan. Stir together glaze ingredients and pour over warm cake.

FARMER'S WASH DAY CAKE
12 servings

2 cups flour
2 teaspoons soda
2 teaspoons cinnamon
¾ teaspoon salt
1 cup sugar
2 eggs
½ cup butter, softened
1 cup raisins, soaked in warm
water and drained
1 cup chopped nuts
2 teaspoons vanilla
1 21-ounce can pie filling:
apple, peach, cherry or
apricot

Sift flour, soda, cinnamon, salt and sugar into a large bowl. Add rest of ingredients and mix until no more flour is visible. Put into a greased 9x13-pan. Mix together sugar and cinnamon; sprinkle over batter. Bake in 350 degree oven for 35 to 50 minutes.

TOPPING
¾ cup sugar
2 teaspoons cinnamon

BLUEBERRY FILLED COFFEE CAKE
12 servings

½ cup margarine, softened
1 cup sugar
2 eggs
1 cup sour cream
2 cups flour
½ teaspoon salt
1½ teaspoons baking powder
½ teaspoon baking soda
1 teaspoon vanilla
1 21-ounce can blueberry pie
filling

Cream together margarine and sugar. Add eggs and sour cream. Sift together flour, salt, baking powder and baking soda. Stir into creamed mixture. Add vanilla. Mix topping ingredients together until crumbly. Pour half the batter into a greased 9x14-inch pan. Spread with pie filling. Add remaining batter. Sprinkle with topping and bake at 350 degrees 40 to 50 minutes.

TOPPING
¼ cup margarine, softened
½ cup sugar
1 teaspoon cinnamon
½ cup flour
½ cup chopped nuts

BLUEBERRY BREAKFAST BARS

4 dozen

1¾ cup sugar
1   cup butter
4   eggs
1   teaspoon vanilla
3   cups flour
1½ teaspoons baking powder
½   teaspoon salt
1   21-ounce can blueberry pie
      filling

FROSTING
1¼ cups confectioners' sugar,
      sifted
1   tablespoon butter, melted
2   tablespoons lemon juice
      Sprinkle of nutmeg

Cream together sugar and butter. Add eggs and vanilla; beat well. Stir together flour, baking powder and salt. Add to creamed mixture, stirring until blended. Spread ½ of the dough in an ungreased 15x10-inch jelly roll pan. Carefully spread with blueberry filling. Sprinkle with a little nutmeg. Drop remaining dough from teaspoon over pie filling. Bake at 350 degrees for 45 minutes. Combine frosting ingredients and drizzle over warm bars.

APPLE COFFEE CAKE

12 servings

1¼ cups sugar
1   cup butter, minus 2 table-
      spoons
2   eggs
1   cup sour cream
1   teaspoon vanilla
2   cups flour, sifted
½   teaspoon baking soda
½   teaspoon baking powder
3   apples, peeled and sliced thin

TOPPING
½   cup chopped walnuts
½   cup brown sugar
1   teaspoon cinnamon

Cream together sugar and butter. Add eggs and beat well; mix in sour cream and vanilla. Mix soda and baking powder with sifted flour; add to batter. Pour ½ of batter into an ungreased tube pan; lay on sliced apples. Sprinkle on ½ the topping; pour on the rest of the batter. Sprinkle with remaining topping. Bake at 350 degrees for 1 hour. Cool well before removing from pan.

RHUBARB COFFEE CAKE

2 cups rhubarb, cubed
1½ cups brown sugar
½ cup margarine
1 egg
2 cups flour
1 teaspoon baking soda
½ teaspoon salt
1 cup buttermilk
1 teaspoon vanilla

TOPPING
½ cup sugar
1 teaspoon cinnamon

Blend sugar and margarine; beat in egg. Mix together dry ingredients. Beat in alternately with buttermilk. Add vanilla and rhubarb. Spread in 9x13-inch greased pan and sprinkle on topping. Bake at 350 degrees for 30 to 35 minutes. Serve warm or cold. NOTE: You can use 1 cup rhubarb and 1 cup strawberries.

MAPLE CHEESE RING
20 servings

1 cup brown sugar, packed
¾ cup chopped nuts
⅓ cup maple flavored syrup or dark Karo syrup
¼ cup margarine, melted
1 8-ounce package cream cheese
¼ cup confectioners' sugar
2 tablespoons margarine, softened
2 cans Hungry Jack Biscuits

Combine brown sugar, nuts, syrup and margarine. Place in ungreased bundt pan. Blend together cream cheese, confectioners' sugar and 2 tablespoons margarine. Separate biscuit dough into 20 pieces. Press each piece into a 4-inch circle. Spoon 1 tablespoon of the cheese mixture onto center of each piece. Fold over and stand seam side down in bundt pan; cover with syrup mixture. Bake at 350 degrees for 20 to 30 minutes. Cool 3 minutes. Turn onto serving plate.

WORLD'S EASIEST COFFEE CAKE
3 dozen

1 package pound cake mix
½ cup butter or margarine, softened
2 eggs
1 8-ounce package cream cheese, softened
2 eggs
1 pound confectioners' sugar
1 cup chopped nuts

Mix the pound cake, butter and eggs together with a fork. Spread in a greased 9x13-inch pan. Mix cream cheese, eggs and sugar with a mixer until smooth. Pour over first layer. Sprinkle with nuts. Bake at 350 degrees for 35 to 45 minutes. Cool thoroughly before cutting. Cut into 1½ to 2-inch squares.

PLUM COFFEE CAKE

8   Santa Rosa plums, diced with
    skins
½   cup sugar
2   cups flour
2   tablespoons sugar
½   teaspoon salt
⅓   cup shortening
1   tablespoon cider vinegar
1   cup milk
½   teaspoon baking soda
1   cup sugar
½   cup flour
¼   cup butter

Mix plums with ½ cup sugar and set aside. Mix flour, 2 tablespoons sugar and salt together. Mix vinegar with milk and baking soda; blend quickly into dry ingredients. Gently pat cake into a greased and floured 10x15-inch jelly roll pan. Top with plums and sugar mixture. Sprinkle with topping made by mixing together 1 cup sugar, ½ cup flour and ¼ cup butter. Bake at 350 degrees, 50 to 60 minutes, or until brown and bubbly.

CHOCOLATE CHIP COFFEE CAKE   12 servings

½   cup butter, softened
1   cup sugar
2   eggs
2   cups flour
1   teaspoon baking powder
1   teaspoon baking soda
1   cup sour cream
1   teaspoon vanilla

Cream together butter and sugar; add eggs. Beat in dry ingredients. Stir in sour cream and vanilla. Mix topping in separate bowl. Pour half of the batter into greased spring form pan. Add half of the topping. Repeat the procedure. Bake at 350 degrees for 50 to 60 minutes.

TOPPING
½   cup chopped pecans or
    walnuts
⅓   cup brown sugar
1   6-ounce package chocolate
    chips

OATMEAL-RAISIN SODA BREAD   1 loaf

2   cups whole wheat flour
2   cups rolled oats
2   cups buttermilk
1½   cups raisins
1   cup brown sugar
3   eggs
2   tablespoons baking soda
2   tablespoons baking powder

Generously grease 9x5-inch loaf pan. Combine ingredients thoroughly. Spoon into pan, filling ¾ full to allow for rising during baking. Bake about 1 hour at 350 degrees, or until toothpick inserted in center of loaf comes out clean. Remove from pan and place on rack to cool. Serve warm or toasted with cream cheese.

IRISH SODA BREAD

12 servings

3 tablespoons margarine, softened
1 cup sugar
1 egg
2 cups flour
1 cup milk
2 cups flour
Dash salt
3 teaspoons baking powder
½ cup milk
1 cup raisins, plumped in hot water and drained

Cream together margarine and sugar. Add egg and mix well. Add two cups of flour and mix well; add milk. Stir in remaining flour, salt and baking powder; mix well by hand. Batter will be too stiff for mixer at this point. Add the last of the milk and the raisins and stir. Pour evenly into greased angel food cake pan. Bake at 350 degrees for one hour. NOTE: Slice and toast for breakfast.

POPPYSEED BREAD

2 loaves

3 eggs, beaten
1½ cups milk
1⅛ cups oil
2¼ cups sugar
3 cups flour
1½ teaspoons salt
1½ teaspoons baking powder
1½ teaspoons vanilla
3 tablespoons poppyseeds
1½ teaspoons almond flavoring
1½ teaspoons butter flavoring

Combine beaten eggs, milk, oil and sugar in mixing bowl. Combine and sift in flour, salt and baking powder; mix well. Add vanilla, poppyseeds, almond and butter flavorings. Pour into 2 greased loaf pans or 3 small loaf pans. Bake for about 1 hour (adjust time for your oven) at 350 degrees.

RAISIN BROWN BREAD

3 loaves

15 ounces raisins
2 tablespoons baking soda
10 tablespoons butter
2 cups boiling water
4 cups flour
2 cups sugar
2 teaspoons cinnamon
2 eggs

Soak raisins, baking soda and butter in boiling water for 5 hours. Mix with flour, sugar, cinnamon and eggs. Pour into three greased 1-pound coffee cans. Bake 1 hour at 350 degrees.

BEER BREAD

1 loaf

3 cups unsifted, self-rising flour
2 tablespoons sugar
1 12-ounce can of beer, room
temperature or warmer
1 egg, beaten with 1 tablespoon
water
3 tablespoons butter, melted

Place flour, sugar and beer in a bowl. Stir 17 times, making certain dry ingredients are moistened. Turn dough into a well-greased 9x5-inch loaf pan. Dough will be sticky; spread evenly in pan. Brush dough with egg mixture. Bake in preheated oven at 375 degrees for 40 to 45 minutes or until wooden pick comes out clean. Bake on lowest shelf of oven. While bread is still warm brush with melted butter. NOTE: For muffins, use 12 greased muffin pans and bake 30 minutes at 375 degrees.

BANANA WHEAT BREAD

2 loaves

1 cup sugar or ¾ cup honey
½ cup oil
3 ripe bananas, mashed
¼ cup orange juice concentrate
2 eggs, beaten
1 cup whole wheat flour
1 cup flour
1 teaspoon baking soda
¼ teaspoon salt
¼ cup chopped nuts
¼ cup flaked coconut
¼ cup chopped dates (optional)

Combine sugar or honey, oil, bananas, orange juice concentrate and eggs. Add wheat flour, flour, baking soda, salt, nuts, coconut and dates. Pour batter into two greased loaf pans. Bake at 375 degrees for 30 to 40 minutes.

BUTTER BRICKLE BREAD

3 loaves

1 package Butter Brickle cake
mix
¼ cup vegetable oil
1 3-ounce package instant
coconut pudding mix
1 cup hot water
4 eggs, slightly beaten
¼ cup poppy seeds

Mix all ingredients together and pour into three small loaf pans. Bake at 275 degrees for 1 hour. NOTE: Easy bake sale item.

UNIQUE ZUCCHINI BREAD
2 loaves

3 cups flour
3 teaspoons baking powder
1½ teaspoons baking soda
1 teaspoon salt
3 teaspoons cinnamon
2 cups sugar
3 eggs
1 cup oil
2 cups grated and drained
zucchini
1 17-ounce can crushed
pineapple, drained
1 teaspoon almond extract
1 teaspoon butter flavoring

Sift together flour, baking powder, soda, salt and cinnamon. Mix sugar, eggs and oil; add to dry ingredients. The dough will be stiff. Stir in grated zucchini and pineapple. Add almond extract and butter flavoring. Oil and flour 2 medium bread pans and pour mixture into them. Bake at 350 degrees for 45 to 60 minutes.

WHOLE WHEAT CORN MUFFINS
1½ dozen

1 cup flour, sifted
1½ teaspoons baking soda
1 teaspoon baking powder
1 teaspoon ground cinnamon
½ teaspoon ground cloves
½ teaspoon ground nutmeg
½ teaspoon salt
1 cup whole wheat flour
3 eggs
1 cup vegetable oil
1 cup sugar
2 cups fresh corn kernels (about
4 ears)
1 cup chopped walnuts

Sift together flour, baking soda, baking powder, cinnamon, cloves, nutmeg and salt; stir in whole wheat flour. Beat eggs, oil and sugar in large mixer bowl until smooth; stir in corn. Stir in flour mixture and nuts just until moistened. Spoon batter into well-buttered muffin cups, filling ⅔ full. Bake at 400 degrees until tops are golden and sides begin to pull away from cups, 20 to 25 minutes. Remove from cups; cool on wire racks. NOTE: The batter can also be baked in a greased 13x9-inch baking pan at 350 degrees until top is golden and center springs back when lightly tapped, 40 to 45 minutes. Cool in pan on wire rack. Cut into squares.

MOTHER'S OATMEAL MUFFINS
2 dozen

1 cup oatmeal
1 cup buttermilk
½ cup shortening
1½ cups brown sugar
1 egg, beaten
1½ cups flour
½ teaspoon salt
1 teaspoon baking powder
½ teaspoon baking soda

Soak oatmeal in buttermilk for 1 hour. Cream together shortening and brown sugar; add beaten egg. Add oatmeal mixture. Sift together flour, salt, baking powder and soda. Add to oatmeal mixture. Grease and flour muffin tins. Fill muffin tins ⅔ full. Bake at 400 degrees for 20 minutes. Cool on rack.

APPLE MUFFINS
1½ dozen

1 egg
1 cup milk
¼ cup salad oil
⅔ cup sugar
½ teaspoon salt
½ teaspoon cinnamon
1 teaspoon lemon juice
¼ teaspoon vanilla
2 cups flour
1 tablespoon baking powder
1 cup chopped apples

Beat egg; stir in milk, oil, sugar, salt, cinnamon, lemon juice and vanilla. Sift together flour and baking powder. Stir dry ingredients into liquid mixture just until blended. Do not over mix. Fold in apples. Pour into greased muffin cups and bake at 450 degrees for 20 minutes.

LITTLE APPLESAUCE MUFFINS
3 dozen

½ cup butter, softened
½ cup sugar
2 eggs
¾ cup applesauce
1¾ cups flour
1 tablespoon baking powder
½ teaspoon salt

TOPPING
½ cup melted butter
½ cup sugar
½ teaspoon cinnamon

Cream together butter and sugar until light and fluffy. Beat in eggs one at a time. Stir in applesauce. Sift together flour, baking powder and salt. Stir in dry ingredients just until moistened. Fill small greased muffin cups ⅔ full. Bake at 425 degrees for 15 minutes. While warm, dip each muffin into melted butter and roll in cinnamon sugar. NOTE: Makes 18 large muffins.

BUTTER-KA-NUTS

1 dozen

CRUST
⅔ cup salad oil
3 tablespoons milk
2 cups flour
2 teaspoons sugar
¼ teaspoon salt

Whip the salad oil and milk with a fork. Add dry ingredients and mix until damp. Pat crust into individual greased muffin tins.

FILLING
1 cup butter
2 cups sugar
4 eggs
2 cups raisins
2 cups coconut
2 cups chopped walnuts

Cream together butter and sugar; add eggs one at a time. Mix in raisins, coconut and walnuts. Fill muffin tins ¾ full. Bake 10 minutes at 400 degrees. Reduce oven to 350 degrees and watch carefully as you may need to bake them up to 10 minutes longer to set the fillings. Cool for 10 minutes. To remove from tins, slide a knife around each muffin.

EASY DO DONUTS

2½ dozen

⅓ cup sugar
1½ cups flour
½ teaspoon salt
⅛ teaspoon nutmeg
2 tablespoons baking powder
½ cup milk
1 egg
2 teaspoons vegetable oil
½ cup raisins (optional)

TOPPING
¼ cup sugar
½ teaspoon cinnamon

Mix dry ingredients together. Add milk, egg, oil and raisins, if desired. Stir just until mixture is smooth. Preheat 1½ inches of oil in a heavy skillet or electric frying pan to 375 degrees. Drop dough from tablespoon into hot oil. Fry until golden brown on both sides, about 2 or 3 minutes. Drain on paper towels. Roll in cinnamon-sugar mixture.

DILLY APPETIZING BREAD

8 servings

2 tablespoons margarine
1 16-ounce frozen French bread
   dough, thawed
4 ounces shredded Swiss
   cheese
3 strips bacon, cooked and
   crumbled
1 beaten egg
3 tablespoons Dijon mustard
1 tablespoon dill weed
2 tablespoons dill seed
1 small onion, chopped

Brown onion in margarine, using a small skillet; set aside to cool. Roll out bread dough on a floured surface to a 16x18-inch rectangle. Spread dough with Dijon mustard; then sprinkle with cheese, crumbled bacon, 1 tablespoon dill seed and dill weed. Roll up from the long side like a jelly roll; pinch edges to seal. Place roll, seam side down, on a greased cookie sheet. Score top of bread with ¼ inch deep crosswise cuts. Cover; let rise 45 minutes in a warm place until almost double. Brush top with beaten egg; sprinkle with remaining dill seed. Bake at 350 degrees for 25 to 30 minutes. Serve warm.

TOASTED CELERY BREAD

1 loaf

½ cup butter or margarine,
   softened
¼ teaspoon salt
   Dash of cayenne pepper
¼ teaspoon paprika
½ teaspoon celery seeds
1 loaf unsliced white bread

Blend together butter, salt, pepper, paprika and celery seeds. Slice crust from top and sides of bread. Do not remove bottom crust. Slice the loaf down the middle lengthwise, almost to the bottom. Cut crosswise at 2-inch intervals from the top almost through to the bottom. Spread butter mixture generously over the entire cut surface, not the bottom. Place on cookie sheet and refrigerate for several hours. Preheat oven for 10 minutes at 400 degrees. Bake bread on cookie sheet for 18 minutes. Serve hot.

GREEN CHILI CHEESE BREAD

1 loaf

1 loaf French bread, cut
　in half lengthwise
1 stick butter or margarine
1 4-ounce can chopped
　green chilies
2 cups grated Cheddar or
　Colby cheese
½ cup mayonnaise
½ cup Parmesan cheese

Melt butter and add the green chilies. Spread on bread. Mix grated Cheddar and Parmesan cheeses with mayonnaise. Spread on top of buttered bread. Place bread on baking sheet, cheese side up, and bake at 375 degrees for 15 to 20 minutes.

HERB CROUTONS

3 cups

3 cups day old French
　bread, cut in ½ inch cubes
¼ cup butter, melted
½ teaspoon Worcestershire
¼ teaspoon oregano
¼ teaspoon thyme
¼ teaspoon marjoram
¼ teaspoon basil
½ teaspoon garlic powder
1 tablespoon Parmesan cheese

Spread bread cubes in a jelly roll pan. Bake at 300 degrees for 10 minutes. Remove from oven. Combine remaining ingredients and pour over bread cubes. Toss to coat evenly. Bake at 275 degrees for 20 to 30 minutes or until crisp and light brown. Cool and store in a covered jar. Can be frozen.

CRISPY FINGER BREAD

1 loaf

1 loaf sliced white bread
¾ cup of butter
3 tablespoons fresh chives
¾ teaspoon summer savory
¾ teaspoon sweet basil

Cut crusts off bread. Roll slices thin with rolling pin. Combine all ingredients and spread generously on bread. Roll bread corner to corner. Bake at 350 degrees for 20 to 25 minutes on a cookie sheet or shallow pan. NOTE: Different types of loaf bread can be used.

HUGGIN'S HOT BREAD

8 servings

1   **loaf unsliced white bread**
¾   **cup butter or margarine, melted**
2   **cups buttermilk**
    Poppyseeds

Remove crust from bread. Cut bread into finger-size pieces. Mix together butter and buttermilk. Roll bread in mixture. Sprinkle with poppyseeds on all sides. Place on cookie sheet, leaving space between each. Refrigerate overnight. Bake 20 to 30 minutes in 350 degree oven.

PARMESAN SLICES

12 servings

1   **loaf French bread**
½   **cup butter**
    Dash of garlic salt
1   **cup mayonnaise**
½   **cup Parmesan cheese**
¼   **cup finely chopped onion**
    Dash of Worcestershire
    Dash of Tabasco

Cut bread in half, lengthwise. Spread with butter and sprinkle on garlic. Combine mayonnaise, cheese, onion, Worcestershire and Tabasco. Cut bread into thick slices and frost with mixture. Bake 15 minutes at 350 degrees.

EASY APPLE PANCAKE

6 servings

4   **tablespoons butter**
4   **tablespoons brown sugar**
2   **teaspoons cinnamon**
2   **large apples, sliced**
6   **tablespoons flour**
½   **teaspoon baking powder**
    Dash of salt
4   **eggs, separated**
6   **tablespoons milk**
3   **tablespoons sugar**

Melt butter in 10-inch pie plate. Combine sugar and cinnamon; sprinkle evenly on bottom. Arrange apple slices over mixture. Cook slowly for 5 minutes. Preheat oven to 400 degrees. Combine flour, baking powder and salt with egg yolks and milk. Beat egg whites until foamy. Gradually add 3 tablespoons sugar, beat until soft peaks form. Fold into flour mixture. Pour batter over apple slices, spreading evenly. Bake 20 minutes or until golden and puffy. Remove from oven; invert on a large plate. Cut in wedges and serve with sour cream, ice cream, or yogurt.

GERMAN PANCAKE

4 servings

4 eggs, separated
2 tablespoons cornstarch
¼ cup lukewarm milk
¾ teaspoon salt
1 tablespoon sugar
  Grated rind of a large orange
1½ cups thinly sliced apples
2 tablespoons butter

Beat egg yolks and combine with cornstarch, milk, water, salt, sugar and orange rind. Beat the whites until stiff. Fold apples into yolk mixture; then fold in whites. Melt butter in heavy 10-inch skillet. When hot, pour in pancake and cook over medium low heat, partially covered, for about 5 minutes. May also be cooked on top of stove until it begins to set; then put in preheated 400 degree oven until it is puffed and firm. Invert onto heated platter. Sprinkle with cinnamon sugar. Serve immediately with melted butter and maple syrup.

YOGURT PANCAKES

4 servings

1 cup yogurt
2 eggs, separated
1 stick butter, melted and
   cooled
¾ cup sifted flour
1 tablespoon flour
1 teaspoon baking soda
½ teaspoon salt

In a bowl, mix yogurt with egg yolks and cooled melted butter. Combine flour, sugar, salt and baking soda. Stir into yogurt mixture. Beat egg whites until stiff and fold gently into batter. Cook pancakes on a hot greased griddle over medium heat. Serve with maple syrup or blueberry yogurt.

GRAM'S BUTTERMILK PANCAKES

8 servings

4 teaspoons soda
2 teaspoons baking powder
¼ cup warm water
4 eggs
4 cups buttermilk
4 tablespoons sugar
2 teaspoons salt
2½ cups flour or enough to make
   thin batter
12 tablespoons butter, melted

Dissolve baking soda and powder in a small amount of water; set aside. In a large bowl, beat eggs with a fork. Add buttermilk, sugar, salt and enough flour to make a thin batter. Add melted butter, and the baking powder-soda mixture. Pour small amounts onto very hot griddle for small size pancakes. NOTE: Purchase buttermilk a week ahead; old buttermilk works better.

RAY'S RICE PANCAKES

4 servings

1 cup warm cooked rice
1 cup milk
2 eggs, separated
½ teaspoon salt
2 tablespoons butter, melted
½ cup flour, sifted
2 teaspoons baking powder

Combine rice, milk, egg yolks, salt and melted butter. Stir in sifted flour and baking powder. Beat egg whites until stiff; fold into rice mixture. Fry in a little butter and dust with confectioners' sugar. NOTE: Very, very light and special pancakes.

SOUR CREAM WAFFLES

4 servings

1 cup flour
½ tablespoon sugar
1 teaspoon baking powder
¼ teaspoon baking soda
¼ teaspoon salt
1 egg, separated
1 cup sour cream
¼ cup milk
3 teaspoons butter or
        margarine, melted and
        cooled

Sift together all dry ingredients. Beat egg yolk slightly; blend with sour cream, milk and melted butter. Add flour mixture and beat until smooth. Beat egg white until stiff and fold into mixture. Bake in preheated waffle griddle. NOTE: You can prepare the batter up to one hour before baking.

EBLESKIVER

6 servings

3 eggs, separated
2 cups buttermilk
2 cups flour
1 teaspoon baking powder
1 teaspoon baking soda
½ teaspoon salt
3 tablespoons sugar

Beat egg yolks; stir in buttermilk. Sift dry ingredients together, add to egg mixture. Beat egg whites until stiff peaks form. Fold into batter. Heat ebleskiver pan over medium heat. Rub each cup with butter. Fill cups ⅔ full with batter. Cook until center is bubbly. Carefully turn over with a fork and cook to brown the other side. Serve with honey, syrup, jelly or confectioners' sugar. These can be kept in a warm oven until all are cooked. NOTE: Ebleskiver are small round Danish pancakes. Must be made in a special pan.

111

NO-FAIL MATZO BALLS

4 eggs
3 tablespoons water
¼ cup chicken fat (schmaltz),
   melted
1 cup matzo meal
1 teaspoon salt
1 tablespoon chopped parsley
⅛ teaspoon pepper

Beat eggs until light and fluffy. Stir in water, seasoning and chicken fat. Stir in matzo meal, amount depends upon size of eggs. Dough should be semi-loose. Refrigerate for several hours. When ready to cook, dip hands in cold water and roll dough into small egg shape. Drop into large pot of boiling water and cook gently for 45 minutes, covered. Do not peek while cooking. Uncover and drain at once. Serve with chicken soup.

Eggs, Cheese, Pasta & Rice

SHRIMP CURRIED EGGS

8 servings

8   eggs, hard-boiled and
    halved
⅓   cup mayonnaise
½   teaspoon salt
⅓   teaspoon curry powder
½   teaspoon paprika
¼   teaspoon dry mustard
2   tablespoons margarine
2   tablespoons flour
1   10-ounce can condensed
    cream of shrimp soup
½   soup can of milk
1   cup small cooked shrimp
½   cup shredded sharp
    cheese
1   cup fresh bread crumbs
1   tablespoon butter or
    margarine

Push egg yolks through a sieve or mash with fork; mix with mayonnaise, salt, curry powder, paprika and dry mustard. Fill egg whites with mixture and arrange in a 9x13-inch baking dish. In a saucepan, melt butter; add flour gradually. Stir to make a paste. Slowly add soup and milk; cook until thick. Add cheese and cook, stirring, until melted. Add shrimp. Pour sauce over stuffed eggs. Melt butter; mix with bread crumbs. Spread over sauce. Bake in 350 degree oven until thoroughly heated, about 25 minutes.

MEXICAN EGG BRUNCH

8 servings

1   pound bulk sausage, crumbled
½   pound mushrooms, chopped
1   medium onion, diced
    Salt and freshly ground pepper
6   eggs
3   tablespoons sour cream
8   tablespoons tomato
    and yellow chili hot sauce
8   ounces Cheddar cheese,
    grated
8   ounces Mozzarella cheese,
    grated
8   ounces Velveeta cheese,
    grated

Grease 9x13-inch baking dish. Combine sausage, mushrooms and onion in large skillet. Sauté over medium-high heat until sausage is completely cooked. Season to taste with salt and pepper. Drain well. Combine eggs and sour cream in blender and whip 1 minute. Turn into baking dish and bake at 400 degrees until eggs are softly set, 4 to 7 minutes. Spoon hot sauce evenly over top. Add sausage mixture and top with combined grated cheeses. To serve immediately, broil until cheeses are melted. To serve next day, refrigerate until serving time; bake at 325 degrees until cheeses are melted, about 30 minutes.

HUEVOS RANCHEROS

6 servings

1 teaspoon corn oil
1 onion, chopped
1 green pepper, seeded and
   chopped
2 cloves garlic, pressed
1 28-ounce can peeled
   tomatoes, chopped with juice
3 green chilies, chopped with
   vein and seeds removed
1 teaspoon salt
⅓ teaspoon black pepper
1 teaspoon chili powder
½ teaspoon ground cumin
6 eggs, room temperature
1 cup grated Monterey Jack
   cheese
6 corn tortillas, heated

Heat the oil in a skillet, sauté onions, green pepper and garlic until onion is clear. Add tomatoes, chilies and seasonings. Make 6 small depressions in the sauce and carefully place 1 egg in each depression. Sprinkle grated cheese over the top of each egg. Cover and cook for 10 to 12 minutes or until egg whites are set and cheese has melted. Serve each egg on top of hot tortilla, spoon remaining sauce over top or on side. If desired, top each serving with a dollop of sour cream.

BACON AND EGGS MORNAY

6 servings

1 pound bacon
¼ cup diced onion
¼ cup flour
1½ teaspoons paprika
2 cups milk
1 cup shredded mild cheese
2 tablespoons Dijon mustard
   Pinch dried red pepper
   flakes
⅔ cup croutons
10 hard-boiled eggs, sliced

Cook bacon until crisp. Drain well. Save 8 strips to top casserole, crumble rest into large pieces. Partially drain bacon grease from pan. Sauté onions in remaining grease until transparent. Stir in flour, paprika and salt to taste. Gradually add milk; cook, stirring, until thick. Add cheese, red pepper and mustard. Grease a 1½-quart casserole. Layer ½ of the eggs, ½ of the bacon and ½ of the croutons. Repeat the layers. Top with remaining sauce and reserved bacon slices. Cover and refrigerate until baked. Bake, covered, 20 to 30 minutes at 350 degrees.

AFTER EASTER EGGS

8 servings

¼ cup butter
¼ cup flour
1 cup half-and-half
1 cup milk
½ teaspoon thyme
¼ cup margarine
¼ teaspoon basil
1 pound Cheddar cheese, grated
18 hard-boiled eggs, thinly sliced
1 pound bacon, cooked and
    crumbled
¼ cup parsley

Melt butter in saucepan; blend in flour, half-and-half and milk. Cook slowly until thick; add herbs and cheese. Stir until melted. In a 3-quart casserole, layer ⅓ of the egg slices. Sprinkle with ⅓ of the bacon and ⅓ of the parsley. Top with ⅓ of the cheese sauce. Repeat layers twice. Bake at 350 degrees for 30 minutes, until bubbly.

BAKED PANCAKES 'N SAUSAGE

8 servings

2 eggs
1 cup milk
1¼ cups sifted flour
3 teaspoons baking powder
1 tablespoon sugar
½ teaspoon salt
2 tablespoons shortening,
    melted
2 8-ounce packages regular
    brown 'n' serve sausage links

Beat eggs with rotary beater until light and fluffy. Combine with milk. Sift together flour, baking powder, sugar and salt. Add the dry ingredients and shortening to the milk mixture. Beat until the batter is smooth. Pour into 2 greased 8-inch pie pans. Arrange sausage links on the batter in spoke fashion. Bake 15 minutes at 450 degrees. Serve wedges with heated syrup.

CANADIAN BACON AND EGGS

8 servings

8 slices Canadian bacon
8 ounces Swiss cheese, grated
8 eggs
    Heavy cream
    Grated Swiss cheese
4 English muffins

In a 9x13-inch pan, place a layer of Canadian bacon topped with a layer of Swiss cheese. Break eggs on top as if you were frying them. Drizzle cream so that the yolks peek out. Bake 10 minutes at 450 degrees. Sprinkle with more grated cheese. Bake 8 to 10 minutes more. Let cool until set. Cut into squares. Serve on toasted English muffins.

MUSHROOM QUICHE

9-inch quiche

CRUST
1¼ cups whole wheat cracker
     crumbs (24 crackers)
⅓ cup butter, melted

Combine crumbs and butter in medium bowl and blend well. Pat into 9-inch pie plate and chill while preparing filling.

FILLING
¼ cup butter
1½ pounds mushrooms, sliced
4 green onions, chopped
1 garlic clove, minced
2 teaspoons oregano
2 teaspoons basil
1½ teaspoons salt
1½ teaspoons freshly ground
     pepper
1 teaspoon marjoram
½ teaspoon thyme
½ teaspoon dry mustard
5 eggs
1 cup half-and-half
     Juice and finely grated peel
     of ½ lemon

Position rack in lower third of oven and preheat to 375 degrees. Melt butter in large skillet over medium-high heat. Add mushrooms, onion and garlic; sauté until liquid is evaporated, 10 to 15 minutes. Stir in oregano, basil, salt, pepper, marjoram, thyme and mustard; cook 2 minutes. Let cool 5 minutes. Combine eggs, half-and-half, lemon juice and peel in a large bowl; beat well. Fold in the mushroom mixture. Turn into prepared crust. Bake 25 minutes. Remove from oven and let cool slightly.

TOPPING
1½ cups mayonnaise
2 teaspoons dried dill weed
     (optional)
⅓ cup half-and-half

Combine mayonnaise, half-and-half and dill weed in small bowl. Spoon evenly over the quiche. Continue baking until top is set, 20 to 25 minutes.

BEEF-MUSHROOM QUICHE

8 servings

1 9-inch unbaked pastry shell
¾ pound ground beef
1 10½-ounce can condensed
     cream of mushroom soup
½ cup milk
2 eggs, slightly beaten
2 tablespoons chopped chives
¼ teaspoon salt
     Pinch of pepper
     Dash of Tabasco
1 4-ounce can mushrooms,
     drained
¾ cup shredded Swiss cheese or
     combination of Swiss and
     Cheddar

Prick bottom and sides of pastry shell. Bake 12 to 15 minutes at 450 degrees. Remove shell from oven. Reduce oven heat to 350 degrees. Brown beef in a skillet. Drain and set aside. Mix soup, milk, eggs, spices and Tabasco. Add beef, mushrooms and cheese. Pour into pie shell. Cover edges of pie shell with foil. Bake for 60 minutes. Test with knife.

COMPANY QUICHE

8 servings

1 9-inch unbaked deep dish
   pie shell
½ cup mayonnaise
2 tablespoons flour
½ teaspoon prepared mustard
4 eggs, beaten
½ cup milk
1 7-ounce can Alaskan crab,
   drained and flaked
8 ounces Swiss cheese, grated
⅓ cup sliced green onions
1 14-ounce can artichoke
   hearts, quartered
1 15-ounce can white asparagus,
   cut in small pieces
½ cup sliced almonds
   Ground nutmeg

Combine mayonnaise, flour, mustard, eggs and milk; stir in crab, cheese, onions, artichokes and asparagus. Pour mixture into pie shell. Sprinkle lightly with nutmeg and cover with sliced almonds. Bake at 350 degrees for 50 to 60 minutes, or until toothpick inserted in middle comes out clean. NOTE: You may have an excess of some ingredients. These can be used to make 2 small individual quiches if desired.

SPINACH QUICHE

10 servings

1 onion, chopped
1 tablespoon butter
1 pound bacon
2 10-ounce packages frozen,
   chopped spinach
8 eggs
2 cups heavy cream
½ teaspoon salt
   Pinch nutmeg
   Dash cayenne pepper
¾ pound Monterey
   Jack cheese, shredded
½ pound Swiss cheese,
   shredded
1 unbaked pastry shell in
   11-inch quiche pan

Sauté onion in butter until clear. Cook bacon until very crisp; crumble into small pieces. Beat eggs; add cream and spices; beat again until well mixed. Sprinkle onions on unbaked crust. Top with crumbled bacon. Squeeze liquid out of spinach and spread on top of bacon. Pour ⅓ of egg mixture on spinach and top with both cheeses. Pour remaining egg mixture over cheese. Liquid should almost cover other ingredients. It is easier to add the last of the liquid to the pan after it is on the oven rack, to prevent spilling. Bake at 425 degrees for 45 minutes, or until golden brown and set. Note: This recipe fills a porcelain quiche pan (11x1½-inch) to the brim. If you do not have one you can use two smaller pie pans.

CHICKEN QUICHE IN LEMON PASTRY SHELL   8 servings

PASTRY

1½ cups sifted flour
½ teaspoon salt
3 tablespoons ice water
9 tablespoons butter
1 heaping teaspoon shortening
Grated rind and juice of ½
lemon

Sift flour and salt, cut in butter and shortening until crumbly. Add lemon rind, juice and water. Mix lightly. Form a ball, adding a small amount of extra flour, if needed. Roll out on lightly floured board. Roll 1½ inches larger than 10-inch pan. Roll edge of crust under and flute, hooking onto edge of pie plate. Prick crust with fork. Bake at 425 degrees for 10 minutes. Crust will be partially baked.

FILLING

2 whole chicken breasts, skinned, boned and cut into 1-inch cubes
1½ teaspoons salt
⅛ teaspoon white pepper
¼ cup corn oil
1 large onion, thinly sliced and separated into rings
1 large firm tomato, seeded, peeled, cut into cubes and drained
3 large eggs
¾ cup milk
¾ cup half-and-half
4½ to 5 ounces Gruyere or aged Swiss cheese, cut in small pieces
¼ cup freshly grated Parmesan
Pinch of ground nutmeg
1 teaspoon butter, cut in pieces

Add ½ teaspoon salt and pepper to chicken. Sauté slowly, 5 to 6 minutes in heated oil. Remove chicken, add onion and cook until nearly tender. Add tomato, cover and cook 7 minutes or until moisture evaporates. Beat eggs. Add milk, cheeses, cream, nutmeg and remaining salt. Arrange onion, tomato and chicken on bottom of pastry shell. Pour in egg mixture and dot with butter. Bake in preheated 375 degree oven, 35 to 40 minutes. If knife inserted 3 inches from side comes out clean, it is done. Let stand 10 minutes before cutting.

SAUCE

10 small mushrooms
3 tablespoons butter
Salt and pepper to taste
2 tablespoons flour
½ cup half-and-half
2 tablespoons chutney
½ pint sour cream
¼ cup dry sherry

Chop mushrooms and sauté in butter. Season with salt and pepper. Add flour and blend. Stir in cream and cook until thick, stirring constantly. Add chutney, sour cream and sherry. Heat through. Serve over sliced quiche.

CABBAGE PATCH QUICHE

8 servings

1	small head of cabbage
2	tablespoons butter
½	pound bacon, chopped
1	medium onion, chopped
¾	cups shredded Gruyere cheese
¼	cup grated Parmesan cheese
3	eggs
1	cup heavy cream
1	9-inch unbaked pastry shell

Quarter cabbage. Cook in boiling, salted water for 20 to 25 minutes, until crisp, but tender. Drain well, squeezing to dry. Core and shred cabbage to make 3 cups. Sauté bacon until brown, but not crisp. Drain on paper towels. Reserve 2 tablespoons of bacon drippings. Sauté onion in reserved bacon drippings for 5 minutes. Combine bacon, onion and shredded cabbage. Cook on low for 15 minutes. Place in unbaked 9-inch pastry shell. Combine cheeses and sprinkle on top of mixture in pie shell. Beat eggs; add heavy cream. Pour over cheeses. Bake in preheated 350 degree oven for 30 to 40 minutes, until set. Serve immediately.

SWISS CHEESE SOUFFLÉ

8 servings

½	cup butter
6	tablespoons flour
2	cups milk
2	cups grated Swiss cheese
8	egg yolks
1½	teaspoons Dijon mustard
⅛	teaspoon cayenne pepper
1	teaspoon salt
8	egg whites
	Parmesan cheese (optional)

Melt butter. Add flour and cook slowly. Stir in milk and bring to boil. Cook, stirring, until sauce is smooth and thick. Remove from heat and add cheese; stir until blended. Cool slightly. Beat yolks and add to mixture. Add mustard, cayenne and salt. Let mixture cool. Beat egg whites until stiff, but not dry. Gently stir ¼ of whites into mixture. Fold in remaining whites until well blended. Butter a 2½ to 3-quart soufflé dish and sprinkle lightly with Parmesan cheese. Pour in cheese mixture and bake in a 350 degree oven for 30 to 40 minutes. Serve immediately.

SAUSAGE ZUCCHINI STRATA

8 servings

16 ounces pork sausage
16 ½-inch slices French or
    Sourdough bread
8 ounces jalapeno pepper
    cheese, shredded
1½ cups thinly sliced zucchini
4 eggs
1 cup milk
1⅓ cups tomato sauce
    Butter

Cook sausage, crumble and drain. Line 9x11-inch casserole with 12 slices of bread. Sprinkle with cheese. Layer zucchini on top of cheese. Cover with sausage. In another bowl, beat eggs, milk and tomato sauce. Pour over casserole. Butter remaining slices of bread, cut into cubes; and sprinkle on top. Let stand at room temperature for 1 hour or in refrigerator for several hours. Bake for 40 minutes at 325 degrees. Remove and let stand 10 minutes before serving.

CHILIES 'N GRITS

10 servings

4 cups boiling water
1 cup grits
1⅓ teaspoons salt
1⅓ teaspoons Lawry's seasoning
    salt
⅔ stick butter or margarine
10 ounces sharp Cheddar
    cheese, grated
2 eggs
1 4-ounce can chopped green
    chilies or jalapeno peppers
    Dash cayenne pepper

Cook grits, following package directions. Beat eggs well. Combine all ingredients with cooked grits, adding grated cheese last. Place in slightly greased 2 or 3-quart oblong dish. Bake at 300 degrees for approximately 1 hour, or until firm. Serve as a side dish instead of potatoes.

SOUR CREAM TORTILLAS

10 servings

½ cup chopped onion
2 tablespoons vegetable oil
12 tortillas
¾ cup chopped onion
1 pound Monterey Jack cheese,
    grated
2 cups sour cream
1 teaspoon seasoned salt
    Pepper
    Paprika

SAUCE
1 28-ounce can tomatoes
1 package enchilada seasoning
    mix
2 tablespoons chopped jalapeno
    peppers

Sauté onion in oil until tender. Add tomatoes, seasoning mix and jalapeno peppers. Simmer 15 to 20 minutes. Set aside to cool. Fry tortillas lightly, in small amount of oil, for 10 to 15 seconds on both sides. They should not be crisp. Pour ½ cup sauce in bottom of 9x13-inch pan. Arrange layer of 4 tortillas over sauce (they can overlap). Top with ⅓ of the sauce, ⅓ of the onions and ⅓ of the cheese. Repeat procedure 2 times, making 3 layers. Combine sour cream and seasoned salt. Spread over cheese, sealing edges of dish. Sprinkle lightly with pepper and paprika. Bake 25 to 30 minutes, uncovered, at 350 degrees. Cut into squares to serve. This can be made ahead and frozen; thaw slightly before reheating.

LINGUINI WITH SPRING VEGETABLES
8 servings

2 tablespoons olive oil
1 stick unsalted butter
1 medium onion, minced
2 large garlic cloves, minced
½ pound mushrooms, thinly
   sliced
1 medium zucchini, sliced
1 medium carrot, julienned
1 pound fresh thin asparagus
1 cup frozen peas, thawed or
   1 cup broccoli florets
½ cup chicken broth
1 cup heavy cream
2 teaspoons dried basil
3 scallions, thinly sliced
  Salt and pepper
1 pound Linguini, cooked,
   drained and kept warm
½ cup freshly grated Parmesan
   cheese
¼ cup minced fresh parsley

Preheat wok or large skillet over medium-high heat. Add some oil and butter and sauté onions and garlic until softened. Add mushrooms, zucchini, carrot and asparagus; stir-fry 2 to 3 minutes. Add more oil and butter as needed. Stir in broth and cream; cook several minutes to reduce. Add basil, peas and scallions and season to taste with salt and pepper. Cook 1 minute. Add hot pasta and cheese; mix well. Sprinkle with parsley.

SUMMERTIME PASTA
4 servings

½ pound fettuccini
½ cup olive oil
1 heaping teaspoon dried basil
1 tablespoon chopped fresh
   parsley
½ cup margarine
10 fresh mushrooms, sliced
2 small cloves garlic, minced
½ cup broccoli florets
¼ cup frozen peas
2 teaspoons olive oil
2 cups cooked chicken, cubed
  Salt and pepper to taste
1 ripe tomato

Cook pasta and rinse. Transfer to mixing bowl. Toss with olive oil, basil and parsley. Sauté mushrooms and garlic in margarine until lightly browned. Remove from pan. Lightly stir-fry broccoli in same pan; reduce heat, cover and simmer for 2 minutes. Remove from pan. Stir-fry chicken pieces in a few teaspoons olive oil until lightly browned. Toss chicken with pasta. Add vegetables carefully. Chill for 1 hour. Toss again before serving. Garnish with ripe tomato cut into thin wedges. Bring to room temperature before serving.

121

CANNELLONI

12 servings

1   8-ounce box manicotti shells
2   tablespoons olive oil
¼   cup finely chopped onion
1   teaspoon finely chopped garlic
1   10-ounce package frozen
      chopped spinach, thawed,
      squeezed dry and chopped
      again
2   tablespoons butter
1   pound ground round steak
2   chicken livers
5   tablespoons freshly grated
      Parmesan cheese
2   tablespoons heavy cream
2   eggs, lightly beaten
½   teaspoon dried oregano,
      crumbled
2   tablespoons Parmesan cheese
2   tablespoons butter

Heat olive oil in skillet and cook onion and garlic until soft but not brown. Stir in spinach and cook 3 to 4 minutes, stirring constantly. When all moisture has boiled away, transfer to a mixing bowl. Melt 1 tablespoon butter in the same skillet and lightly brown the beef. Add to onion-spinach mixture. Melt 1 tablespoon butter and cook chicken livers 3 to 4 minutes until lightly browned but still pink inside. Chop coarsely. Add to spinach mixture along with 5 tablespoons Parmesan, cream, eggs and oregano. Mix together and set aside. Cook manicotti shells according to package directions. In a 9x13-inch casserole dish, pour a small amount of tomato sauce to cover bottom of dish. Stuff noodles with meat-spinach mixture and arrange in dish. Pour white sauce over stuffed noodles. Spread tomato sauce over white sauce. Scatter 2 tablespoons Parmesan cheese over top and dot with 2 tablespoons butter, cut in small bits. Bake uncovered at 375 degrees for 20 minutes or until cheese is melted.

WHITE SAUCE

6   tablespoons butter
6   tablespoons flour
1   cup milk
1   cup heavy cream
1   teaspoon salt
⅛   teaspoon pepper

Melt butter and add flour. Whisk in milk and cream. Stir constantly and simmer until thick enough to coat the wire of the whisk. Season with salt and pepper.

TOMATO SAUCE

4   tablespoons olive oil
1   cup finely chopped onion
4   cups canned tomatoes,
      undrained and coarsely
      chopped
6   tablespoons tomato paste
2   teaspoons dried basil
1   teaspoon salt
2   teaspoons sugar

Heat oil in skillet; cook onion until soft but not brown. Add remaining ingredients and simmer, partially covered, about 40 minutes. Press the sauce through a sieve or mash with a potato masher.

STUFFED JUMBO SHELLS

SAUCE

1   pound pork spare ribs
4   15-ounce cans whole tomatoes
1   6-ounce can tomato paste
1   small onion, chopped
3   garlic cloves, chopped
1   tablespoon oregano
1   tablespoon basil
2   bay leaves
    Salt and pepper to taste
2   tablespoons sweet Marsala
    wine
2   tablespoons olive oil

In large saucepan, brown ribs in oil. Remove ribs and sauté onion and garlic in remaining oil. Mix in tomato paste. Purée whole tomatoes in blender and add to sautéed onions and garlic. Add rest of seasonings and pork ribs. Mix well and simmer at least 3 hours. Remove meat from ribs; mince and add to sauce.

MEATBALLS

1   pound ground beef
1   pound ground pork
2   cups bread crumbs
2   eggs
1   cup grated Romano cheese
½   onion, chopped
3   small garlic cloves, minced
2   teaspoons salt
2   teaspoons pepper
1   teaspoon oregano
1   teaspoon basil

Mix beef, pork, bread crumbs, eggs, cheese, onion, garlic, salt, pepper, oregano, and basil together. Form into meatballs and place on cookie sheet. Bake in 350 degree oven for 50 to 60 minutes. Add meatballs to sauce and simmer for at least 1 hour before serving.

CHEESE FILLING

2   pounds Ricotta cheese
½   pound Mozzarella cheese, diced
2   eggs
½   cup or more grated Romano cheese
1   tablespoon fresh parsley, chopped
1   box jumbo pasta shells
1   cup grated Romano cheese

Mix together cheeses, eggs and parsley. Cook shells according to package directions. Stuff with cheese filling and place in one 9x13-inch pan and one 9x9-inch pan. Pour tomato sauce with meatballs over stuffed shells. Sprinkle with 1 cup Romano cheese. Bake in 350 degree oven for 20 minutes or until hot.

SPINACH LASAGNE

8 servings

FILLING

2   packages fresh spinach
4   tablespoons Parmesan cheese
1½ cups Ricotta cheese
½   teaspoon nutmeg, salt and
      pepper

Wash spinach thoroughly. Chop and put in covered pan with small amount of water. Cook until soft, 2 to 3 minutes. Squeeze out excess liquid and mix with cheese, nutmeg, salt and pepper. Set aside.

SAUCE

1   28-ounce can tomatoes,
      chopped
1   12-ounce can tomato paste
½   cup chopped onions
2   cloves garlic, crushed
1   tablespoon oil
2   teaspoons basil, oregano and
      salt
2   cups tomato juice

Brown onion and garlic in oil. Stir in tomatoes, tomato paste, basil, oregano, salt and pepper to taste. Thin sauce with tomato juice until it is the consistancy of a thick soup. Simmer 30 minutes.

PASTA

1   pound package lasagne
      noodles, cooked
1   pound Mozzarella cheese,
      grated
      Parmesan cheese

To assemble; alternate layers of sauce, noodles and spinach filling, ending with sauce. Sprinkle Parmesan and Mozzarella cheese on each layer. Bake in 350 degree oven for 30 minutes or until heated through.

FETTUCCINI MILANO

6 servings

1   pound mild Italian sausage
3   cups sliced mushrooms
2   cloves garlic, minced
1   large bell pepper, chopped
1   cup chopped parsley
1   teaspoon basil
½   teaspoon oregano
¼   teaspoon rosemary
½   cup olive oil
½   cup butter
1   pound fettuccini or spaghetti,
      cooked and kept warm
      Parmesan cheese

Brown sausage; drain and set aside. Sauté mushrooms, garlic, green pepper, onion, parsley and seasonings in oil and butter, until green pepper is soft. Remove from heat and stir in sausage. Toss with hot fettuccini and sprinkle generously with Parmesan.

PASTA WITH WHITE CLAM SAUCE   4 servings

4   tablespoons butter
½   cup chopped onion
4   cloves garlic, minced
2   6½-ounce cans minced clams
4   tablespoons minced fresh
    parsley
½   cup milk
    Salt and pepper to taste
    Shell-shaped macaroni,
    cooked, rinsed and kept
    warm
    Freshly grated Parmesan or
    Romano cheese
    Fresh coarse ground black
    pepper

Melt butter in medium skillet. Add onions and garlic, sauté until transluscent. Add clams with juice and parsley. Simmer for 10 minutes; add milk, salt and pepper. Cook until slightly thickened. Serve hot sauce over cooked pasta. Sprinkle with cheese and freshly grated black pepper.

SPAGHETTI CARBONARA   4 servings

¼   pound bacon
1   pound spaghetti
1   egg, beaten
1   cup freshly grated Parmesan
    cheese
1   cup heavy cream
¼   cup butter, cut in thin slices
2   tablespoons chopped parsley
¼   teaspoon pepper

Cook bacon until crisp. Drain, crumble and reserve. Cook spaghetti according to package directions. Mix egg, cheese, cream parsley, salt and pepper in small bowl. When spaghetti is done, drain and toss with butter. Add egg mixture and toss. Serve with bacon sprinkled on top.

NORFOLK NOODLES   10 servings

12   ounces wide noodles
1   cup chopped fresh parsley
1   pint large curd cottage cheese
1½   pints sour cream
1   tablespoon Worcestershire
     Dash Tabasco
1   bunch green onions, chopped
1   teaspoon salt
½   cup grated sharp Cheddar
     cheese
½   teaspoon paprika

Cook noodles according to package directions. Drain. While noodles are still hot, mix in all of the remaining ingredients except the grated cheese and paprika. Place in shallow baking dish. Refrigerate. When ready to bake, top with cheese and paprika. Place in 350 degree oven, uncovered, for 40 minutes.

NOODLE-ONION PIE

9-inch pie

CRUST
1   cup grated Cheddar cheese
3/4   cup flour
1/4   teaspoon dry mustard
1/4   cup butter, melted
1/2   teaspoon salt

Combine all crust ingredients and knead about 1 minute. Press into the bottom and sides of a 9-inch pie pan. Set aside.

FILLING
1 1/2   cups cooked medium egg noodles
2   cups thinly sliced onions
1/4   teaspoon pepper
1/2   teaspoon salt
1   cup milk, scalded
1   cup grated Cheddar cheese
2   tablespoons butter
2   eggs, beaten

Sauté onions in butter until tender, but not brown. Remove from heat; add noodles and toss lightly. Combine milk, eggs, salt, pepper and cheese. Place noodle mixture in pie shell and pour milk mixture over noodles. Bake at 325 degrees for 30 to 35 minutes. Can be served as an appetizer or side dish.

BRAISED SAFFRON RICE WITH PEAS

8 servings

6 1/2   cups chicken stock (canned)
4   tablespoons butter
1/2   cup finely chopped onions
2   cups long grain white rice
1/2   cup dry white wine or dry vermouth
1/8   teaspoon powdered saffron
1/2   10 1/2-ounce package frozen peas, cooked until just tender
1/2   stick butter, softened
1/2   cup shredded fresh Parmesan cheese

Bring stock to a simmer in a large saucepan and keep it simmering over low heat. In a heavy, large casserole or frying pan, melt butter over low heat. Cook onions in butter, stirring frequently, for 7 to 8 minutes. Do not brown. Add rice and cook 1 to 2 minutes more, until grains glisten with butter and are somewhat opaque. Pour in wine and boil until it is almost absorbed. You may need to transfer to a larger pot at this point. Add 2 cups of the simmering stock to the rice and cook, uncovered, stirring occasionally until all liquid is absorbed. Add 2 more cups of stock and cook, stirring occasionally. Meanwhile, stir the saffron into 2 of the remaining 2 1/2 cups of stock and let it steep for 1 minute. Pour it over the rice; cook until rice is tender and stock is completely absorbed. If the rice is still not tender, add the last 1/2 cup of stock a little at a time. Combine the butter, cheese and peas and stir in just before serving.

VEGETABLE FRIED RICE

10 servings

1 cup brown rice
2 stalks celery
2 carrots
½ pound fresh mushrooms
1 medium onion
1 green pepper
1 16-ounce can bean sprouts
Garlic powder
¼ teaspoon ginger
Seasoned salt
Pepper
1 tablespoon soy sauce
3 tablespoons peanut oil
2 eggs, scrambled
Shredded lettuce

Cook brown rice according to package directions. Thinly slice the fresh vegetables on the diagonal (Chinese-style). Stir-fry vegetables and seasonings in peanut oil until warm. Vegetables should be crisp. Place vegetables in a bowl and mix in the eggs and lettuce. Serve warm. Any quantity of diced, cooked meat or seafood may be added. Heat in pan with vegetables.

TANNER WILD RICE

8 servings

1 4-ounce package wild rice
2 tablespoons butter
1½ cups quartered fresh mushrooms
10 strips bacon, cooked and crumbled (reserve grease)
1 onion, chopped
2 teaspoons Worcestershire
½ cup slivered almonds, toasted
Salt and pepper
1 cup chicken broth

Cook wild rice according to package directions. Sauté mushrooms in butter. Sauté onion in a little of the bacon grease. In a greased 2-quart casserole, combine rice, mushrooms, onion, bacon, Worcestershire, almonds, salt and pepper. Pour ½ cup chicken broth over mixture. Cover and bake at 300 degrees for 30 minutes. Check casserole occasionally and add more broth if mixture appears dry.

MUSHROOM-RICE RING

15 servings

½ cup cooked rice
⅔ cup cooked brown rice
2 pounds mushrooms, finely chopped
¼ pound butter
1 small onion, chopped
Garlic salt
Salt and pepper

Sauté mushrooms in butter with onion. Drain. Mix white and brown rice with mushrooms and onions. Season with garlic salt, salt and pepper. Pack in well-buttered ring mold and place in pan of water. Bake 1 hour at 350 degrees. Unmold to serve.

127

WILD RICE CASSEROLE

6 servings

1 cup wild rice
1 cup chopped ripe olives
1 cup chopped mushrooms
1 cup grated American
    cheese
1 16-ounce can stewed
    tomatoes
½ cup olive oil
1 cup hot water

Soak rice overnight. Drain well. Mix olives, mushrooms, cheese, tomatoes, oil and water with rice. Pour into a greased 2-quart casserole. Bake at 350 degrees for 1 hour. NOTE: You may substitute one 6-ounce box whole grain and wild rice mix.

BUFFET RICE

10 servings

2 6-ounce packages Uncle
    Ben's Original Long
    Grain and Wild Rice
2 10½-ounce cans condensed
    beef consomme
1 10-ounce can condensed
    cream of mushroom soup
1 medium onion, chopped
¼ cup salad oil
1 cup water
1 cup chopped cashews
2 4-ounce cans button
    mushrooms

Use only one of the rice seasoning packets. Mix the rice with seasoning packet, consommé, mushroom soup, onion, salad oil, water and mushrooms. Pour into a 2-quart casserole and bake for 1½ hours, covered, at 350 degrees. Add nuts, bake 30 minutes longer.

DILLY RICE

6 servings

1½ cups water
2 chicken boullion cubes
1½ cups Minute rice
½ cup chopped black olives
1 cup sour cream
1 teaspoon dill weed
1 cup shredded Cheddar
    cheese

In a saucepan, bring water to a boil. Stir in chicken cubes until dissolved. Add rice. Remove from heat and let sit until all water has evaporated, about 10 minutes. Add black olives, sour cream and dill weed. Pour mixture into a greased 2-quart casserole. Sprinkle with cheese. Bake at 325 degrees for 25 minutes.

CHEESE AND CHILE RICE

10 servings

¼ cup butter
1 cup chopped onion
4 cups cooked white rice
1 large bay leaf, crumbled
½ teaspoon salt
⅛ teaspoon pepper
3 4-ounce cans green chilies, drained and halved
2 cups sour cream
1 cup cream-style cottage cheese
2 cups grated sharp Cheddar cheese
Parsley, chopped

Lightly grease a 2-quart or 8x12-inch baking dish. Sauté onion in butter. Remove from heat and stir in rice, sour cream, cottage cheese, bay leaf, salt and pepper. Toss lightly to mix well. Layer ½ of the rice mixture, then ½ of the chiles; sprinkle with ½ of the cheese. Repeat. Bake, uncovered, for 30 to 35 minutes at 375 degrees, or until bubbly. Sprinkle with chopped parsley.

SPINACH-RICE SOUFFLÉ

12 servings

4 eggs, beaten
⅔ cup milk
½ cup minced onion
¼ cup butter or margarine, melted
2 tablespoons minced parsley
1 teaspoon Worcestershire
2 teaspoons salt
½ teaspoon thyme
½ teaspoon nutmeg
Dash pepper
2 10-ounce packages frozen chopped spinach
2 cups cooked rice
⅔ cup milk
2 cups shredded American cheese

Add to beaten eggs; milk, butter, onion, parsley, Worcestershire, and seasonings. Cook spinach according to package directions. Squeeze and drain well. Mix cooked rice with ⅔ cup milk and combine with egg mixture. Stir in spinach and cheese. Pour into greased 9x13-inch baking dish. Bake at 350 degrees for 45 minutes. Let rest a few minutes before cutting into squares and serving.

129

MEXICAN RICE

10 servings

1 large onion, chopped
4 tablespoons olive oil
2 cloves garlic, minced
2 cups long grained rice
1½ cups peeled and finely
    chopped tomatoes
4 cups beef consommé
1½ teaspoons cumin
    Salt to taste

In a large skillet, sauté onion in oil until tender, but not browned. Add garlic and rice; cook 3 to 5 minutes, stirring often, until rice is pale yellow. Stir in tomatoes, consommé, cumin and salt. Bring the mixture to a boil. Cover and simmer over low heat, until liquid is absorbed and rice is tender, approximately 20 minutes.

APPLE-ALMOND RICE

6 servings

½ cup chopped celery
½ cup chopped onion
1 tablespoon margarine
⅛ teaspoon allspice
⅛ teaspoon cinnamon
  Salt
  Pepper
1 tablespoon brown sugar
3 cups cooked rice
½ cup raisins
1 tart cooking apple, cored and
    chopped
½ cup sliced almonds, toasted

Cook celery and onions in margarine until tender crisp. Stir in seasonings, rice and raisins. Heat thoroughly. Stir in apple. Remove from heat; cover and let stand in refrigerator until ready to serve. Reheat in microwave oven. The microwave adds moisture to this dish. Cover with clear plastic wrap while warming. Add toasted almonds just before serving.

Salads &
Salad Dressings

GREEN GODDESS SALAD

DRESSING
1   cup mayonnaise
⅓   cup chopped parsley
3   tablespoons anchovy paste
1   tablespoon lemon juice
½   cup sour cream
3   tablespoons finely chopped
        chives
3   tablespoons tarragon vinegar
     Dash of freshly ground
        pepper

SALAD
1   head romaine lettuce
1   head curly endive
½   cup sliced pitted ripe olives
1   2-ounce can rolled anchovy
        fillets
2   medium tomatoes, cut in
        wedges

Combine all the dressing ingredients by hand; chill at least 3 hours. To serve the salad, combine all the ingredients for the salad and top with the dressing. Toss and serve.

ANCHOVY-ARTICHOKE SALAD

DRESSING
½   cup olive oil
1   2-ounce can anchovy fillets,
        drained
2   tablespoons lemon juice
2   tablespoons white wine
        vinegar
½   teaspoon salt
½   teaspoon sugar
¼   teaspoon onion salt
¼   teaspoon dried oregano
        leaves
¼   teaspoon dry mustard
¼   teaspoon paprika
⅛   teaspoon dried thyme leaves
1   clove garlic, crushed

SALAD
1   8½-ounce can artichoke
        hearts, drained
1   can pitted ripe olives, drained
2   heads lettuce, not iceberg

Place all ingredients in a blender. Cover and blend on medium until very smooth and creamy. Chill at least 2 hours. Pour the dressing into a large container and add ripe olives and artichoke hearts. In a large salad bowl, tear lettuce into bite-size pieces and top with the dressing. Toss and serve.

POLYNESIAN SALAD

8 servings

DRESSING
½ cup salad oil
¼ cup white wine tarragon
    vinegar
1½ teaspoons sugar
½ teaspoon tarragon
¼ teaspoon salt
⅛ teaspoon pepper
    Dash Tabasco

SALAD
1 large head romaine lettuce,
    torn
2 heads Bibb lettuce, torn
1 bunch scallions, finely
    chopped
1 3½-ounce can shredded
    coconut
1 11-ounce can mandarin
    oranges, drained
2 packages slivered almonds,
    toasted or glazed in sugar

Prepare almonds in advance. For toasted almonds; sauté in butter in a frying pan and drain on a paper towel. To glaze; bring ¼ cup water and ½ cup sugar to a boil and continue boiling until the mixture is thick and syrupy. Add almonds, stirring to coat completely. Remove and cool on a plate. Chip off. Almonds should be kept in a sealed bag until used, to retain freshness and crispness. Place all dressing ingredients in a bowl and whisk together. Pour into a jar and chill overnight. Mix together lettuces, chopped scallions, coconut, mandarin oranges and toasted or glazed almonds. Dress with chilled salad dressing.

SUMMER SALAD

8 servings

SALAD
2 heads iceberg lettuce, broken
    up
1 package fresh spinach
2 cucumbers, thinly sliced
½ cup white vinegar
3 tomatoes, peeled and
    quartered
    Capers for garnish
½ teaspoon salt
    Dash of Accent (optional)
    Ground pepper to taste

Marinate cucumbers in vinegar and seasonings for 2 hours. Drain and combine with spinach and lettuce. Gently toss with sour cream dressing. Arrange tomato quarters on plates, add greens and top with capers.

SOUR CREAM DRESSING
1 cup sour cream
1 clove garlic, minced
1 teaspoon lemon juice
¼ teaspoon cayenne pepper
2 green onions, minced
1 teaspoon dill weed
½ teaspoon salt
    Dash of Accent (optional)

Combine all ingredients and chill until needed.

CAESAR SALAD SUPREME

8 servings

1 cup salad oil
1 egg yolk, lightly beaten
1 teaspoon salt
1 teaspoon pepper
1 tablespoon Worcestershire
3 garlic cloves, crushed
1 6-ounce can mushrooms, drained
3 ounces Blue cheese, crumbled
1 head romaine lettuce
  Croutons
  Grated Parmesan or Romano cheese

Blend salad oil, beaten egg yolk, salt, pepper and Worcestershire. Add crushed garlic and mushrooms. Stir in crumbled Blue cheese. Toss dressing with romaine lettuce just before serving. Top with croutons and grated cheese.

PINE CREEK SALAD

4 servings

2 large avocados
½ lemon
1 tablespoon olive oil
1 tablespoon lemon juice
1½ cups watercress leaves, firmly packed
1 cup seeded, chopped tomatoes
¼ cup minced red onion
¼ cup minced celery
  Salt and pepper

Halve the avocados lengthwise and scoop out the pulp leaving a ¼-inch shell. Rub the shell with the lemon. Cut the pulp into ½-inch cubes and toss with olive oil and lemon juice. Combine avocado with watercress leaves, tomatoes, onion and celery. Mix well, adding salt and pepper to taste. Divide the salad among the avocado halves, mounding the mixture into the shells. Chill and serve.

GLEN SALAD

6 servings

2 medium heads of lettuce
¾ cup Blue or Roquefort cheese salad dressing
1 3-ounce package Blue cheese
6 slices bacon, fried and crumbled

Heat oven to broil. Cut 3 1-inch slices from center of each head of lettuce. Reserve ends for some later use. Secure outside leaves with toothpicks. Place lettuce slices on ungreased baking sheet. Spread 2 tablespoons dressing on each; sprinkle with crumbled Blue cheese. Broil lettuce, 2 to 3 inches from heat, until dressing bubbles and begins to brown, about 45 seconds. Place on serving plates and sprinkle with bacon bits.

KOREAN CRUNCH

8 servings

DRESSING
¾ cup sugar
¼ cup vinegar
1 cup oil
2 tablespoons Worcestershire
⅓ cup catsup
1 small onion, finely chopped
Salt and pepper

SALAD
1 bag spinach
1 cup fresh bean sprouts
1 can sliced water chestnuts
½ pound fresh mushrooms,
 sliced
2 hard-boiled eggs, chopped
6 slices bacon, cooked and
 crumbled
2 small green onions, chopped

Combine dressing ingredients in blender or processor. Toss together all salad ingredients. Pour dressing on salad just before serving.

ALL OR NOTHING SALAD

8 servings

1½ pounds fresh spinach
½ pound fresh mushrooms,
 sliced
1 bunch scallions, minced
2 hard-boiled eggs, sieved
4 or more slices of bacon, fried
 (reserve grease)
¼ cup vinegar
½ teaspoon salt
2 cloves garlic, minced
¼ teaspoon freshly ground
 pepper
1 teaspoon sugar
 Pinch dry mustard
¼ teaspoon oregano
¼ teaspoon basil
 Small balls of Blue cheese,
 rolled in chopped nuts
1 avocado, sliced

Wash, drain and tear spinach greens. Chill and crisp. Add mushrooms, scallions and eggs. Crumble crisp bacon into greens. Combine vinegar, seasonings and sugar. Add to bacon drippings in pan. Warm over medium heat. Pour over spinach mixture and toss well. Garnish with Blue cheese balls and avocado. Serve immediately after dressing and garnishing. Serves 4 as a luncheon main dish or 8 as a dinner salad.

PINK SPINACH BOWL

8 servings

1 10-ounce package raw fresh
   spinach
1 cup Marzetti coleslaw
   dressing
1 6-ounce can diced beets
1 bunch green onions, chopped
4 hard-boiled eggs, chopped
1 teaspoon Beau Monde
   seasoning
½ pound bacon, cooked and
   crumbled or 1 can bacon
   bits

Wash spinach and tear for salad. Mix all ingredients for dressing, adding a little beet juice to the dressing to give it a pink color. Just before serving, pour dressing over salad of spinach, beets, eggs and bacon.

SALADE ÉLÉGANT

8 servings

DRESSING
¾ cup salad oil
¼ cup red wine vinegar
2 egg yolks
1 tablespoon parsley
1 tablespoon onion
1 clove garlic, minced
1 teaspoon chopped shallots
2 teaspoons Dijon mustard
⅛ teaspoon tarragon
  Dash of pepper
¼ teaspoon Worcestershire
1½ cups fresh, sliced mushrooms

SALAD
1 head Boston lettuce
4 cups fresh spinach
½ head romaine
½ head French endive
1 14-ounce can artichoke
   hearts, quartered
1 14-ounce can hearts of palm,
   quartered
1 avocado, peeled and sliced
   lengthwise
2 tablespoons chopped walnuts

Combine dressing ingredients and shake vigorously. Add mushrooms to dressing. Chill. Wash and dry greens and place in salad bowl. Add hearts of palm, artichokes and avocado. Toss with dressing. Sprinkle walnuts on top.

COLUMBUS SALAD

6 servings

DRESSING
4 tablespoons sugar
3 teaspoons salt
2 teaspoons Accent
1 teaspoon black pepper
½ cup oil
6 teaspoons white vinegar

SALAD
5 slices bacon, fried and
    crumbled
1 head lettuce, torn
4 green onions, finely chopped
¾ cup chow mein noodles
3 ounces almonds
4 tablespoons sesame seeds

Mix together all dressing ingredients, whisk and pour into a bottle to chill overnight. Take out of the refrigerator and bring to room temperature before dressing salad. Toast almonds and sesame seeds in 325 degree oven for 10 to 15 minutes. Combine all salad ingredients at the last minute. Toss and dress with accompanying dressing. It is very important that the chow mein noodles not be allowed to become stale or soggy.

SWISS GRAPE SALAD

4 servings

BACON DRESSING
¼ cup cider vinegar
½ cup vegetable oil
2 teaspoons Dijon mustard
2 teaspoons brown sugar
1 teaspoon seasoned salt
¼ teaspoon pepper
4 slices bacon, cooked crisp
    and crumbled
2 tablespoons sliced green
    onion

SALAD
6 cups fresh spinach, torn and
    lightly packed
6 ounces Swiss cheese,
    julienned
6 ounces Cheddar cheese,
    julienned
2 cups seedless grapes

In a small bowl, whisk together all ingredients for Bacon Dressing, except bacon and onion. Blend thoroughly. Stir in crumbled bacon and onion. Cover and chill several hours or overnight. Just before serving, mix dressing thoroughly. Arrange spinach, cheeses and grapes on platter or individual serving plates. Spoon dressing over salad.

HOLD-THE-MEAT TACO SALAD   8 servings

1   head lettuce, torn
2   medium tomatoes, chopped in
    large pieces
1   cup chopped green onions
1   cup crushed Fritos
1   cup shredded sharp Cheddar
    cheese
1   package prepared Buttermilk
    salad dressing

Mix lettuce, tomatoes and onions together. May be refrigerated at this point until serving time. When ready to serve, add Fritos, cheese and dressing; toss.

SPRINGTIME SALAD   6 servings

2   bunches fresh spinach,
    washed and dried
1   pint fresh strawberries,
    washed, hulled and halved

DRESSING
½   cup sugar
2   tablespoons sesame seeds
1   tablespoon poppy seeds
1½ teaspoons minced onion
¼   teaspoon Worcestershire
¼   teaspoon paprika
½   cup vegetable oil
¼   cup cider vinegar

Arrange spinach and strawberries in a large bowl. Place sugar, seeds, onion, Worcestershire and paprika in blender. With blender running, add oil and vinegar in a slow, steady steam until thoroughly mixed and thickened. Drizzle over berries and spinach. Serve immediately.

APPLE BACON SALAD   8 servings

¼   teaspoon garlic powder
⅔   cup oil
½   pound bacon, fried and
    crumbled
1   head lettuce, torn
3   red apples, sliced
2   teaspoons lemon juice
½   cup grated Parmesan cheese
3   green onions, sliced
1   cup croutons
½   teaspoon pepper
¼   teaspoon salt
1   egg

Combine oil, lemon juice and garlic powder. Stir in apples. Add remaining ingredients. Toss until all traces of egg disappear. Serve immediately.

MARINATED ASPARAGUS

8 servings

2 14-½ ounce cans asparagus
   spears or same amount
   fresh
1 green pepper, chopped
1 small bunch green onions,
   chopped
½ cup wine vinegar
½ cup sugar
¾ cup salad oil
½ clove garlic
¼ teaspoon paprika

Drain asparagus and lay in shallow pan. Fresh asparagus should be cooked first; do not overcook. Mix remaining ingredients and pour over asparagus. Chill at least 5 hours.

ZUCCHINI APPLE SALAD

6 servings

⅓ cup salad oil
1 tablespoon lemon juice
2 tablespoons white wine
   vinegar
1 teaspoon sugar
1 teaspoon dry basil
¾ teaspoon salt
¼ teaspoon pepper
3 Red or Golden Delicious
   apples, diced
½ medium mild red onion
1 green pepper
1 pound zucchini

In large bowl combine the oil, lemon juice, vinegar, sugar, basil, salt and pepper. Add the unpeeled, diced apples and coat well with the dressing. Thinly slice the onion lengthwise; distribute over the apples. Remove seeds from the green pepper, cut into matchstick-size pieces and arrange over the onion. Thinly slice zucchini and distribute over top. Mix all together gently but thoroughly. Cover and chill. Just before serving, mix again.

MAKE AHEAD SALAD

8 servings

1½ cups mayonnaise
¼ cup Italian salad dressing
2 tablespoons lemon juice
1 tablespoon sugar
   Salt and pepper to taste
2 bunches green onions,
   chopped
½ pound Swiss cheese,
   julienned
1 10-ounce box frozen peas,
   thawed
1 bunch broccoli, cut into
   florets
1 head cauliflower, cut into
   florets

Combine all ingredients in serving bowl. Cover and chill overnight.

BEST CAULIFLOWER SALAD

12 servings

1 head cauliflower, broken into
   florets
1 cup celery, sliced diagonally
   into chevrons
½ cup thinly sliced and
   separated onion
1 14-ounce can artichoke
   hearts drained and
   quartered
1 bunch broccoli, broken into
   florets
1 cup pitted black olives
½ pound fresh mushrooms,
   sliced
1 8-ounce bottle Italian dressing
1 cup mayonnaise
2 teaspoons lemon juice
¼ cup chili sauce
2 teaspoons dill
1 teaspoon salt
   Cherry tomatoes, halved

In large bowl, combine cauliflower, celery, onion, quartered artichoke hearts, broccoli, black olives and mushrooms. Pour bottled dressing over vegetables and marinate in refrigerator overnight. Stir occasionally. In the morning, drain excess oil from vegetables. Combine mayonnaise, lemon juice, chili sauce, dill and salt. Pour over drained vegetables. Toss gently. Do not overdress. Chill in refrigerator several hours. Garnish with tomato halves.

VICTORY GARDEN

20 servings

1 16-ounce can french cut
   green beans
1 14-ounce can bean sprouts
1 4-ounce can mushrooms
1 10-ounce can white whole
   corn
1 4-ounce can pimiento,
   chopped
1 8-ounce can sliced water
   chestnuts
3 grated carrots
1 large onion, chopped
1 small head cauliflower,
   beaded
1 cup diced celery
1 cup diced green pepper

DRESSING
1⅔ cups cider vinegar
1½ cups sugar
¾ cup oil
3 teaspoons salt (amount
   optional)

Open, drain and combine all vegetables. Use a very large bowl. To make the dressing, combine vinegar, sugar, oil and salt in a saucepan and bring to a boil. Pour over the vegetables. Let cool. Refrigerate. This salad will last under refrigeration for 4 weeks.

MEXICAN WINTER SALAD

10 servings

2 cups sliced zucchini
1 10-ounce package frozen
   corn, cooked
1 cup canned roasted, sweet
   red peppers
¾ cup light salad oil
¼ cup vinegar
2 teaspoons salt
   Garlic powder
1 teaspoon sugar
1 16-ounce can garbanzo
   beans, drained
1 16-ounce can black olives,
   drained
1 medium avocado, sliced
   Lettuce leaves

Combine all ingredients, except avocado, and marinate for 3 to 4 hours. Add avocado and drain. Serve on lettuce leaves. Great to serve with any Mexican dish.

PEA-NUT SALAD

12 servings

2 10-ounce packages frozen
   baby peas
2 cups diced celery
1 cup chopped green onion
1 pound bacon, fried and
   crumbled
1 teaspoon Beau Monde
1 cup dry roasted peanuts,
   chopped
1 8-ounce container sour cream

Break up frozen pea packages. Combine peas, celery, onions, bacon, and Beau Monde. Refrigerate. Just before serving, add peanuts and sour cream.

HOT CARAWAY SLAW

6 servings

1¼ cups chopped onion
3 tablespoons butter or
   margarine
1 very tart apple, pared, cored
   and thinly sliced
1 head cabbage, shredded
⅓ cup Dekuyper's Kümmel
¼ cup white wine vinegar
1 teaspoon sugar
½ teaspoon salt
½ teaspoon caraway seeds
¼ teaspoon pepper

Sauté onions in butter over medium heat until tender but not brown. Stir in apple. Sauté 3 minutes. Add cabbage and sauté for 2 minutes. Cover and steam for 3 to 4 minutes. Add remaining ingredients. Reduce heat to low and steam another 5 minutes. Cabbage should be crisp-tender. Do not overcook.

COUNTRY SLAW

8 servings

1 head cabbage, shredded
1 small white onion, chopped
1 green pepper, diced
1 carrot, shredded
Salt and pepper to taste
½ cup sugar
1 cup mayonnaise
¼ cup vinegar

Toss together all vegetables. Mix mayonnaise with vinegar, sugar, salt and pepper. Combine with vegetables and chill before serving.

GERMAN COLESLAW

8 servings

4 slices bacon
¼ cup vinegar
1 teaspoon salt
1 tablespoon brown sugar
1 tablespoon finely chopped
   onion
4 cups shredded cabbage
½ cup chopped parsley

Cook bacon until crisp; remove from skillet and crumble. Add vinegar, salt, sugar and onion to the fat in the skillet. Return bacon to the pan and heat dressing thoroughly. Pour over cabbage and parsley; toss and serve.

CAESAR POTATO SALAD

8 servings

DRESSING
½ cup salad oil
1 teaspoon Worcestershire
1 teaspoon salt
⅛ teaspoon pepper
⅛ teaspoon garlic powder
¼ cup lemon juice
1 egg
¼ cup minced onion

SALAD
4 cups cooked, diced potatoes
1 large head romaine
2 cups cubed bread
2 tablespoons butter, melted
   Pinch of garlic powder
¼ cup grated Parmesan cheese
¼ cup crumbled Roquefort
   cheese
8 anchovies
½ cup sliced black olives

Prepare dressing by combining salad oil, Worcestershire, salt, pepper, garlic powder, lemon juice, egg and onion. Toss with potatoes and chill overnight. Clean and prepare romaine. Toss together bread, butter and pinch of garlic and add to romaine. Add Parmesan, roquefort, olives and anchovies. Add potatoes to salad; toss and serve.

CONFETTI POTATO SALAD

6 servings

2 **pounds red potatoes**
½ **cup salad oil**
¼ **cup white wine vinegar**
1 **tablespoon sugar**
1½ **teaspoons chili powder**
1 **teaspoon seasoned salt**
½ **teaspoon garlic salt**
¼ **teaspoon ground cumin**
¼ **teaspoon Tabasco**
1 **12-ounce can corn with sweet red & green peppers, drained**
1 **2-ounce can sliced ripe olives, drained**
⅔ **cup thinly sliced green onions Lettuce leaves**

Clean potatoes and cook in boiling water until just tender, 20 to 30 minutes. Drain. When cool enough to handle, peel and cut into ½ to ¾-inch cubes. While potatoes are cooking, mix together; oil, vinegar, sugar, chili powder, salts, cumin and Tabasco. Pour over warm potates and mix well. Cover and refrigerate until cold. Add the olives, corn and green onions. Cover and refrigerate up to 2 days. Stir well before serving. Serve on lettuce leaves.

COTTAGE POTATO SALAD

8 servings

3 **cups mayonnaise**
6 **medium red potatoes, boiled, peeled and thinly sliced**
1 **large red onion, thinly sliced**
2 **cups small curd cottage cheese**
Salt

Generously spread bottom and sides of a large bowl with part of the mayonnaise. Add a layer of potatoes. Sprinkle lightly with salt. Spread with mayonnaise. Add layer of onion and push down into mayonnaise. Next add a layer of cottage cheese and press into mayonnaise. Repeat with potatoes, salt, mayonnaise and onion; end with cottage cheese. Cover and refrigerate 12 hours or longer if possible.

SUZETTE D'AVOCADO

6 servings

6 **slices bacon**
2½ **cups cubed, warm, cooked potatoes**
2 **hard-boiled eggs, chopped**
¼ **cup minced onion**
1 **tablespoon thinly sliced scallion tops**
1 **tablespoon sliced pimiento Salt and pepper**
½ **cup mayonnaise**
2 **tablespoons lime juice**
2 **avocados, peeled, seeded and cubed**

In a skillet, sauté bacon until crisp. Drain the bacon on paper towels and crumble into a salad bowl. Add cubed potatoes, eggs, onion, scallion tops and pimiento. Salt and pepper to taste. Toss and chill, covered, for 1 hour. In a small bowl, combine the mayonnaise and lime juice. Fold the dressing into the potato mixture and add cubed avocados.

MOSTACCIOLI SALAD

1   pound box Mostaccioli
     Oil
1½   cups sugar
2   cups vinegar
1   cup water
1   teaspoon salt
1   tablespoon coarsely ground
     pepper
1   tablespoon Accent
½   teaspoon garlic powder
1   teaspoon parsley flakes
1   medium red onion, thinly
     sliced
2   cucumbers, thinly sliced

Cook Mostaccioli 12 to 15 minutes in water. Drain. Rinse in cold water. Coat lightly with oil. Add sugar, vinegar, water, salt, pepper, Accent, garlic powder, parsley flakes, onion and cucumbers. Chill several hours.

TROPICAL TOSS

12 servings

2   cantaloupes, cubed
4   avocados, cut in ¼-inch slices
2   14-ounce cans hearts of palm,
     sliced 1-inch thick
4   tablespoons lemon juice
     Lettuce leaves
2   heads curly endive
½   cup toasted, slivered almonds

TANGY CITRUS DRESSING
6   tablespoons lemon juice
6   tablespoons lime juice
½   teaspoon each: salt, white
     pepper, ground ginger,
     ground coriander and
     ground allspice

Combine cantaloupe, avocado and hearts of palm in a large bowl. Sprinkle with lemon juice and chill for 1 hour. Make citrus dressing by combining all ingredients. Line a large bowl with lettuce leaves. Tear endive into bite-size pieces and place in bowl. Spoon fruit mixture into center. Pour dressing over salad. Sprinkle with nuts. Toss before serving.

HOT FRUIT COMPOTE

8 servings

10   macaroon cookies, crumbled
4   cups canned, drained fruit
     (peaches, pears, apricots or
     pineapple)
½   cup toasted, slivered almonds
¼   cup light brown sugar
½   cup cooking sherry
¼   cup butter, melted

Butter 2½-quart casserole. Cover the bottom with crumbled macaroons. Alternate fruit and macaroons. Sprinkle with almonds, brown sugar, sherry and butter. Bake uncovered at 350 degrees for 30 minutes.

PEACH AMBROSIA

8 servings ... 12 servings

1   13¼-ounce can pineapple
      tidbits, drained
1   11-ounce can mandarin
      orange segments, drained
1   cup seedless grape halves
1   cup miniature marshmallows
1   cup flaked coconut
1   cup dairy sour cream
2   16-ounce cans peach halves,
      drained and chilled
½   cup toasted, slivered almonds

Combine pineapple, mandarin oranges, grapes, marshmallows and coconut; stir in sour cream. Cover and refrigerate overnight. Mound in peach halves and sprinkle with almonds. This may also be served as a dessert.

LUNCHEON GRAPEFRUIT WEDGES

8 servings

1   3-ounce package lemon
      gelatin
1   cup boiling water
2   large, fresh grapefruit
2   cups crushed pineapple,
      undrained

Pour boiling water over gelatin. Cool until mixture begins to thicken slightly. Cut the grapefruit in half and remove all sections from the grapefruit rind. Clean the shells. Drain grapefruit sections and reserve the juice. Combine grapefruit sections with crushed pineapple. Add the gelatin mixture and spoon into grapefruit shells. Refrigerate.

DRESSING

½   cup fruit juice (you may use
      the juice from the
      grapefruit)
3   tablespoons flour
½   cup sugar
1   scant teaspoon salt
2   egg yolks, beaten
3   marshmallows
⅛   cup lemon juice
½   cup chopped pecans
2   egg whites, whipped
½   cup heavy cream, whipped

Heat fruit juice. Combine flour, salt and sugar; blend with just enough heated fruit juice to make a smooth paste. Add to remaining heated fruit juice and cook for 15 to 20 minutes or until smooth and thickened. Stir in slightly beaten egg yolks and cook for 5 minutes longer. Remove from heat; add marshmallows and cool. Add nuts and lemon juice. Fold in stiffly beaten egg whites and whipped cream. Refrigerate. When ready to serve, cut grapefruit shells in half again. Serve with dressing.

TUNA SALAD PUFF

4 servings

PASTRY SHELL

¾ cup milk
4 tablespoons butter
¾ cup flour
½ teaspoon salt
3 eggs
1 tablespoon butter, softened

In a medium saucepan, cook milk and butter over medium heat until butter melts and milk almost boils. Remove mixture from heat; with a wooden spoon, beat in flour and salt all at once. Return to low heat; stir vigorously until batter leaves sides of pan and clings to spoon, about 1 minute. Remove from heat and cool 3 to 4 minutes. Add eggs, one at a time, beating well after each addition. Use electric mixer or wire whisk. Batter will be smooth and glossy. Grease a 9-inch pie plate with the softened butter. Spoon in batter and spread evenly. Bake at 400 degrees for 30 to 35 minutes. Remove from oven and cool for 10 minutes. Carefully remove shell from pie plate and let cool completely before filling.

SALAD

1 cup loosely packed parsley
½ cup whole walnuts
1 clove garlic, chopped
½ teaspoon salt
⅓ cup olive oil
2 7-ounce cans tuna, drained
1 tablespoon lemon juice
1 avocado
Lettuce leaves

Break stems from parsley and discard. Put parsley in a food processor or blender along with walnuts, garlic, salt and half of the oil. Whirl several seconds. Scrape down sides and whirl again while pouring in the remaining oil. In a mixing bowl, break up tuna, leaving some chucks. Sprinkle with lemon juice. Toss with dressing from blender. Cut avocado in half and remove pit. Peel and slice lengthwise. Line cooled shell with lettuce leaves. Place avocado slices around the edge and spoon salad in the center. Cut into pie-shaped wedges.

SENSATIONAL SEAFOOD SALAD

8 servings

1 loaf sliced, white sandwich
   bread
Butter
1 medium onion, finely chopped
4 hard-boiled eggs, chopped
2 4¼-ounce cans of shrimp,
   rinsed and drained
1 6-ounce can crab meat,
   rinsed and drained
1 cup finely chopped celery
2 cups mayonnaise
Salad greens
Cucumber slices
Cherry tomatoes

Cut crust from bread; spread slices lightly with butter. Cut each slice into small cubes. Combine onion and eggs with the bread cubes. Refrigerate overnight. Add shrimp, crab meat, celery and mayonnaise. Blend. Cover and let stand 3 to 4 hours in the refrigerator before serving. To serve; pile mixture on salad greens and garnish with cucumber slices and cherry tomatoes.

SHRIMP-RICE SALAD

10 servings

1½ cups uncooked rice
1 pound shrimp
¼ package Shrimp Boil
½ cup chopped green pepper
⅓ cup chopped onion
1½ cups cauliflower, cut in
   florets
¼ cup stuffed green olives,
   sliced
½ cup mayonnaise
Dash of Tabasco
Juice of 1 lemon
Lettuce leaves

Cook rice. Cook shrimp in water with Shrimp Boil until tender. Drain and shell. Combine all ingredients except lemon juice. Chill several hours. One hour before serving, stir in lemon juice. Serve on lettuce-lined plates.

CHINESE TAKE-OUT

6 servings

DRESSING
¼ cup cider vinegar
¼ cup salad oil
2 tablespoons sugar
1 teaspoon salt
¼ teaspoon pepper
Seasonings from noodle
   package

SALAD
1 head lettuce
1 4½-ounce can shrimp
   or

Mix salad dressing ingredients in order given. Shake well and set aside. Break apart lettuce and put in salad bowl. Add shrimp, chicken, or cooked bacon pieces and oranges. Set aside. Melt margarine. Over medium-low heat, add broken pieces of noodles. Stir until lightly tan. Add sesame seeds. Continue to sauté until all are medium to dark brown. When ready to serve, add noodles to lettuce. Toss with dressing and serve.

1 cup cooked, cubed chicken
or
½ pound bacon, cooked and
crumbled
1 11-ounce can mandarin
oranges, drained
1 package Ramen noodles,
broken
2 tablespoons margarine or
butter
2 tablespoons sesame seeds

DAGWOOD DINNER
8 servings

3 poppy seed rolls
3 tomatoes, chopped
1 head lettuce, chopped
1 onion, chopped
6 ounces Swiss cheese,
julienned
¼ pound shaved ham
¼ pound salami, sliced into
thin strips

Pull apart rolls into walnut-sized pieces. Combine tomatoes, lettuce, onion, cheese and meat. Toss together in a bowl. Mix dressing, shake well and pour over salad. Put garlic powder, salt, pepper and oregano on the table for people to add extra. Any cheese or meat combinations may be substituted.

DRESSING
¾ cup oil
¼ cup tarragon vinegar
½ teaspoon dried oregano
⅛ teaspoon pepper
1 teaspoon salt
¼ teaspoon garlic powder

FONDULOHA CHICKEN
24 servings

6 large pineapples
7½ cups cooked cubed chicken
2½ cups diced celery
2½ cups sliced bananas
1 cup salted peanuts or
cashews
2½ cups mayonnaise
6 tablespoons chopped chutney
or 1½ teaspoons salt and
1 teaspoon pepper
1½ teaspoons curry powder
1½ cups shredded or flaked
coconut
3 11-ounce cans mandarin
oranges

Leaving green tops on, cut pineapple into fourths lengthwise. Remove fruit and cube. Drain fruit and shells on paper towels. Mix pineapple, chicken, celery, bananas and nuts. Blend together mayonnaise, chutney and curry powder. Toss mayonnaise mixture with pineapple mixture. Fill each pineapple shell with the fruit mixture, sprinkle with coconut and garnish with mandarin orange sections.

CHRISTMAS BRUNCH SALAD

10 servings

1 16-ounce can jellied cranberry
    sauce
2 tablespoons lemon juice
½ cup unsweetened pineapple
    juice
  Rind of 1 lemon, finely
    grated
1 egg white
2 tablespoons confectioners'
    sugar
  Foil baking cups
  Whole cranberries
  Parsley

Crush jelly and add lemon juice, pineapple juice and rind. Freeze until mushy, stirring frequently. Beat egg white until stiff, gradually adding confectioners' sugar. Fold egg white into jelly mixture. Pour into foil baking cups and freeze until firm. Serve in the foil cups. Garnish with a few whole cranberries and parsley.

APRICOT SALAD

12 servings

3 3-ounce packages orange
    gelatin
2 cups boiling water
1 cup pineapple juice
1 cup apricot nectar
1 30-ounce can apricots,
    cut up and drained
1 15¼-ounce can crushed
    pineapple, drained
10 large marshmallows, cut
    in small pieces

TOPPING
½ cup apricot nectar
½ cup sugar
2 tablespoons flour
1 egg
2 tablespoons lemon juice
2 tablespoons butter
2 cups non-dairy whipped
    topping

Mix together gelatin, water, pineapple juice and apricot nectar. Let cool. Add apricots, pineapple and marshmallows. Pour into a 9x13-inch pan and refrigerate until set. To prepare topping; mix apricot nectar, sugar and flour in a saucepan. Cook until thickened. Add small amount of hot liquid to egg and mix before adding egg to pan. Cool; add lemon juice and butter. Fold in whipped topping. Spread over set gelatin.

PECK O' CUCS SALAD

8 servings

5 medium cucumbers, peeled
1 envelope unflavored gelatin
2 tablespoons sugar
¾ teaspoon salt
⅔ cup boiling water
3 tablespoons lemon juice
1 cup mayonnaise
¼ cup minced onion
¼ cup fresh, minced parsley
(optional)
1 8-ounce package cream
cheese, softened

DRESSING
1 cup sour cream
1 cup mayonnaise
½ cup fresh or frozen chives
1 tablespoon cider vinegar
1 teaspoon lemon juice
1 teaspoon salt
1 teaspoon pepper
1 clove garlic (optional)
2 ounces Blue cheese

Cut cucumbers in half and scrape seeds. Chop; making about 2¼ cups of drained cucumber. Thoroughly mix gelatin, sugar and salt. Add the boiling water and stir to dissolve sugar. Add lemon juice. Combine cucumber, onion, parsley and mayonnaise with the cream cheese. Mix well and stir into gelatin mixture. Pour into a 9-inch ring mold or serving dish and refrigerate for at least 8 hours.

To prepare dressing, combine all ingredients in blender and mix until smooth. Unmold salad and place dressing in a bowl that will fit into the center hole.

SPINACH SWINGER SALAD

6 servings

2 envelopes unflavored gelatin
1 10-ounce can condensed
beef broth
¼ cup water
½ teaspoon salt
2 tablespoons lemon juice
1 cup Miracle Whip
1 10-ounce package frozen,
chopped spinach, thawed
¼ cup chopped green onion
4 hard-boiled eggs, chopped
½ pound bacon, cooked and
crumbled
Pimiento strips

Soften gelatin in broth. Stir over low heat until dissolved. Stir in water, salt and lemon juice. Gradually add gelatin to Miracle Whip and mix well. Chill until slightly thickened. Fold in well-drained spinach, onion, eggs and bacon. Pour into a 1½-quart mold. Unmold when set and garnish with pimiento strips.

TOMATO ASPIC WITH SHRIMP

4 servings

2 envelopes unflavored gelatin
3½ cups tomato juice
½ teaspoon salt
6 tablespoons bottled chili
  sauce
2 tablespoons lemon juice
3 tablespoons horseradish
2 teaspoons sugar
2 4½-ounce cans tiny shrimp
  Mayonnaise
  Lemon slices
  Asparagus spears (optional)

Soak gelatin in ½ cup tomato juice. Bring to a boil 3 cups tomato juice, salt, chili sauce, lemon juice, horseradish and sugar. Add gelatin and stir until gelatin is dissolved. Add shrimp and stir. Pour into an 8x8-inch pan and refrigerate. Serve each portion on a bed of lettuce leaves. Garnish with mayonnaise and lemon slices or asparagus spears.

PRETZEL SALAD

20 servings

3 tablespoons sugar
2 cups crushed pretzel crumbs
¾ cup butter or margarine,
  melted
½ cup confectioners' sugar
1 8-ounce package cream
  cheese, softened
1 package Dream Whip
2 cups miniature marshmallows
1 16-ounce box strawberry
  gelatin
2½ cups boiling water
1 10-ounce box frozen
  strawberries

Mix sugar, pretzel crumbs and melted butter. Press into a 9x13-inch pan and bake 15 minutes at 350 degrees. Cool. Mix confectioners' sugar with cream cheese. Prepare Dream Whip according to package directions and add it and the marshmallows to the cheese. Spread mixture in pan. Dissolve gelatin in boiling water, stir in strawberries. Cool and allow to thicken slightly. Spread over cheese layer, refrigerate overnight.

BACON AND EGG SALAD DRESSING
3 cups

½ cup red wine vinegar
2 tablespoons mayonnaise
8 slices bacon, chopped and
    cooked crisp
1 hard-boiled egg, chopped
⅓ cup sugar
1 tablespoon salt
½ tablespoon garlic powder
3 cups light salad oil

Combine salt, pepper, egg, bacon, sugar, garlic powder, vinegar and mayonnaise. Stir until salt and sugar dissolve. Stir in oil and blend well. Good over fresh spinach.

SUNNY'S DRESSING
1 pint

1 3-ounce package cream
    cheese, softened
3 ounces Blue cheese,
    crumbled
5 tablespoons water
1 egg
1 tablespoon plus 1½ teaspoons
    lemon juice
1 cup salad oil
¼ cup red wine vinegar
¼ teaspoon prepared sharp
    mustard
¾ teaspoon paprika
¾ teaspoon salt
¼ teaspoon garlic powder
¼ teaspoon white pepper
1 tablespoon sugar
2 tablespoons snipped chives
1½ tablespoons Worcestershire
2 tablespoons prepared salad
    and sandwich sauce

Combine cheese and beat until smooth. Beat in water, 1 teaspoon at a time, until mixture is of pouring consistency. Set aside. Combine egg, lemon juice and ¼ cup oil in container of blender. Blend on medium speed for 15 seconds. Turn to high speed and slowly add remaining oil. Turn off blender; add vinegar and seasonings. Blend at high speed for 30 seconds. Add cheese mixture and blend until well combined.

LEMONADE DRESSING
1½ cups

2 eggs, slightly beaten
½ cup sugar
1 6-ounce can lemonade
    concentrate
1 cup heavy cream, whipped

Combine eggs, sugar and lemonade concentrate in a small saucepan. Cook over medium heat, stirring, until thick; cool. Refrigerate for several hours until well chilled. Fold in whipped cream. Refrigerate until needed. Serve on any fruit salad. May also be served as a dip for a fruit tray.

CAROL'S SALAD DRESSING
1 pint

1⅓ cups salad oil
⅓ cup honey
⅓ cup tarragon vinegar
⅔ cup catsup
1 teaspoon salt
½ teaspoon Worcestershire
  sauce
1 clove garlic, minced

Blend all ingredients well. Keeps several days refrigerated.

TANGY HONEY DRESSING
2 cups

½ cup honey
½ teaspoon salt
⅓ cup chili sauce
⅓ cup vinegar
1 tablespoon grated onion
1 teaspoon Worcestershire
1 cup salad oil

Mix together honey, salt, chili sauce, vinegar, onion and Worcestershire. Slowly add salad oil, beating constantly until well blended. Can be made in a blender or food processor.

BISTRO VINAIGRETTE
1 cup

1 teaspoon salt
½ teaspoon freshly ground
  pepper
1 teaspoon Dijon mustard
⅔ cup refined olive oil
⅓ cup red wine vinegar

Mix together salt, pepper and mustard. Slowly add olive oil; blend well. Add vinegar and blend.

TART MAYONNAISE
1 cup

4 teaspoons Dijon mustard
4 teaspoons red wine vinegar
1 egg yolk
½ teaspoon Worcestershire
  Tabasco
½ cup peanut or olive oil
  Salt and freshly ground
  pepper
4 teaspoons heavy cream

Place mustard, vinegar, egg yolk, Worcestershire and a few drops of Tabasco in a bowl. Using a wire whisk, start beating the mixture rapidly. Gradually add the oil; beating constantly. The mixture should be like a thin mayonnaise. Add salt and pepper to taste and the heavy cream; blend. To make a thinner dressing, beat in a little water or lemon juice.

THOUSAND ISLAND DRESSING
2 cups

1 cup mayonnaise
¼ cup chili sauce
¼ cup sour cream
2 tablespoons ketchup
2 tablespoons lemon juice
1 hard-boiled egg
2 tablespoons minced green
   pepper
2 tablespoons minced celery
2 tablespoons minced green
   onion
2 tablespoons minced
   cucumber
1 tablespoon chopped parsley
1 teaspoon salt
1 teaspoon sugar
½ teaspoon paprika
¼ teaspoon pepper

Mix all ingredients together. Serve on lettuce salad or Crab Louis. Can be made ahead and kept refrigerated.

BLUE CHEESE VINAIGRETTE
1 quart

2 cups imported olive oil
1 cup vinegar
   Juice of 1 lemon
2 teaspoons paprika
   Dash Worcestershire
1 tablespoon grated onion
1 tablespoon cayenne pepper
1 teaspoon salt
8 ounces Blue cheese, mashed

Combine oil and vinegar in quart jar with lid. Add remaining ingredients, including Blue cheese, and shake to blend. Keeps refrigerated indefinitely. Flavor improves with time. Shake well before serving.

PARMESAN DRESSING
4 servings

¼ cup vegetable oil
¼ teaspoon pepper
1 garlic clove, minced
½ teaspoon salt
1 tablespoon lemon juice
   Pinch of dry mustard
2 rounded tablespoons
   Parmesan cheese

Combine all ingredients in a glass jar and shake vigorously until thoroughly blended. Enough for 2 quarts of salad greens.

BLUE CAESAR DRESSING

¾ cup

3 ounces Blue cheese
2 tablespoons white vinegar
1 teaspoon anchovy paste
Dash of Worcestershire
1 tablespoon lemon juice
½ cup olive oil
2 small cloves garlic, minced

Combine all ingredients except, Blue cheese, in a jar and shake well. Before serving, crumble Blue cheese over lettuce salad; toss with dressing.

ROQUEFORT DRESSING

1 quart

2 cups Roquefort cheese, crumbled
1 cup cottage cheese
2 tablespoons lemon juice
½ teaspoon crushed garlic
½ cup mayonnaise
1 cup half-and-half

Mix all ingredients together. Thin as desired with additional cream. For smaller cheese pieces, put ingredients into food processor and mix. For more color, top the salad dressing with chopped green onions.

CLIFF'S DRESSING MIX

1 pint

4 teaspoons salt
1¾ cups cider vinegar
1¼ cups sugar
⅞ cup water
Salad oil
Garlic cloves (optional)

Combine all ingredients, except oil, and garlic, in a small saucepan. Cook, stirring, over medium heat until sugar is dissolved. Store in refrigerator until needed. To serve; lightly toss lettuce with salad oil. You may add 1 to 2 peeled garlic cloves to oil several hours before serving. Toss oiled lettuce with small amount of refrigerated dressing mix. Toss again and taste; correct the amounts if needed. Rough proportions are: ⅓ dressing mix to ⅔ oil.

AVOCADO FRUIT TOPPING

1 cup

2 ripe avocados
⅓ teaspoon salt
Juice of 3 limes
1 tablespoon lemon juice
½ teaspoon grated lemon rind
⅓ cup honey

Peel avocado and press through strainer. Add remaining ingredients. Blend. Pour into small bowl and freeze 3 hours. Stir to slush before serving. Serve over fresh peaches, pears, thinly sliced bananas or any combination of fresh fruit.

MOM'S SALAD DRESSING MIX
1½ cups

2	tablespoons butter
2	tablespoons flour
½	teaspoon dry mustard
4	egg yolks
½	cup sugar
½	cup vinegar
1	cup water
1	teaspoon salt

Melt butter; stir in flour and mustard. Mix together yolks, sugar, vinegar, water and salt. Stir into butter mixture. Cook until thick; cool, then refrigerate. This dressing mix keeps in the refrigerator for weeks. For potato salad: add 2 parts dressing mix to 1 part mayonnaise. For fruit salad: whip 1 cup of whipping cream and add 2 tablespoons or more of dressing mix.

SEEDED FRUIT DRESSING
1½ cups

¾	cup sugar
1	teaspoon dry mustard
1	teaspoon salt
⅓	cup cider vinegar
1	cup salad oil
1	tablespoon minced onion (optional)
1	teaspoon poppy seeds
1	teaspoon sesame seeds

Combine ingredients and shake well. Serve over fresh fruit salad.

FRUIT SALAD HONEY DRESSING
1 pint

⅔	cup sugar
1	teaspoon dry mustard
1	teaspoon paprika
¼	teaspoon salt
1	teaspoon celery seed
⅓	cup honey, warmed
5	tablespoons white vinegar
1	tablespoon lemon juice
1	teaspoon grated onion
1	cup salad oil

Mix together sugar, mustard, paprika, salt and celery seed. Add honey, vinegar, lemon juice and onion to above mixture. Add salad oil and shake well. Serve over fresh fruit salad. This can be made ahead and refrigerated. Warm to room temperature before using.

Entrees

MEATBALLS WITH TOMATO SAUCE

12 servings

SAUCE
1   small onion, chopped
1   14½-ounce can stewed
       tomatoes
4   6-ounce cans tomato paste
4   cans of water for each can of
       paste
1   pound spareribs

Brown onion in small amount of cooking oil; remove from pan. Cut ribs apart and brown in same pan. Remove ribs from pan. Place tomatoes in pan and mash down with slotted spoon or potato masher. Simmer tomatoes for ½ hour over low heat; don't burn. In separate kettle, place 4 cans of tomato paste, water and the simmered tomatoes. Stir well and add the browned ribs. Simmer or cook slowly for a minimum of 3 hours. Stir occasionally. Remove ribs; take off meat; mince and return to sauce.

MEATBALLS
1   pound each ground beef and
       chuck
2   eggs
1   cup freshly grated Parmesan
       cheese
½   cup freshly chopped parsley
1   clove garlic, finely chopped
1   cup bread crumbs, soaked in
       milk to make mushy paste
2   teaspoons salt
⅛   teaspoon pepper
     Oil
     Spaghetti

Combine ground beef, chuck, eggs, cheese, parsley, garlic, bread crumbs, salt and pepper; form meatballs. Brown in small amount of oil. Add the meatballs to sauce and simmer for 1 hour. Serve over 1 pound cooked spaghetti.

QUICKIE MOUSSAKA

8 servings

1   pound eggplant
4   zucchini
1   medium onion, sliced
2   tablespoons chopped parsley
3   tablespoons salad oil
1   7½-ounce jar roasted
       pimientos, drained
1   4½-ounce jar sliced
       mushrooms, drained
1½ pounds ground chuck
1   teaspoon salt
1   teaspoon dried oregano
1   6-ounce can tomato paste
6   drops Tabasco
1   10-½-ounce can condensed
       Cheddar cheese soup
¼   cup Parmesan cheese, grated

Wash and dry eggplant and zucchini. Do not peel. Cut eggplant lengthwise into quarters and slice crosswise. Cut zucchini into ¼-inch slices. In skillet, heat oil and add eggplant, zucchini, onion and parsley. Cook, covered, over medium heat 15 minutes. Stir in mushrooms and pimiento. Sauté ground chuck. Stir in salt, oregano, tomato paste and Tabasco. Cool several minutes. Heat cheese soup. In large round casserole, arrange vegetables around edge. Place meat in center and cover with heated soup. Sprinkle grated Parmesan cheese over all and put under the broiler 2 to 3 minutes.

ITALIAN DELIGHT

12 servings

2 7-ounce packages spaghetti,
    cooked and drained
2 pounds ground beef
2 tablespoons butter
1 6-ounce can mushrooms
    with juice
½ cup butter, melted
1 16-ounce can cream-style
    corn
1 16-ounce can tomatoes
    with juice, chopped
1 cup chopped celery
1 small green pepper, chopped
1 medium onion, chopped
2 teaspoons Worcestershire
1 teaspoon chili powder
    Salt
1 cup grated American or
    Cheddar cheese

Brown ground beef in butter. Combine with cooked spaghetti, mushrooms, melted butter, corn, tomatoes, celery, green pepper, onions and seasonings. Stir in ¾ cup cheese. Place in large 3-quart casserole and top with reserved ¼ cup cheese. Bake 1½ hours at 325 degrees.

PARTY LASAGNE

12 servings

1½ pounds lean ground beef
¼ cup olive oil
1 cup chopped onion
1 garlic clove, minced
3½ cups tomatoes, canned
1 6-ounce can tomato paste
2 6-ounce cans tomato sauce
1 pound Mozzarella cheese,
    sliced
½ cup grated Parmesan
1 8-ounce package lasagne
    noodles
12 ounces cottage cheese or
    Ricotta
2 teaspoons salt
1 teaspoon basil
½ bay leaf
½ teaspoon oregano
½ teaspoon pepper
1 cup sliced ripe olives
1 egg, beaten
6 ounces frozen spinach
1 teaspoon sugar
¼ teaspoon nutmeg

Brown meat in hot oil; add onion and garlic. Drain excess moisture. Add to meat; tomatoes, tomato paste and sauce, salt, basil, oregano, pepper and bay leaf. Cover and simmer for 1 hour. Stir in olives. Meanwhile, cook lasagne noodles in boiling water for 20 minutes; drain. Cook spinach as directed on package; drain. Mix sugar, egg and nutmeg in saucepan with spinach. In shallow baking dish, spread ⅓ of the meat sauce and cover with a layer of ½ of the noodles, arranging them lenthwise in dish. Add a layer of ½ of the cottage cheese or Ricotta, and a layer of ½ of the Mozzarella; then all of the spinach and ½ of the Parmesan. Repeat with rest of the noodles, another ⅓ of sauce, rest of cottage cheese and Mozzarella. Finish with remaining sauce and Parmesan. Bake at 350 degrees, uncovered, for 40 minutes or until bubbly.

SPAGHETTI PIE

1 10-inch pie

6 ounces spaghetti, broken up
2 eggs, beaten
1 cup Parmesan cheese
2 tablespoons margarine
½ cup chopped onion
½ cup chopped green pepper
1 cup sour cream
  or
1 cup cottage cheese
½ pound bulk Italian sausage
¼ pound hamburger
1 6-ounce can tomato paste
1 cup water
4 ounces Mozzarella cheese,
  grated

Break up spaghetti and cook; drain. While still warm, add Parmesan cheese and beaten eggs. Make a crust with this mixture by patting it into a 10-inch pie pan. Melt margarine. Sauté green pepper and onion. When cool, add to sour cream. Pour over the spaghetti crust. Cook and drain meats. Add tomato paste and water; simmer 10 minutes uncovered. Pour over sour cream mixture. Top with Mozzarella cheese. Bake at 350 degrees for 30 minutes or until heated throughout. Freezes well.

ITALIAN STUFFED ZUCCHINI

2 servings

½ pound ground beef
½ cup chopped onion
1 clove garlic, minced
1½ tablespoons olive oil
2 eggs, beaten
¼ cup chopped parsley
¼ cup grated Romano cheese
½ teaspoon salt
½ teaspoon garlic salt
⅛ teaspoon pepper
1½ teaspoons Italian seasoning
½ teaspoon oregano, crumbled
1½ teaspoons spaghetti sauce
  seasoning
1 teaspoon basil, crumbled
2 medium zucchini
¼ pound Mozzarella cheese,
  sliced
  Spaghetti sauce (optional)

Cook beef, onion and garlic in oil in large skillet; remove and place in bowl. Stir beaten eggs with parsley, Romano cheese, salt, garlic salt, pepper, Italian seasoning, oregano, spaghetti sauce seasoning and basil. Mix with ground beef. Cut each zucchini in half and scoop out seeds; fill with beef mixture. Place on baking sheet; bake at 350 degrees for 5 minutes. Remove and top with Mozzarella cheese; return to oven until cheese melts. Can be topped with spaghetti sauce.

SICILIAN MEATLOAF

8 servings

2 eggs, beaten
¾ cup soft white bread crumbs
    (1 slice)
½ cup tomato juice
2 tablespoons snipped parsley
½ teaspoon dried oregano,
    crushed
¼ teaspoon salt
¼ teaspoon pepper
1 small clove garlic, minced
2 pounds lean ground beef
8 thin slices boiled ham
1½ cups grated
    Mozzarella cheese
3 slices Mozzarella cheese,
    halved diagonally

Combine eggs, bread crumbs, tomato juice, parsley, oregano, salt, pepper and garlic. Stir in ground beef; mix well. On foil, pat meat into a 12x10-inch rectangle. Arrange ham slices atop meat, leaving a small margin around edges. Sprinkle grated cheese over ham. Starting at short end, carefully roll up meat using foil to lift. Seal edges and ends. Place roll, seam side down, into a pan. Bake at 325 degrees for 1 hour and 15 minutes. Center of meat will be pink because of ham. Place cheese wedges over top of roll and return to oven for 5 minutes or until cheese melts.

SUNDAY MEATLOAF

6 servings

2 cups sliced fresh mushrooms
1 cup chopped onion
2 tablespoons butter or
    margarine
½ cup sour cream
2 eggs
½ cup milk
1½ pounds ground beef
¾ cup bread bread crumbs
2 teaspoons salt

SAUCE
1 tablespoon Worcestershire
1 cup sour cream
1 tablespoon Dijon mustard
1 teaspoon horseradish
½ teaspoon salt
    Pinch of nutmeg
    Pinch of white pepper

Sauté mushrooms and onion in butter. Remove from heat and stir in sour cream. Set aside. Combine remaining ingredients, except sauce, and put ½ of mixture in a 9-inch loaf pan. Make a shallow trough down the center and fill with ½ of the mushroom mixture (reserving the second ½ for top). Shape the rest of the meat over the filling, making sure the filling is covered. Seal the sides carefully. Top with remaining mushrooms. Bake 1 hour at 350 degrees. Serve with sour cream sauce made by combining ingredients and heating thoroughly.

REUBEN MEATLOAF

6 servings

1 pound ground beef
1 egg
¼ cup pickle relish
1 tablespoon Worcestershire
½ cup caraway rye bread
   crumbs
½ cup chopped onion
¼ cup Russian dressing
1½ teaspoons salt
¼ teaspoon pepper
8 ounces sauerkraut, drained
8 ounces sliced Swiss cheese

Mix ground beef, egg, relish, Worcestershire, bread crumbs, onion, dressing, salt and pepper. Turn out on waxpaper. Shape into 6x14-inch rectangle. Sprinkle with sauerkraut and cheese, reserving 2 slices. Roll up like a jelly-roll and place reserved cheese on top. Put in loaf pan. Bake at 350 degrees for 45 minutes.

MOCK TOURNEDOS

4 servings

1 1¼ to 1½ pound flank steak
½ cup cooking oil
¼ cup lemon juice
1 tablespoon grated onion
1 teaspoon coarsely ground
   pepper
4 slices of bacon, partially
   cooked
   Herb-seasoned hollandaise
   sauce

Score steak diagonally in diamond-shaped cuts. Cut lengthwise into 4 strips. Combine oil, lemon juice, grated onion and pepper in a deep bowl. Cover and refrigerate overnight. Drain. Roll each strip to form a "fillet". Wrap bacon slice around each steak and secure with string or skewer. Broil 3 inches from the heat for 7 to 8 minutes per side. If done on outside grill, adjust time according to distance from coals. Top with herb-seasoned hollandaise sauce.

BAR-B-QUE STEAK

6 servings

1 3-pound chuck roast
1 small onion, minced
1 clove garlic, crushed
¼ cup oil
6 tablespoons lemon juice
2 cups beer
2 cups chili sauce
1 tablespoon Worcestershire
1 teaspoon salt

Sauté onion and garlic in oil. Add lemon juice, beer, chili sauce, Worcestershire and salt. Cook over medium heat until boiling. Place roast in a shallow pan. Cover with sauce. Let marinate overnight. Grill chuck roast 6 inches above hot coals, about 20 minutes on each side. Baste with sauce while grilling. Serve with sauce.

MEXICAN SAUSAGE-STUFFED STEAK
6 servings

1 4½-pound flank steak
2 cloves garlic, cut
½ cup flour
3 tablespoons oil

SAUSAGE STUFFING
8 whole chopped scallions
½ cup chopped parsley
¾ cup walnuts, chopped
4 teaspoons red chili powder
¾ cup bread crumbs
4 slices fresh ginger, minced
2 eggs, beaten
1 pound chorizo sausage,
    chopped
1 teaspoon salt
½ teaspoon pepper

STEAK SAUCE
1½ cups tomato purée
½ cup dry red wine
½ cup beef broth
1 bay leaf

Have the butcher butterfly and pound the steak so that it is not more than ¼-inch thick. You may find it easier to make 2 small steak rolls rather than one large one. Rub the steak well with the cut cloves of garlic. Mix all the stuffing ingredients together and spread the filling evenly on the steak. Roll up the steak, jelly-roll fashion, and tie with string. Dredge with flour and brown in heated oil. Combine all sauce ingredients in a pan and simmer for 5 minutes. Place the meat in an uncovered casserole or baking dish large enough to hold the rolls without bending. Pour sauce over meat and bake at 350 degrees for 1½ hours. NOTE: Chorizo sausage cannot always be found in grocery stores. A Mexican food supply store would carry it.

YANKEE POT ROAST
8 servings

1 4-pound chuck or arm roast
1 tablespoon instant minced
    onion
2 teaspoons salt
2 teaspoons sugar
½ teaspoon freshly ground
    pepper
⅛ teaspoon ground cloves
1 bay leaf
1 cup dry red wine
2 tablespoons vegetable oil
1 cup sliced celery
1 10-ounce can condensed
    onion soup
2 tablespoons flour
¼ teaspoon garlic powder

Trim excess fat from roast. Pierce meat all over with fork. Place in a bowl and sprinkle with onion, salt, sugar, pepper and cloves. Add wine and bay leaf to bowl. Let stand at least 1 hour, turning meat several times. Heat oil in large heavy pan or dutch oven and brown roast. Add marinade, celery, garlic powder and onion soup. Cover and heat to boiling. Lower heat and simmer about 3 hours or until meat is tender. Remove meat and keep warm. Skim fat from liquid, remove bay leaf and thicken broth with flour for gravy. Or serve sliced meat au jus with cooked whole carrots and whole peeled red potatoes. For a small family, add whole carrots and peeled potatoes to pot the last 30 to 45 minutes of cooking and serve with broth. NOTE: For a second meal: Remove meat and cube. Lift off congealed fat and discard. Thicken remaining broth with flour and water mixture. Add cubed beef and mushroom to gravy. Just before serving over rice or noodles, add sour cream or yogurt for stroganoff.

SESAME BEEF

4 servings

⅛ cup thinly sliced green onions
4 cloves garlic, crushed
½ cup sesame oil
2 tablespoons sesame seeds, crushed
½ cup soy sauce
2 tablespoons sugar
1 teaspoon pepper
1 pound boneless beef sirloin, sliced paper thin
2 tablespoons cornstarch
⅔ cup cold water
4 tablespoons cooking oil
1½ cups julienned carrots
2 cups julienned green cabbage
2 cups broccoli florets
Rice

Combine onion, garlic, oil, sesame seeds, soy sauce, sugar and pepper. Place meat in bowl and cover with sauce. Marinate at room temperature for 30 minutes. Drain meat, reserving marinade. Add cornstarch and cold water to marinade and blend well. Heat 2 tablespoons of cooking oil in wok over medium-high heat. Add carrots and cook for 3 minutes. Add cabbage and broccoli and cook for 2 minutes, stirring. Cook until tender. Remove to bowl. Add 2 more table-spoons of cooking oil and add beef, cooking and stirring until meat is browned, about 2 minutes. Return vegetables to wok. Stir marinade mixture and add to wok. Cook and stir until sauce thickens. Serve with rice or oriental noodles.

ORIENTAL BEEF TOMATO

6 servings

2 pounds beef sirloin, cut into ½-inch strips, 3 inches long
2 tablespoons soy sauce
2 tablespoons cornstarch
2 teaspoons sugar
2 teaspoons wine
1 teaspoon ginger
Oil
1 cup sliced onions
1 cup cubed green pepper
1 cup celery, sliced diagonally in ⅛-inch pieces
1 cup sliced tomatoes
1 teaspoon salt
4 teaspoons sugar
4 tablespoons soy sauce
1 cup water
2 tablespoons cornstarch
Rice

Season sliced beef 10 to 15 minutes in a mixture of 2 tablespoons soy sauce, 2 tablespoons cornstarch, 2 teaspoons sugar, wine and ginger. Heat enough oil to cover bottom of pan and sauté beef, stirring quickly, to medium-rare. Remove meat from pan. Add more oil and fry onions, green peppers and celery. When al-most done, add tomatoes. Add salt, 4 teaspoons sugar, 4 tablespoons soy sauce, water and 2 tablespoons cornstarch; bring to a boil. Mix in beef. Serve immediately on a bed of rice.

OYSTER SAUCE BEEF

4 servings

1 pound flank, sirloin or round
   steak, partially frozen
1 medium onion, cut in wedges
1 medium green pepper, cut
   into 1-inch chunks
3 tablespoons oil
½ teaspoon salt
1 tablespoon chicken stock
2 cloves garlic, crushed
4 tablespoons oyster sauce

MARINADE
1 tablespoon cornstarch
1 teaspoon sugar
½ teaspoon salt
½ teaspoon sherry
2 tablespoons light soy sauce
   Rice or oriental noodles

Cut partially frozen steak across grain into ⅛-inch slices. Mix marinade ingredients and marinate meat for 15 minutes. Heat wok. Pour in 1 tablespoon oil and heat. Stir fry onion and green pepper together for 1 minute. Add salt and stock; stir fry until liquid has evaporated. Remove vegetables and set aside. Pour 2 tablespoons oil into wok. Brown garlic for 45 seconds; discard. Add beef, stir fry until ¾ done, about 1 minute. Add oyster sauce and mix well. Add vegetables; warm a few seconds. Serve with rice or oriental noodles.

SZECHWAN COLD BEEF

12 servings

½ cup vegetable oil
2 bunches fresh broccoli, cut in
   flowerets
2 sweet red peppers, cut in
   strips
4 cups sliced fresh mushrooms
½ cup white vinegar
¼ cup soy sauce
2½ teaspoons salt
5 dried red peppers, crushed
2 pounds thin-sliced roast beef,
   cut in strips
1 8-ounce can sliced water
   chestnuts, drained
1 8-ounce can bamboo shoots,
   drained

Heat oil in large skillet or wok. Sauté each vegetable on one side only until lightly browned but crisp. Drain off oil. In a large bowl, combine vegetables with remaining ingredients. Cover and refrigerate 4 hours or overnight. Serve chilled.

CROCK POT CHINESE BEEF

4 servings

1 pound round steak
1 10½-ounce can condensed
   beef consommé
¼ cup soy sauce
1 bunch green onions, sliced
1 7-ounce package frozen pea
   pods, partially thawed
2 tablespoons cornstarch
2 tablespoons cold water
   Rice

Thinly slice round steak in strips. In slow-cooker pot, combine strips with beef consommé, soy sauce and sliced green onion. Cover, cook on low for 6 or 7 hours. Turn control to high. Stir in cornstarch dissolved in cold water. Cook on high for 10 to 15 minutes or until thick. Drop in partially thawed pea pods the last 5 minutes. Serve over rice.

BARBECUE PINWHEELS

6 servings

3 pounds round steak,
   tenderized by the butcher
   Salt and pepper
8 slices bacon
4 wooden skewers

BEST EVER BARBECUE SAUCE
1 cup finely chopped onion
1 clove garlic, crushed
1 cup catsup
1 cup maple syrup
2 tablespoons Worcestershire
¼ teaspoon Tabasco
½ cup vinegar
¼ cup light molasses
2 teaspoons dry mustard
1 teaspoon paprika
1 teaspoon salt
⅛ teaspoon pepper

Mix ingredients for Best Ever Barbecue Sauce and simmer 10 minutes. Sprinkle meat with salt and pepper. Lay bacon slices on meat along the short side. Roll up starting at long side. Tie string at each bacon strip. Cut into 8 pieces. Place 2 pinwheels on each skewer. Grill over medium coals or use a gas grill. Cook 25 to 30 minutes. Baste frequently. The sauce may be prepared early in the day and the pinwheels marinated in the sauce and refrigerated until needed.

BEER BRISKET

10 servings

1   4-pound beef brisket
1   onion, sliced
¼   cup chili sauce
2   tablespoons brown sugar
1   clove garlic, minced
1   12-ounce can beer
3   tablespoons flour

Season meat with salt and pepper. Cover the top of the meat with the sliced onion. Place in a 13x9-inch pan. Combine chili sauce, sugar, garlic and beer. Pour over meat. Cover with foil and bake at 300 degrees for 4 to 5 hours. Uncover and bake for 30 more minutes, basting with juice. Remove and slice meat. Skim fat from liquid and add water to make 1 cup. May use more juice and flour for a larger quantity of gravy. Blend flour and ½ cup cold water. Add to juice in saucepan. Cook until it thickens. Serve gravy over meat.

BEST EVER BRISKET

10 to 20 servings

1   4 to 7-pound beef brisket
4   tablespoons liquid smoke

The day before serving, rub brisket with liquid smoke and wrap in heavy-duty foil. Roast at 350 degrees for 30 minutes per pound. Reserve cooking juices. Cool; remove fat from meat and slice very thin. Place in foil and pour sauce, mixed with at least ½ cup of cooking juices, over meat. Separate slices to allow sauce to run between. Rewrap in foil. Refrigerate overnight. Reheat at 275 degrees for 1 hour.

SAUCE
18 ounces ketchup
¼   cup brown sugar
¼   cup light molasses
1   tablespoon liquid smoke
2   tablespoons red wine
1½ teaspoons garlic salt
½   teaspoon Tabasco
½   teaspoon salt
¼   teaspoon pepper

Combine all ingredients in saucepan. Bring to a boil; reduce heat and simmer 15 minutes. Refrigerate until needed.

EASY ELEGANT BEEF TENDERLOIN 10 servings

Olive oil
1 whole beef tenderloin, trimmed
¼ pound Blue cheese
1 stick butter
½ teaspoon garlic powder
1 tablespoon Worcestershire
1 teaspoon onion salt
¼ teaspoon caraway seeds
2 4-ounce cans buttom mushrooms
Cherry tomatoes
Parsley

Rub meat with olive oil. Place meat in preheated 500 degree oven. Immediately reduce heat to 350 degrees. Roast until medium-rare (135 to 140 degrees internal temperature). Combine all remaining ingredients in a saucepan over low heat. Stir until cheese and butter melt and are well blended. Keep warm over very low heat. When meat is done, allow resting time. Slice meat in thin portions and pour sauce over it on serving platter. Garnish with cherry tomatoes and parsley.

MARINATED TENDERLOIN 4 to 8 servings

1 envelope Italian salad dressing mix
½ cup water
½ cup catsup
1 teaspoon prepared mustard
¼ teaspoon Worcestershire
1 beef tenderloin, 2 to 4 pounds

Combine salad dressing mix, water, catsup, mustard and Worcestershire. Pierce meat with fork on all sides. Place meat in a plastic bag and set in a bowl. Add marinade to bag. Close bag tightly around meat so marinade covers all sides. Chill 24 hours. Remove meat from bag and place in preheated 500 degree oven. Immediately reduce heat to 350 degrees. Roast 15 to 20 minutes. Tenderloin will be rare when internal temperature reaches 120 degrees.

VEAL AMELIO 8 servings

2 pounds veal fillets, cut into 1½-ounce scallops
Flour
Salt and pepper
2 tablespoons olive oil
2 sticks butter
6 tablespoons dry white wine
1 tablespoon lemon juice
1 pound fresh mushrooms, sliced

Pound veal gently with mallet. Season with flour, salt and pepper. Heat oil and 2 tablespoons butter in skillet. Sauté veal without browning. Remove meat and keep warm. Add wine to pan. Heat slightly. Add remaining butter and lemon juice. Sauté mushrooms briefly. Place veal slices on each plate and top with mushrooms and sauce.

VEAL PRINTEMPS
6 servings

12 veal scallops
½ cup sherry
2 tablespoons butter
2 tablespoons oil
¼ pound mushrooms, thinly
    sliced
1 teaspoon lemon juice
1 tablespoon tomato paste
1 tablespoon flour
2 tablespoons beef broth
1½ cups chicken broth
1 tablespoon currant jelly
½ cup white wine
1 10-ounce package frozen
    asparagus spears
½ cup grated Parmesan cheese
    Butter

Brush scallops with ¼ cup sherry. Melt butter and oil in heavy skillet over medium-high heat. When foaming, add veal. Quickly brown, turning after 2 minutes on each side. Remove from heat. In a saucepan, heat ¼ cup sherry and ignite. Pour over scallops. Remove scallops from pan to warm plate; reserve cooking juices. Toss mushrooms in lemon juice. Set aside. Return pan with cooking juices to medium heat. Stir in tomato paste, flour and beef stock. Blend well. Add currant jelly, wine and chicken broth. Cook, stirring, until thick. Add mushrooms. Return veal to pan. Cook asparagus until just tender. Remove scallops from sauce and overlap in a long pan. Arrange asparagus in a row on top. Pour on sauce. Sprinkle with Parmesan cheese. Dot with butter. Broil 8 to 10 minutes until cheese melts and is lightly browned.

VEAL MARSALA SICILIANO
4 servings

4 tablespoons butter
¾ pound fresh mushrooms,
    sliced
2 pounds veal scallops
½ cup flour
1 teaspoon salt
¼ teaspoon white pepper
1 cup Marsala wine
    Minced parsley
    Noodles

Melt 2 tablespoons of butter in large frying pan. Add mushrooms and cook over medium-high heat until mushrooms are limp. Remove and set aside. Cut veal into strips 1 inch wide, 2 to 3 inches long. Dredge veal in flour seasoned with salt and pepper. Place remaining butter in frying pan and melt. Brown meat over medium-high heat. When veal is light brown, it is done. Set meat aside. Add wine to frying pan and cook rapidly, stirring all bits in pan into liquid. Return mushrooms and meat to pan and heat until entire mixture is heated. A sprinkle of flour into Marsala mixture while cooking will thicken sauce, if needed. Garnish with parsley and serve with buttered noodles.

VEAL PICCATA

4 servings

1½ pounds veal scallops
   Salt
   Pepper
   Flour
3   tablespoons butter
1   tablespoon olive oil
2   cloves garlic, minced
½   pound fresh mushrooms,
       sliced
2   tablespoons fresh lemon juice
½   cup dry white wine
2   teaspoons capers
3   tablespoons minced parsley
1   lemon, thinly sliced

Sprinkle veal with salt and pepper; dust lightly with flour on both sides. Heat butter and olive oil in large skillet. Add veal. Brown on both sides. Remove from skillet. Add garlic and mushrooms to pan; cook 1 minute. Return veal to pan. Add lemon juice and wine; cover and simmer 20 minutes or until veal is tender. Add capers. Remove to warm platter. Sprinkle with parsley and garnish with lemon slices.

VEAL À LA BOURGUIGNONNE

6 servings

2   pounds veal cutlets, cut to
       playing card size
   Flour
   Margarine
1   10¾-ounce can condensed
       cream of chicken soup
1   10¾-ounce can condensed
       cream of celery soup
1   cup burgundy wine
2   tablespoons brandy
1   2⅛-ounce can french-fried
       onion rings
1½ cups grated Cheddar cheese

Flour veal and brown in margarine. Remove meat from pan and set aside. Mix in the pan, soup, burgundy and brandy. Place meat in a casserole and cover with the sauce. Layer onion rings with cheese. Bake, covered, 1½ hours at 350 degrees.

PORK

GRILLED MANDARIN PORK   4 to 6 servings

1   whole pork tenderloin

MARINADE
½   cup vegetable oil
1   cup soy sauce
1   clove garlic, minced
3   tablespoons honey
1   tablespoon Accent
1   tablespoon ginger
1   tablespoon dry mustard

Combine marinade ingredients. Pour over pork tenderloin and cover tightly with plastic wrap. Refrigerate 24 hours, turning and basting occasionally. Grill over hot coals until done; time will depend on size of the loin. Slice and serve on rolls for appetizers or with rice for dinner.

POLYNESIAN PORK ROAST   8 servings

1   2½ to 3 pound pork tenderloin
     Rosemary
     Salt
     Pepper
½   cup honey
½   cup soy sauce
½   cup catsup
2   large garlic cloves, crushed

Place roast on a rack. Rub roast with crushed rosemary, salt and pepper. Combine honey, soy sauce, catsup and garlic. Roast at 350 degrees for 2 to 2½ hours until tender. Baste frequently with sauce.

PORK TENDERLOIN CORDON BLEU   6 servings

12   pork tenderloin slices,
       ½ inch thick
6   slices Emmenthaler or Swiss
       cheese
6   thin slices smoked ham
     Flour
1   egg, beaten
2   tablespoons water
1½   cups cracker crumbs
2   10¾-ounce cans condensed
       cream of mushroom soup
⅔   cup heavy cream

Pound the meat slices until thin. Top 6 of the slices with a slice of cheese and a slice of ham. Top with remaining tenderloins. Press together. Dip into flour on both sides and then into egg, which has been mixed with 2 tablespoons water. Press firmly into cracker crumbs. Fry slowly about 45 minutes. Pork should be well cooked and browned. Combine soup and cream in a saucepan. Heat and pour over tenderloins just before serving.

CRANBERRY BARBECUE

4 servings

4 cups fresh cranberries, well drained
1 cup sugar
½ cup commercial barbecue sauce
½ cup orange juice
4 thick pork chops
   Salt
   Flour
   Vegetable oil
   Orange slices for garnish

Combine fresh cranberries, sugar, sauce and orange juice in a large saucepan, mixing well. Bring to a boil over medium heat, stirring constantly. Continue boiling without stirring for 5 minutes. Set aside. Sprinkle pork chops with salt and dredge in flour. In a skillet, brown on both sides in a small amount of hot oil. Remove from skillet and place in baking dish. Cover with the berry sauce. Bake, covered, at 350 degrees for 70 minutes or until done.

CHERRY CHOPS

6 servings

6 pork chops
½ cup cherry preserves
2 tablespoons light corn syrup
2 tablespoons red wine
   Salt
   Cinnamon
   Nutmeg
   Ground cloves
2 tablespoons slivered almonds

Brown pork chops on both sides. Drain; salt and pepper. Add 1 tablespoon water to pan. Cover and cook chops slowly for 30 minutes. In a saucepan, combine cherry preserves, corn syrup, red wine and dashes of salt, cinnamon, nutmeg and ground cloves. Bring to a boil. Add almonds. Glaze cooked pork chops with cherry sauce. Cover and cook for 15 minutes, basting with sauce several times.

ITALIAN PORK CHOPS

6 servings

12 pork chops
½ cup chopped onion
2 tablespoons butter
½ cup water
1 cup stuffing mix
½ teaspoon oregano
1 16-ounce can tomato sauce with cheese
6 slices Mozzarella cheese

Sauté onion in butter until soft. Add water, stir in stuffing mix and oregano. Put stuffing mix between 2 pork chops. Arrange in shallow baking pan. Pour tomato sauce into pan. Cover tightly with foil. Bake 2 hours at 300 degrees. Uncover pan and top each pork chop with a slice of Mozzarella. Bake until cheese is melted.

WINE BRAISED PORK CHOPS   4 servings

1   teaspoon dried sage
1   teaspoon dried rosemary
1   teaspoon finely chopped
       garlic
1   teaspoon salt
     Fresh ground pepper
4   center cut loin chops,
       1 inch thick
2   tablespoons butter
1   tablespoon olive oil
¾   cup dry white wine
1   tablespoon finely chopped
       parsley

Combine herbs, garlic and seasonings; press into chops. In heavy skillet, melt butter with olive oil over moderate heat. When foam subsides, place chops in hot fat and brown for 2 to 3 minutes on each side. Remove from pan when chops are golden brown. Pour off all but a thin film of fat; add ½ cup of wine and bring to a boil. Return chops to pan, cover and reduce heat to simmer. Basting with pan juices occasionally, cook chops for 25 to 30 minutes or until tender. Transfer chops to heated serving platter; skim off fat from braising liquid and pour in remaining wine. Boil briskly over high heat, reducing liquid to a few tablespoons of syrup glaze. Stir in parsley. Pour over chops.

CANTONESE SPARERIBS   6 servings

¼   cup vinegar
1   onion
2   cloves
1   rib of celery
4   pounds country style
       spareribs

SAUCE
1   cup orange marmalade
½   cup soy sauce
½   teaspoon ground ginger
1½ teaspoons crystallized ginger,
       finely chopped
2   garlic cloves, finely minced

Parboil ribs in water to which the vinegar, onion (stuck with 2 cloves), and the rib of celery have been added. Simmer until nearly fork-tender, approximately 1 hour. Remove from pan and discard the liquid. Put ribs in shallow baking pan. Mix sauce ingredients together and pour mixture over ribs. Bake at 350 degrees for 20 to 30 minutes, basting frequently. Ribs are done when they pierce easily with a fork. Ribs could be cooked in water ahead of time, refrigerated, and baked prior to serving. If started cold, the ribs will need to bake about 45 minutes.

MOTHER'S BAR-B-Q RIBS

8 servings

6	pounds country style ribs
1	lemon, sliced
1	white onion, sliced
1	cup catsup
2	cups water
⅓	cup Worcestershire
1	teaspoon salt
1	teaspoon chili powder
6	dashes Tabasco

Cut ribs into serving pieces. Put 1 slice lemon and 1 slice white onion on each piece. Bake at 450 degrees for 30 minutes. Drain off fat. Combine remaining ingredients and heat to boiling. Pour over ribs. Lower oven to 350 degrees and continue baking for 1½ hours. Baste several times.

SWEET AND SOUR PORK

2 servings

½	pound pork tenderloin or other lean pork, sliced into ¼ x 2-inch pieces
	Peanut oil for frying
¼	cup peanut oil
1	green pepper, parboiled and cut into 1½-inch cubes; or 1 cup pea pods
1	cup canned pineapple, cut into 1½-inch pieces
1	cup firm red tomatoes, cut into 1½-inch pieces; or ⅓ cup pimiento pieces
	Rice

Prepare Cantonese Fritter Batter and Sweet-Sour Sauce. Dip meat into batter. Fry in 350 degree peanut oil, a few pieces at a time, until golden brown. Drain. Pour peanut oil into a large skillet or wok and heat. Add green pepper, pork and pineapple. Cook 2 to 3 minutes, stirring gently. Stir in Sweet-Sour Sauce, cover pan and cook about 5 minutes or until sauce is transparent. Fold in tomatoes and cook 2 minutes. Serve over plain or fried rice.

CANTONESE FRITTER BATTER

1	medium egg
2	tablespoons chicken stock or milk
¼	cup flour, sifted
½	teaspoon salt

Combine all ingredients in a small bowl and beat until smooth. Let stand 10 minutes. If batter is too thin, add a little more flour; if too thick, add more liquid. Batter should be on the thin side.

SWEET-SOUR SAUCE

¼	cup cider or white vinegar
½	cup pineapple juice
⅓	cup brown sugar
1½	tablespoons cornstarch
2	tablespoons water
1	teaspoon salt
¼	teaspoon MSG (optional)

Combine all ingredients in a saucepan and cook to boiling, stirring constantly. Lower heat and simmer about 5 minutes.

HAM AND ASPARAGUS CASSEROLE

6 servings

1 **10-ounce package frozen,
cut asparagus**
1 **cup cubed ham**
¼ **cup grated American cheese**
2 **tablespoons quick cooking
tapioca**
2 **tablespoons chopped green
pepper**
¼ **cup chopped onion**
1 **tablespoon minced parsley**
1 **tablespoon lemon juice**
4 **hard-boiled eggs, sliced**
½ **cup half-and-half**
1 **10¾-ounce can condensed
cream of mushroom soup**
½ **cup dry bread crumbs
Margarine**

Cook asparagus for slightly less time than indicated on the package and place in 1½-quart casserole. Combine ham, cheese, tapioca, green pepper, onion, parsley and lemon juice. Place in a casserole alternate layers of ham mixture, sliced eggs and asparagus, ending with asparagus. Stir together cream and soup. Pour over ingredients. Sprinkle with bread crumbs and dot with margarine. Bake at 375 degrees for 25 to 30 minutes.

HAM AND ARTICHOKE HEARTS

6 servings

4 **tablespoons butter**
¼ **cup flour**
2 **cups milk, warmed**
⅛ **teaspoon seasoned salt**
⅛ **teaspoon cayenne pepper**
½ **teaspoon ground nutmeg
Paprika
Pinch of white pepper**
¾ **cup grated Swiss cheese**
3 **tablespoons cognac or sherry**
2 **8½-ounce cans artichoke
hearts, drained**
12 **thin slices boiled or baked ham**
⅔ **cup buttered bread crumbs**
⅔ **cup grated Parmesan or Swiss
cheese**

Melt butter in saucepan; blend in flour. Gradually blend in warm milk and cook over low heat until thick, stirring constantly. Add seasonings and ¾ cup Swiss cheese; stir until cheese melts. Add cognac or sherry. If artichoke hearts are large, halve and wrap 2 or 3 in a slice of ham. Arrange in buttered baking dish with sides touching. Pour sauce over all and sprinkle with a mixture of bread crumbs and grated cheese. Bake at 350 degrees for 25 to 30 minutes or until brown and bubbly.

SPRING HAM STEAK

4 servings

½ cup dark brown sugar
½ teaspoon cinnamon
⅛ teaspoon nutmeg
1 1-pound 13-ounce can cling peach halves
1 2-pound cooked bone-in ham steak, 1 inch thick
1 cup cranberries, fresh or frozen

Preheat broiler. In a small saucepan, stir brown sugar, cinnamon and nutmeg with ¼ cup of the peach syrup over low heat until hot. Place ham steak on broiler pan. Brush with some of the syrup mixture. Broil 10 minutes, brushing once with syrup mixture. Turn ham; brush with syrup and broil 5 minutes. Arrange 6 to 8 peach halves around the ham. Fill centers with remaining syrup mixture. Scatter cranberries on and around ham. Broil 5 minutes. Transfer to heated platter. Garnish with peach halves and cranberries.

HAM LOAF

8 servings

1½ pounds ground ham
¾ pound ground pork
3 eggs, beaten
1 cup soft bread crumbs
½ 10¾-ounce can tomato soup, undiluted
1 small onion, chopped
Paprika

Mix together ham, pork, eggs, crumbs, soup and onion. Shape into loaf and sprinkle with paprika. Bake at 350 degrees for 1 hour. While loaf is baking; mix together sauce ingredients; chill. Serve ham loaf with chilled sauce.

SAUCE
¾ cup sour cream
½ cup Dijon mustard
Fresh horseradish

SAUSAGE AND WILD RICE

15 servings

2 cups uncooked wild rice
1 6-ounce package Uncle Ben's Wild and White Rice Mix
3 pounds bulk pork sausage
1 large onion, chopped
1 cup sliced mushrooms
3 tablespoons butter
3 10¾-ounce cans condensed cream of chicken soup

Cook rice according to package directions; add packet of seasonings from package. Brown sausage; break into small pieces and drain. Sauté mushrooms and onion in butter; drain. Mix all ingredients together with soup and put in large greased baking dish. Bake at 350 degrees for 45 minutes. May be prepared a day ahead and refrigerated until baking time.

ITALIAN SAUSAGE SUPPER

8 servings

¼ cup olive oil
1 medium onion, thinly sliced
1 clove garlic
3 pounds bulk Italian sausage
2 green peppers, cut in strips
1 small zucchini, cut in
  ½-inch slices
2 quarts tomatoes
2 cups fresh mushrooms
  sautéed
½ teaspoon Italian seasoning
  Mostaccioli or spaghetti

In a deep skillet, sauté the onion and garlic in olive oil until golden brown. In a separate pan, boil sausage in enough water to cover. Drain. Add sausage to sautéed onion mixture. Stir in vegetables and seasoning. Good served with mostaccioli noodles or spaghetti.

SAUSAGE BEAN BAKE

8 servings

2 pounds pork sausage
2 large onions, chopped
1 15-ounce can kidney
  beans
1 16-ounce can butter
  beans
1 15-ounce can navy or
  northern beans
⅓ cup brown sugar
¼ teaspoon garlic salt
¼ teaspoon dry mustard
½ cup ketchup
¼ cup cider vinegar

Mix together brown sugar, garlic, salt, mustard, ketchup and vinegar. Brown sausage; remove from pan. Sauté onions in sausage drippings; drain. Drain navy and butter beans. In large pot, combine sausage, onions and all beans. Add ketchup mixture to beans and bake 50 minutes at 350 degrees covered; bake additional 15 minutes uncovered.

RACK OF LAMB

6 servings

2 racks of lamb
2 cups fresh bread crumbs
1 cup chopped fresh parsley
4 cloves garlic, crushed
2 teaspoons salt
1 teaspoon rosemary
½ teaspoon pepper
½ cup olive oil

Mix together all ingredients, except lamb. Pat mixture onto the lamb with ribs down. Wrap with plastic wrap and refrigerate overnight. Take out of refrigerator 1½ hours before roasting. Roast at 400 degrees until meat thermometer registers 170 degrees. Carve between ribs.

LAMB PAPRIKA

6 servings

2 pounds lean lamb shoulder or leg of lamb
2 onions, sliced
2 teaspoons margarine
1½ cups canned tomatoes
1 clove garlic, minced
1 teaspoon parsley
1 teaspoon salt
1 teaspoon pepper
Paprika to taste
1 cup sour cream
Rice

Trim fat and cut meat into 1-inch cubes or strips. Brown onion in margarine. Add meat and brown well. Drain tomatoes, reserving the juice. Add tomatoes, garlic, parsley, salt, pepper and paprika to meat. Cover. Simmer on top of stove for 1½ hours or bake 1½ hours at 275 degrees. Refrigerate overnight. Before serving, bring sour cream and lamb to room temperature; combine. Reheat over medium heat; do not boil. Serve over brown or wild rice.

LAMB MANCHU

16 servings

4 cloves garlic, peeled and chopped
⅓ cup honey
½ cup boiling water
1 cup soy sauce
1 7-pound leg of lamb
½ cup white wine
Club rolls (optional)

Mix garlic, honey and boiling water. Stir until honey is dissolved; add soy sauce. Pour over lamb. Marinate 4 to 12 hours, turning lamb several times. Put in roasting pan and add ½ cup of the marinade. Cook 30 minutes per pound at 325 degrees, adding wine halfway through. Thinly slice lamb across grain, and pour cooking sauce over meat. Good served on heated club rolls. Place sliced lamb on rolls and pour on sauce.

GRILLED STUFFED LEG OF LAMB   10 servings

2   cups bread crumbs
4   tablespoons butter or
        margarine
1   tablespoon chopped onion
1   9-ounce can crushed
        pineapple, drained
½   cup brown sugar
½   cup chopped pecans
2   tablespoons chopped parsley
½   teaspoon ginger
1   8-pound leg of lamb, boned
        and split
2   tablespoons lemon juice
      Soy sauce

Sauté crumbs in butter; add pineapple, brown sugar, pecans, parsley, onion and ginger. Let stand for 1 hour. Brush cavity of lamb with lemon juice. Stuff with filling and skewer tightly shut, or tie with string soaked in cold water. Brush outside of lamb with soy sauce. Put on spit over medium coals for 2½ hours.

SOUTH AFRICAN LAMB CURRY   8 servings

1   cup dried apples
½   cup dried, pitted prunes
½   cup seedless raisins
1½   cups water
1½   pounds boneless lamb
        shoulder or beef chuck,
        cubed
1   teaspoon salt
2   tablespoons vegetable oil
1   cup finely chopped onion
2   tablespoons curry powder, or
        more to taste
2   tablespoons red wine vinegar
1   tablespoon lemon juice
¼   cup chopped salted peanuts
2   medium bananas, sliced
        ⅛ inch thick
      Rice

Combine apples, prunes, raisins and water. Soak at least 1 hour, stirring frequently. Salt meat and brown in oil. Transfer to a plate. Pour off all but 2 tablespoons fat. Cook onions in fat until soft. Reduce heat and add curry powder. Cook another 2 minutes. Return meat to skillet along with fruits and their liquid, vinegar and lemon juice. Bring to a boil and reduce heat. Simmer, covered, for 1 hour or until lamb is tender. If beef is used, simmer for 2½ to 3 hours. Stir occasionally, add water as needed. To serve, mound meat on platter, sprinkle with peanuts and surround with banana slices. Serve immediately with saffron rice and various garnishes such as: chopped green onions, watermelon pickles, chutney, chopped coconut, chopped nuts, candied ginger, chopped green pepper, mandarin oranges, pimiento, chives, sour cream, chopped bacon, chopped egg yolks, apple butter and marmalade. Garnishes should have a variety of textures and colors. The more, the better. They make this meal.

MOUSSAKA

MEAT SAUCE

2 tablespoons butter of margarine
1 cup finely chopped onion
2½ pounds ground lamb or beef chuck
¼ teaspoon garlic powder
½ teaspoon oregano
1 teaspoon basil
½ teaspoon cinnamon
Dash of pepper
2 8-ounce cans tomato sauce
2 eggplants, washed and dried
Salt
½ cup butter or margarine, melted

Melt butter in 3½-quart Dutch oven. Sauté onion, lamb and garlic, stirring until brown. Add herbs, spices and tomato sauce; bring to boil, stirring. Reduce heat and simmer, uncovered, ½ hour. Halve unpared eggplant lengthwise and slice crosswise into ½-inch slices. Place in bottom of broiler pan; sprinkle lightly with salt and brush with melted butter. Broil, 4 inches from heat, 4 minutes per side, or until golden. Set aside while preparing cream sauce.

CREAM SAUCE

2 tablespoons butter or margarine
2 tablespoons flour
½ teaspoon salt
Dash of pepper
2 cups milk
2 eggs
½ cup grated Parmesan cheese
½ cup grated Cheddar cheese
2 tablespoons dry bread crumbs

In medium saucepan, melt butter. Remove from heat; stir in flour, salt and pepper. Gradually add milk. Bring to a boil, stirring until mixture is thickened. Remove from heat. In small bowl, beat eggs with wire whisk. Beat in some hot cream sauce mixture; return mixture to saucepan, mix well and set aside. In bottom of a shallow 2-quart baking dish, layer half of the eggplant and sprinkle with 2 tablespoons each, Parmesan and Cheddar. Stir bread crumbs into meat sauce. Spoon evenly over eggplant. Sprinkle with 2 tablespoons each, Parmesan and Cheddar. Layer remaining eggplant slices, overlapping as before. Pour cream sauce over all. Sprinkle with remaining cheeses. Bake 35 to 40 minutes, or until golden brown. If desired, brown top a little more under broiler. Cool slightly to serve. Cut in squares.

LAMB KABOBS

6 servings

2 pounds boneless lamb
shoulder or leg, cut into
1½-inch cubes
¼ cup oil
¼ cup lemon juice
1½ teaspoons salt
1 teaspoon marjoram
½ teaspoon oregano
⅓ cup chopped onion
⅛ teaspoon garlic powder
3 green peppers, cut in chunks
24 mushroom caps
3 cups boiling water
24 cherry tomatoes

A day before serving, trim fat from lamb and cube. Mix oil, lemon juice, salt, marjoram, oregano, garlic powder and onion. Pour over lamb and let meat stand in refrigerator 24 hours. Cook pepper pieces in 1 cup boiling water for 5 minutes. Drain. Pour 2 cups boiling water over fresh mushrooms. Cover. Let stand 5 minutes. Drain. Alternate lamb, pepper pieces, tomatoes and mushrooms on skewers. Brush with remaining oil mixture. Broil, turning as needed, 6 to 8 inches from heat. For medium, cook 18 to 20 minutes.

BREAST OF CHICKEN À L'ARCHIDUC
6 servings

8 large chicken breast halves, skinned and boned with a pocket cut in each
1 tablespoon butter
¼ pound mushrooms, sliced
⅓ cup shredded, boiled ham (about 1½ ounces)
1½ teaspoons dry sherry
½ teaspoon fresh lemon juice
¼ teaspoon dried tarragon
½ clove garlic, minced
1 cup grated Swiss cheese
Salt and pepper
Flour
¼ cup butter
2 tablespoons cognac or brandy

Melt 1 tablespoon butter in a large skillet over medium-high heat. Add mushrooms and sauté 3 to 4 minutes. Stir in ham, sherry, lemon juice, tarragon and garlic and cook a few minutes more. Remove from heat and mix in cheese. Season with salt and pepper. Stuff a heaping tablespoon of mixture into each chicken breast. Place chicken on large baking sheet and cover with waxed paper. Place another baking sheet over the chicken and put books on top to press the chicken. Refrigerate overnight. When ready to cook, coat each breast lightly with flour, seasoned with salt and pepper. Grease a 9x13-inch baking dish. Melt ¼ cup butter in a large skillet over medium high heat and sauté chicken until a deep golden-brown on both sides and just cooked through. Warm brandy and pour over chicken, lighting it with a match to flame it. Transfer chicken to the baking dish and set aside. Reserve skillet with pan juices.

SAUCE
1 teaspoon tomato paste
1 teaspoon Dijon mustard
3 tablespoons flour
1¼ cups chicken broth
1 cup heavy cream
2 tablespoons dry white wine
1 tablespoon dry sherry
½ teaspoon white pepper

Preheat oven to 350 degrees. Stir tomato paste and mustard into pan juices. Mix flour with small amount of chicken broth and blend until smooth. Stir in remaining broth, add to the skillet. Place over medium heat and simmer 5 minutes, stirring constantly until slightly thickened. Gradually add cream, stirring to blend well. Add wine, sherry and white pepper. Pour over chicken and bake 15 minutes.

TOPPING
¼ cup butter
8 large mushroom caps
½ cup grated Gruyere cheese

Melt ¼ cup butter in skillet; add mushroom caps and sauté briefly. Place caps on chicken and sprinkle with cheese. Bake 4 to 5 minutes until cheese is melted. Serve.

GOLD COAST CHICKEN

4 servings

6 whole chicken breasts, boned
1 8-ounce bottle lemon juice
  Salt and pepper
6 tablespoons butter, melted
¼ cup butter
¼ cup flour
1 pint heavy cream
2 10-ounce cans condensed
  chicken broth, chilled
¾ cup champagne
  Waxed paper
1 8½-ounce can or 2 packages
  frozen artichoke hearts

Rub chicken breasts on both sides with lemon juice, salt and pepper. Roll breasts in 6 tablespoons of melted butter; place in a large casserole and cover with waxed paper. Bake for 8 minutes in 400 degree oven. Remove chicken; rinse casserole and set aside. Remove fat from top of chicken broth and discard. Simmer broth. In another pan, melt remaining butter and stir in flour. Remove mixture from heat. Heat cream, but do not boil; add to broth along with combined butter and flour mixture. Stir in ¾ cup champagne. Pour sauce mixture over chicken breasts and artichokes in large casserole; cover and refrigerate overnight. Remove from refrigerator and let warm to room temperature, about 2 hours. Heat at 250 degrees for 2 hours before serving.

POLLO ALLA FIORENTINA

6 servings

6 chicken breast halves
  or
1 chicken, cut up
1 cup seasoned bread crumbs
2 tablespoons olive oil
2 tablespoons butter
2 cups Marinara sauce
½ cup dry red wine
1½ cups chicken stock, boiling
1 cup uncooked long-grain rice
1 2½-ounce can sliced black
  olives, drained
2 10-ounce packages frozen
  chopped spinach, thawed
  and squeezed
1 cup Ricotta cheese
2 tablespoons minced onion
½ teaspoon crushed majoram
¼ teaspoon nutmeg
½ teaspoon salt
2 eggs, beaten
  Parmesan cheese, grated

Coat chicken with crumbs, sauté in oil and butter until brown. Remove from skillet. Mix together Marinara sauce and wine. Combine 1 cup of the mixture with stock, rice and olives. Pour into lightly oiled 3-quart casserole or 11x13-inch pan. Place chicken, skin side down on rice. Cover with foil and bake at 350 degrees for 20 minutes. Turn chicken; cover and bake additional 25 minutes. Combine spinach, onion, Ricotta, eggs and seasonings. Spoon around edge of casserole. Pour remaining sauce over chicken; sprinkle with Parmesan. Bake uncovered 10 to 15 minutes. NOTE: May be refrigerated after baking chicken and rice. Spoon spinach mixture around edge and bake 15 to 20 minutes longer.

MARINARA SAUCE

1 clove garlic, minced
2 tablespoons olive oil plus oil
  from anchovies
2½ cups canned Italian tomatoes
6 anchovies, finely chopped
½ teaspoon oregano
1 tablespoon chopped parsley

Sauté garlic in oils. Drain and press tomatoes; add to garlic. Stir in anchovies, oregano and parsley. Simmer, uncovered, for 15 to 20 minutes, stirring occasionally.

BIRTHDAY CHICKEN BREASTS

4 servings

4 chicken breasts, split and
  boned
3 tablespoons flour
½ pint sour cream
1 10-ounce can condensed
  cream of chicken soup
½ cup white wine
¼ cup bacon bits

Arrange chicken, skin-side-up, in shallow baking dish. Combine flour, sour cream, soup, wine and bacon bits. Pour over chicken. Bake for 2 hours at 300 degrees. NOTE: Amount of chicken may be doubled or tripled without increasing other ingredients.

CHICKEN BOSOMS

8 servings

8 chicken breasts
3 tablespoons tarragon
  Garlic powder
  Salt and pepper
  Powdered rosemary
  Basil
  Powdered ginger
¼ pound butter
  Olive oil
1 bunch green onions, chopped
2 medium onions, sliced
2 29-ounce cans peach halves
1 3-ounce package sliced
  almonds
  Parmesan cheese

Wash and dry chicken. Season well with tarragon, garlic powder, salt, pepper, rosemary, basil and ginger. Melt 3 tablespoons butter in skillet; add 1 tablespoon olive oil. Sauté chicken a few pieces at at time, until golden. Add more butter and oil as necessary. Arrange chicken, meat side down, in a large baking dish. Cover with chopped green onions and sliced onion rings. Pour the juice from both cans of peaches over chicken; cover pan with foil. Refrigerate overnight. Remove from refrigerator 1 hour before baking. Bake covered, at 350 degrees, for 35 minutes. Remove foil; turn breasts and bake 25 minutes longer. Sprinkle with almonds and arrange peach halves on top of chicken. Sprinkle with Parmesan cheese and place under a preheated broiler until cheese is brown and bubbly.

SWISS SHERRY CHICKEN
6 servings

3	chicken breasts, split and skinned
¼	cup flour
2½	teaspoons salt
1	teaspoon paprika
¼	cup butter
½	cup water
2	teaspoons cornstarch
½	cup half-and-half
¼	cup cooking sherry
1	teaspoon lemon peel
1	tablespoon lemon juice
1½	cups grated Swiss cheese
	Fresh parsley

Blend flour, salt and paprika. Coat chicken in mixture and sauté in butter. Add water and simmer, covered, for 30 minutes until tender. Lay pieces in long, shallow pan. Mix cornstarch with ¼ cup half-and-half; stir into drippings and cook over low heat. Stir in remaining half-and-half. Add cooking sherry, lemon peel and lemon juice. Cook, stirring constantly, until thickened. Pour sauce over chicken pieces; sprinkle with Swiss cheese. Cook at 350 degrees for 30 minutes. Garnish with parsley. NOTE: This dish freezes well.

CHERRY SAUCED CHICKEN
6 servings

6	chicken breasts, boned
¾	cup Italian dressing
	Salt and pepper
	Garlic powder
½	cup red currant jelly
½	cup frozen concentrated orange juice
1	16-ounce can pitted Bing cherries, drained

Wash chicken; pat dry. Marinate chicken in dressing for 2 to 4 hours at room temperature. Drain chicken; reserve marinade. Place chicken, skin-side-up, in shallow baking dish. Season with salt, pepper and garlic powder. Bake 1¼ hours in 350 degree oven, basting once or twice with marinade. Melt jelly in saucepan; blend in juice. Pour sauce over chicken and continue baking 10 minutes. Add cherries last 5 minutes. Serve over rice.

CURRIED CHICKEN DIVAN
8 servings

4	whole chicken breasts
3	10-ounce cans condensed cream of chicken soup
1½	cups mayonnaise
3	teaspoons lemon juice
1½	teaspoons curry powder
3	10-ounce packages frozen broccoli spears or 2 bunches fresh broccoli
½	pound sharp Cheddar cheese, grated
1	8-ounce package herb stuffing mix
	Butter

Cook chicken in water to cover or in a microwave. Skin, bone and cut into bite-size pieces. Cook broccoli and cut into generous pieces. Line the bottom of a 3-quart baking dish with broccoli. Cover broccoli with chicken pieces. Combine soup, mayonnaise, lemon juice and curry powder. Pour over chicken and broccoli. Top with grated cheese. Generously cover with stuffing mix. Dot with butter. Bake at 350 degrees for 45 to 60 minutes. NOTE: You can make this ahead and refrigerate. Bring to room temperature before baking.

GRILLED VERMOUTH CHICKEN

6 servings

3 whole chicken breasts, halved
¼ cup dry vermouth
1 tablespoon leaf rosemary,
   crumbled
1 teaspoon salt
½ teaspoon pepper
¼ cup butter, melted
¼ cup frozen concentrated
   orange juice, thawed

Combine vermouth, rosemary, salt and pepper; pour over chicken. Marinate for 2 hours or more in refrigerator, turning occasionally. Remove chicken from marinade. Combine marinade with butter and orange juice. Grill chicken 5 inches from hot coals about 30 minutes, turning and basting frequently with orange mixture. Serve chicken with any remaining marinade.

MEXICAN CHICKEN OLE

6 servings

3 whole chicken breasts, boned,
   skinned and split
1½ tablespoons butter
1½ tablespoons oil
½ cup onion, chopped
1 clove garlic, minced
2 stalks celery, thinly sliced
1 4-ounce can chopped green
   chilies
1 1-pound can stewed tomatoes
½ cup chicken broth
¼ teaspoon oregano
½ teaspoon cumin
¼ teaspoon sugar
   Salt and pepper to taste
1½ cups shredded Cheddar
   cheese

Pound chicken breasts to ¼-inch thickness. Heat butter and oil in fry pan over medium-high heat; brown chicken breasts 2 minutes on each side. Remove chicken from pan and add onion, garlic and celery. Cook until onion is limp. Add chilies, stewed tomatoes, broth, cumin, oregano and sugar and cook for 10 minutes. Season with salt and pepper; pour over chicken and continue cooking for 20 minutes. Sprinkle with grated cheese and place under broiler until cheese melts. NOTE: You can serve this over rice.

MANDARIN PLUM CHICKEN

4 servings

2 chicken breasts, split,
   skinned and boned
1 cup plum jam
3 tablespoons soy sauce
1 teaspoon dry sherry
¼ teaspoon garlic powder
¼ teaspoon ground ginger
1 20-ounce can pineapple
   chunks
2 large green peppers, cut into
   24 chunks

Cut chicken into 24 chunks. Combine plum jam, soy sauce, sherry, garlic powder and ginger to make marinade. Marinate chicken several hours. Alternate chicken with green pepper and pineapple pieces on skewers. Brush with marinade and broil or grill until chicken is cooked.

185

MICROWAVE CORDON BLEU

4 servings

CHICKEN:

4   chicken breasts, boned and
     split
¼   pound shredded ham
4   slices Monterey Jack cheese
2   tablespoons butter or
     margarine
2   tablespoons flour
1   cup grated Monterey Jack
     cheese
¼   cup milk
½   cup sliced mushrooms
¼   cup sliced green onions

Pound each breast ¼-inch thick. Place ¼ of ham and one slice of cheese on each breast half. Fold sides together; secure with toothpicks. Set aside. In a 8x12-inch glass dish, microwave butter on high for 30 seconds. Dip chicken in butter and place in dish with thick side of breasts towards the outside of the dish. Cover with waxed paper; cook at 70 percent power for 20 minutes. Cook at 30 percent power for an additional 5 minutes or until done. Remove chicken from dish; keep covered. Stir flour into drippings, making a smooth paste. Add cheese; mix well. Stir in milk and microwave on high 3 to 4 minutes until mixture comes to a boil. Add mushrooms and onions and cook on high for another 1½ minutes. Pour sauce over chicken.

CHICKEN TETRAZZINI

8 servings

4   white meat chicken quarters
1   teaspoon celery salt
1   tablespoon dry seasoned
     chicken bouillon
1   teaspoon Beau Monde
     seasoning
2   tablespoons butter
1   cup fresh mushrooms, sliced
½   yellow onion, finely chopped
½   cup dry vermouth
½   pound fettuccini
2   tablespoons olive oil
1   cup grated Swiss cheese
     Paprika
     Fresh parsley, minced

Cover chicken quarters with water in a 5-quart dutch oven. Add celery salt, bouillon and Beau Monde seasoning. Cook until tender. Remove chicken from water and cool. Skin, bone and cut into bite-size pieces. Continue to boil seasoned chicken water until it is reduced to less than 1 cup and is thick and yellow. In another pan, brown mushrooms and onion in butter. Add cooked chicken pieces and toss to coat with browned butter. Add juice from chicken and vermouth. Cook fettuccine until just done; do not overcook. Drain, rinse and toss with olive oil. Put fettuccini in bottom of a 9x13-inch baking dish. Layer with chicken and mushroom mixture. Top with grated cheese. Bake for 30 to 40 minutes at 350 degrees, or until cheese is brown and bubbly. Garnish with paprika and parsley.

LAYERED CHICKEN CASSEROLE

12 servings

9 slices white bread, crusts
   removed
4 cups diced cooked chicken
1 4-ounce can mushrooms,
   drained
2 5-ounce cans sliced water
   chestnuts
½ cup mayonnaise
1 cup condensed cream of
   mushroom soup
1 cup condensed cream of
   celery soup
4 eggs
2 cups milk
1 teaspoon salt
9 slices Cheddar cheese
   Bread crumbs
¼ cup melted butter

Line 9x13-inch buttered casserole with bread. Layer chicken, mushrooms and water chestnuts. Combine mayonnaise and soups; spread over top layer. Beat together eggs, milk and salt. Pour over soup layer. Top with cheese and refrigerate 24 hours. Bake 1 to 1½ hours at 350 degrees. If cheese gets too brown, cover with foil. Mix crumbs with melted butter and sprinkle on during the last 15 minutes of baking time.

GREEN CHILI CHICKEN

12 servings

2 6-ounce packages long-grain
   and wild rice, cooked
3 cups diced cooked chicken
1 pound Monterey Jack cheese,
   shredded
2 12-ounce cartons sour cream
2 4-ounce cans chopped green
   chilies, drained
   Parmesan cheese

Mix together sour cream and chilies. Layer ingredients in a 9x13-inch pan in the following order: ½ rice, ½ sour cream mixture, ½ chicken and ½ cheese. Repeat layering. Sprinkle liberally with Parmesan cheese. Bake 30 to 40 minutes at 350 degrees until brown and bubbly.

CURRIED CHICKEN IN ACORN SQUASH

4 servings

4 acorn squash
1 yellow onion, thinly sliced
8 mushrooms, sliced
2 teaspoons butter
2 cups diced cooked chicken
1 10-ounce condensed
   mushroom soup
1 teaspoon curry powder
   Salt and pepper to taste
   Parmesan cheese
   Bread crumbs

Wash squash and bake on a rimmed cookie sheet at 350 degrees for 45 minutes. Halve the squash and discard seeds. Place on cookie sheet, cleaned-side up. Sauté onion and mushroom in butter until soft. Add chicken, soup, curry, salt and pepper. Fill squash with mixture. Sprinkle Parmesan cheese and bread crumbs on top. Bake at 350 degrees for 30 minutes.

CHICKEN WITH COCONUT CURRY RICE
8 servings

1½ cups uncooked rice
3 cups chicken broth
1½ teaspoons salt
1 teaspoon curry
½ teaspoon nutmeg
  Pinch cayenne
6 tablespoons toasted almonds
½ cup flaked coconut
6 tablespoons butter, melted
1 medium onion, chopped
1 green pepper, chopped
4 tablespoons butter
4 tablespoons flour
5 cups milk
4 cups diced, cooked chicken
4 tablespoons chopped
    pimiento
2 teaspoons salt
¼ teaspoon pepper

Mix together rice, broth, salt, curry, nutmeg and cayenne. Cook until rice is tender; add almonds, coconut and melted butter. Spoon into 4-quart casserole. Sauté onion and green pepper in butter; stir in flour. Add milk to make a thin white sauce. Mix in pimiento, salt, pepper and chicken. Pour sauce over rice. Bake in 375 degree oven for 35 minutes.

CHINESE CHICKEN NUGGETS
1 serving

1 9-ounce chicken breast,
    boned and cut into chunks
1 ounce pea pods
½ ounce dried Chinese black
    mushrooms
¼ teaspoon salt
⅓ cup chicken broth
1 teaspoon sugar or honey
1 tablespoon oyster sauce
1 tablespoon soy sauce
1 teaspoon Saki or dry white
    wine

Soak mushrooms for 1 hour or until soft; squeeze dry. In very hot wok or skillet, sauté chicken meat with oil for about ½ minute. Stir in mushrooms and pea pods. Add salt, broth and sugar. Cook for about 3 minutes or until chicken is done. Add oyster sauce, soy sauce and Saki. Mix all ingredients well. Correct seasonings with salt and pepper. If the sauce is too thin, transfer the chicken nuggets onto a heated plate using a slotted spoon. Add ½ to 1 teaspoon cornstarch dissolved in a little cold water. Bring sauce to a boil. Pour over chicken nuggets. Serve with rice and fresh fruit. NOTE: Recipe multiplies easily to serve more. Taste before increasing salt.

CHICKEN CHEESE CRÊPES

CRÊPES
4   eggs
2   cups milk
2   teaspoons margarine
1½   cups flour
1   teaspoon salt

Beat eggs until foamy; stir in milk and 2 teaspoons margarine. Beat in flour and salt until smooth. Heat a crêpe pan very hot. Pour in batter. Cook until edges of crêpe are brown. Remove and roll, jelly-roll fashion.

CHICKEN FILLING
2   chickens, about 2½ pounds
       each
3   cups water
1   medium onion, sliced
2   teaspoons salt
6   peppercorns
       Handful of celery tops

Combine chicken, water, onion, celery, salt and peppercorns in kettle. Heat to boiling, lower heat; cover and simmer 45 minutes or until chicken is tender. Remove meat from broth; reserve broth. Remove chicken from bones and dice.

SAUCE
⅓   cup margarine
⅓   cup flour
1   13-ounce can evaporated milk
1   teaspoon salt
¼   teaspoon pepper
⅔   cup grated Parmesan cheese

Combine margarine and flour in large saucepan. Cook, stirring constantly for 3 minutes over medium heat. Remove from heat. Strain reserved broth into a 4-cup measure and add water, if necessary, to make 3 cups. Stir into saucepan with evaporated milk, salt and pepper. Cook, stirring constantly, until mixture thickens and bubbles. Add 1½ cups of sauce to chicken. Stir ⅓ cup cheese into remaining sauce and reserve. Unroll 1 crêpe at a time and spread with ¼ cup of chicken mixture. Place filled crêpes in pan and pour over each set of 2 crêpes ¼ cup reserved sauce; sprinkle with remaining cheese. Bake at 400 degrees; 30 minutes covered and 10 minutes uncovered.

CHICKEN À LA SUCCESS

1   pound Kielbasa sausage,
       sliced into chunks
4   boned chicken breasts, cut
       into bite-size pieces
¼   pound butter
1   clove garlic, finely minced
1   15-ounce can garbanzo
       beans, drained

Sauté sausage and chicken pieces in melted butter. Add garlic, beans, peanuts, onion, raisins and gravy. Place in greased casserole and bake at 350 degrees for 20 minutes.

1 **large onion, chopped**
1 **cup white raisins**
1½ **cups raw peanuts**
2 **10-ounce cans chicken gravy**

HOT CHICKEN AND DRESSING DISH   8 servings

4 **cups chicken, poached,**
   boned and cut in large
   pieces (reserve stock)
2 **tablespoons butter**
½ **cup chopped celery**
½ **cup chopped onion**
1 **10¾-ounce can condensed**
   cream of mushroom soup
1 **10¾-ounce can condensed**
   cream of chicken soup
1 **8-ounce package stuffing mix**
½ **cup butter, melted**
   Salt and pepper to taste

Sauté celery and onion in 2 tablespoons butter. Add soups and ½ cup of chicken stock. Add chicken pieces. Turn into 9x13-inch buttered casserole and set aside. Combine stuffing, 1 cup chicken stock, butter, salt and pepper. Spread on top of casserole. Cover and refrigerate overnight. Before baking, let stand at room temperature for 1 hour. Bake at 350 degrees for 1 hour; cover for the first 15 minutes.

PARTY CHICKEN LASAGNE   10 servings

12 **ounces lasagne noodles**
1 **10¾-ounce can condensed**
   cream of mushroom soup
½ **teaspoon salt**
⅔ **cup milk**
½ **teaspoon poultry seasoning**
1 **16-ounce carton cream-style**
   cottage cheese
⅓ **cup chopped onion**
¼ **cup minced parsley**
2 **3-ounce packages cream**
   cheese, softened
⅓ **cup sliced green olives**
⅓ **cup chopped green pepper**
4 **cups cooked chicken, diced**
   Pimiento for garnish

Cook noodles in boiling salted water, until tender. Drain and rinse in cold water. Mix soup, milk, salt and seasoning together in a saucepan and heat. Beat cheeses together; stir in olives, onion, parsley and green pepper. Place ½ of noodles in a 9x12-inch baking dish. Spread with ½ of cheese mixture, then ½ of the chicken and ½ of the soup mixture. Repeat layers and top with one of the toppings. Bake at 375 degrees for 30 minutes. Let stand 10 minutes. Garnish with pimiento.

TOPPING I
5 **ounces grated Parmesan**
   cheese
¼ **cup fine bread crumbs**
2 **tablespoons butter, melted**

TOPPING II
1½ **cups buttered soft bread**
   crumbs

DAY AHEAD CHICKEN CASSEROLE
8 servings

1 8-ounce package noodles,
   cooked and drained
6 cups diced cooked chicken
   (5 whole breasts)
1 14-ounce can artichoke
   hearts, chopped
1 6-ounce can pitted black
   olives, sliced
½ green pepper, chopped
1 4-ounce can pimientos, diced
1 medium onion, diced
¾ cup white wine
2 10-ounce condensed cream
   of chicken soup
1 cup sour cream
1 cup grated Parmesan cheese

Butter 3-quart casserole. Layer noodles, chicken, artichokes, olives, green pepper, pimiento and onion. Combine wine, soup and sour cream; pour over top layer. Sprinkle with Parmesan cheese. Refrigerate overnight. Remove from refrigerator 2 hours before baking. Bake at 325 degrees for one hour.

JERUSALEM CHICKEN
4 servings

1 small frying chicken
   Seasoned flour
2 tablespoons oil
½ pound sliced fresh
   mushrooms
1 6-ounce jar marinated
   artichoke hearts, undrained
2 cloves garlic, minced
1 teaspoon salt
¼ teaspoon oregano
½ teaspoon pepper
1 1-pound can tomatoes,
   undrained and cut up
½ cup sherry

Dredge chicken pieces in seasoned flour and brown in hot oil. Place browned chicken in a casserole. Combine mushrooms, artichoke hearts, garlic, salt, oregano, pepper and tomatoes and pour over chicken. Bake covered for 1 to 1½ hours at 350 degrees. Add the sherry 15 minutes before serving and finish baking.

POLISH POULTRY
4 servings

1 3-pound chicken, cut up
6 inches Kielbasa Polish
sausage
2 cups sauerkraut, drained
1 onion, diced
1 clove garlic, peeled
Salt
Pepper
Thyme
Caraway seeds

Slice Kielbasa into coins and line bottom of roasting dish. Add onion, garlic and sauerkraut. Sprinkle kraut with caraway seeds. Top with chicken. Sprinkle chicken with salt, pepper and thyme. Bake at 325 degrees for an hour. Baste with pan juices at least 4 times.

POLYNESIAN BAKED CHICKEN
6 servings

2 whole chickens
1½ teaspoons salt
1 cup butter
Flour

SAUCE
1 cup orange juice
2 tablespoons lemon juice
½ cup brown sugar
1 tablespoon cornstarch
1 tablespoon soy sauce
2½ cups cubed fresh pineapple

Melt butter in large pan. Lightly flour and salt chicken. Bake chicken for 50 minutes at 350 degrees. Baste frequently with juices. Bake until chicken is slightly browned. Pour off fat. Mix together all sauce ingredients except pineapple. Boil until clear; add fruit. Pour sauce over chicken and bake 10 minutes longer.

TURKEY WILD RICE CASSEROLE
8 servings

1 6-ounce package long-grain
and wild rice
1 10-ounce can condensed
cream of chicken soup
3 cups diced cooked turkey
1 cup chopped celery
¼ cup chopped onion
1 5-ounce can water chestnuts,
drained and sliced
2 tablespoons soy sauce
1 cup water
1¼ cups buttered bread crumbs

Cook rice according to package directions; stir in soup. Add turkey, celery, onion, water chestnuts, soy sauce and water. Pour into a 3-quart casserole. Sprinkle with bread crumbs. Bake at 350 degrees for 1 hour.

TURKEY FLORENTINE

10 servings

4 ounces fettuccini noodles
   (or your favorite pasta)
8 slices bacon, fried and
   crumbled; reserve drippings
1 cup chopped onion
1 10-ounce package frozen
   chopped spinach, cooked
   and drained
½ cup thinly sliced celery
¼ cup chopped pimiento
2 10-ounce cans condensed
   cream of mushroom soup
1 cup sour cream
1½ teaspoons salt
4 cups cubed cooked turkey or
   chicken
1 cup bread crumbs
3 tablespoons melted butter
   Slivered almonds

Cook noodles as directed on package. Drain. Cook onion in bacon drippings. Combine bacon pieces, onion, noodles, celery and pimiento. Combine soup with sour cream and salt; stir half into noodle mixture. Pour into a buttered 9x12-inch baking dish. Arrange turkey pieces on top and pour remaining soup mixture over turkey. Top with crumbs mixed with melted butter and almonds. Bake at 350 degrees for 35 to 40 minutes. NOTE: Microwave cooking requires about 6 minutes covered with waxed paper. Cook 3 minutes; rotate half a turn and cook 3 minutes more. Test.

CHESTNUT TURKEY STUFFING

15-pound turkey

2 pounds fresh or canned
   chestnuts
1 stick butter
2 onions, coarsely chopped
¾ pound bulk sausage, cooked
   and drained
2 teaspoons salt
½ teaspoon each sage, thyme,
   rosemary and oregano
1 teaspoon pepper
2 pounds bread, cubed and
   toasted
6 large eggs, beaten
1 quart milk

Chestnuts may be prepared up to 2 days ahead. Slash a "t" in the outer skin and bake at 350 degrees for 20 minutes. Peel; then boil for 30 minutes. You can also prepare them by slashing and cooking in a microwave until tender. (It takes about 4 minutes for a batch of 24 chestnuts.) Peel. Chop the nuts when cooled. Melt butter in a 10-inch skillet; sauté onions until soft. Add chestnuts and cook 3 minutes. Add sausage and seasonings; refrigerate. Just before stuffing turkey, combine bread cubes with eggs, milk and chestnut mixture.

ROCK CORNISH GAME HENS

8 servings

STUFFING:

1	small onion, chopped
¼	cup butter
8	ounces mushrooms, chopped
2	cups cooked rice
10	dried apricots, chopped
¼	cup dried currants, chopped
½	teaspoon thyme
1	teaspoon salt
1	teaspoon pepper
8	game hens
3	tablespoons butter, melted

BASTING SAUCE:

½	cup lemon juice
¼	cup butter
½	cup seedless raspberry jam or currant jelly
½	cup cognac

Sauté onions in butter for 3 minutes. Add mushrooms and cook 1 minute. Add rice; toss gently. Add apricots, currants, thyme, salt and pepper. Set aside. Rinse and dry hens. Salt and pepper cavities and stuff with rice mixture. Brush hens with melted butter. Season with salt and pepper and bake at 450 degrees for ½ hour. In the meantime, combine all of the basting ingredients. Turn oven down to 350 degrees and bake hens an additional hour, basting every 10 minutes. If hens get too brown, reduce heat to 325 degrees.

VENISON STEW

8 servings

3 pounds venison, cubed
2 tablespoons oil
2 onions, sliced
1 carrot, grated
½ pound mushrooms, sliced
2 tablespoons flour
1 cup water or beef broth
1 sprig rosemary
1 bay leaf
1½ teaspoons salt
½ teaspoon pepper
2 tablespoons minced
   parsley

Prepare marinade. Pour over venison cubes and marinate overnight. Drain, reserving marinade. Brown meat cubes in oil. Add onions, carrot and mushrooms; sauté 2 to 3 minutes. Sprinkle with flour and cook, stirring, for 3 minutes. Add reserved marinade, broth, herbs and seasonings. Bring to a boil. Cover and reduce heat; simmer 1 hour.

MARINADE

2 cups red wine
½ teaspoon each rosemary,
   thyme and peppercorns
3 whole cloves
1 teaspoon sugar
2 sprigs parsley
½ cup celery tops

Combine all ingredients in a saucepan. Heat just to boiling. Remove from heat and cool.

HARVEST QUAIL

6 servings

½ cup butter
6 quail
1 carrot, diced
1 small onion, diced
2 tablespoons chopped
   green pepper
½ cup sliced mushrooms
3 small slices blanched
   almond peel
1 tablespoon flour
1 cup chicken stock
   Salt and pepper
½ cup white wine

Melt butter in large skillet. Sauté quail until browned; remove to large buttered casserole. In same skillet, sauté carrot, green pepper, mushrooms and almond peel for 5 minutes. Stir in flour and cook for 1 to 2 minutes. Gradually add chicken stock and season with salt and pepper. Simmer 10 minutes. Set aside. Pour wine over quail and roast at 350 degrees for 20 minutes. Pour stock mixture over quail and continue roasting until birds are tender, about 40 minutes. NOTE: This can be prepared ahead up to the final roasting. Refrigerate until 1 hour before serving. May take a little longer to cook.

SOURED CREAM DOVE

4 servings

14 doves
1 quart heavy cream
4 tablespoons vinegar
  Salt
  White pepper

Clean and skin birds. Remove legs; leave breasts whole. Combine cream and vinegar in a pitcher. Set aside, unrefrigerated, for 36 hours. Place doves, breast side down, in a large casserole. Season with salt and white pepper. Cover with cream mixture. Cover casserole and bake at 375 degrees for 1 hour.

PEPPY'S GOOSE

8 servings

2 geese
½ teaspoon salt
½ teaspoon pepper
1 teaspoon thyme
8 apples, cored and quartered
2 oranges
2 28-ounce cans sauerkraut
2 cups raw cranberries
½ cup dark corn syrup
½ cup sugar
1 cup Madeira wine

Clean and wash geese. Rub inside and out with salt, pepper and thyme. Stuff apple quarters into geese. Squeeze juice from 1 orange into each cavity. Cut orange peel into strips and place in geese with apples. Close geese with skewers. Roast on a rack in a roasting pan at 350 degrees for 1 hour. Pour off grease and reduce oven to 325 degrees. Roast 1 hour. Pour off grease and remove geese. Place sauerkraut and cranberries in bottom of roaster. Sprinkle with sugar and corn syrup. Lay geese, breast side down, on top of sauerkraut. Pour wine over geese. Roast 1½ hours at 235 degrees. To serve, place quartered geese on a bed of sauerkraut and cranberries.

SLOW-COOKED GOOSE

4 servings

1 small goose or 2 lean ducks
¾ cup red wine
1 tablespoon grated orange peel
2 tablespoons honey
1 tablespoon soy sauce
  Flour
  Water

Skin and quarter birds. Place skin side up in a slow-cooker. In small bowl, combine all other ingredients. Pour over birds and cook on low setting for 9 to 10 hours. Remove meat and skim fat off liquid in pan. Turn heat to high and slowly add a paste made of equal parts flour and water. Serve gravy over meat.

FAISAN EN ORANGES

4 servings

1½ cups water
    Pheasant necks and giblets
1   small onion, chopped
¾   teaspoon salt
½   teaspoon pepper
¼   cup butter
1   tablespoon olive oil
2   pheasants, trussed
4   slices bacon
½   cup brandy
    Juice and grated rind of 1
      orange
1   bay leaf
1   teaspoon cornstarch
      dissolved in 1
      tablespoon water
1   orange, sliced

Prepare stock by combining water, necks, giblets, onion, ½ teaspoon salt and ¼ teaspoon pepper. Bring to a boil; cover and reduce heat. Simmer 30 minutes. Strain into bowl and reserve. Melt butter with olive oil in large oven-proof casserole. Brown pheasants, turning frequently, for 6 to 8 minutes. Remove casserole from heat and place 2 bacon slices on breast of each pheasant. In a small bowl, combine brandy, orange juice, rind and the remaining salt and pepper. Pour over pheasants; crumble bay leaf on top. Roast at 375 degrees for 1 hour or until pheasants are done. Remove from oven. Carve pheasants and keep hot on heated platter covered with foil. Pour juices from casserole through a strainer into a small saucepan. Add stock and bring to a boil. Boil rapidly for 3 to 5 minutes or until sauce has reduced by ⅓. Reduce heat and add cornstarch mixture. Stirring constantly, bring sauce back to a boil and cook for 2 to 3 minutes. Pour sauce over pheasants. Garnish with orange slices.

HEAVENLY HUNTER'S PHEASANT

4 servings

2   pheasants, cut up
1   stick butter
    Flour
1   8-ounce carton sour cream
1   package onion soup mix
1   10¼-ounce can cream of
      mushroom soup
    Sherry to taste

Melt ½ stick butter in oven-proof casserole or Dutch oven. Flour pheasant pieces and sauté until browned. Add more butter as needed. Combine sour cream, soups and sherry. Pour mixture over pheasant. Cover and bake at 300 degrees for 2½ hours. Add milk or water during cooking if gravy looks dry.

WILD DUCK WITH GAME SAUCE

4 servings

2 ducks, cleaned
2 apples, peeled and chopped
2 onions, chopped
2 stalks celery, chopped
1 10½-ounce can beef
   consomme
1 cup orange juice
½ cup sherry

Combine apple, onion and celery. Stuff ducks with mixture and place breast side down in roasting pan. Combine consomme, orange juice and sherry. Pour ½ over ducks; reserve rest for basting. Cover pan and roast in 350 degree oven for 3 hours. Baste frequently. Just before serving, remove cover from roaster. Remove liquid and reserve for gravy if desired. Return ducks to oven and continue to bake until browned. Birds brown quickly, so watch carefully. Serve with Game Sauce.

GAME SAUCE

1 8-ounce jar red currant
   jelly
   Grated rind from 1 orange
½ cup sherry or vermouth
2 teaspoons cornstarch

In small saucepan, heat jelly until melted. Add orange rind. Combine sherry or vermouth with cornstarch. Stir into jelly and cook until thickened. Good with any game.

SHRIMP CURRY

4 servings

1 coconut
1½ tablespoons vegetable oil
1½ onions, diced
4 stalks celery, diced
½ green pepper, chopped
2 cups chicken stock
2 tablespoons peanut
butter
1 cup sour cream
1 8-ounce can tomato
sauce
3 garlic cloves, crushed
1½ teaspoons sugar
1 tablespoon lemon juice
3 tablespoons curry powder
½ teaspoon salt
4 cups shrimp, cooked

CONDIMENTS
Raisins
Cashews
Bananas
Chutney
Flaked Coconut
Mandarin orange
segments

Pierce coconut and drain the liquid into small pan. Break open and peel about ¼ cup of meat into the pan with the liquid. If necessary, add enough water to equal 1¼ cups. Bring to a boil; remove from heat and strain. Reserve milk; discard meat. In large skillet sauté onions, celery and green pepper in oil. Add 1 cup coconut milk, chicken stock, peanut butter, sour cream, tomato sauce, garlic, sugar and lemon juice. Simmer 30 minutes, covered. Remove 1 cup of sauce and add the curry powder to it. Bring this to a boil in small saucepan and cook until slightly thickened. Add to the rest of sauce; season with salt. Stir in shrimp. Heat well and serve over rice. Serve with condiments in individual bowls. May be made ahead and reheated. NOTE: Substitute chicken for shrimp.

LUNCHEON SHRIMP PIE

6 servings

1 pound small shrimp,
cleaned and shelled
1 cup water
½ cup chopped onion
3 tablespoons butter
1½ cups fresh tomatoes,
peeled and chopped
½ cup sliced fresh
mushrooms
4 tablespoons flour
1 teaspoon seasoned salt
¼ teaspoon black pepper
1 hard-boiled egg, chopped
12 black olives, pitted
and sliced
1 egg, beaten
1 recipe for 2 crust
pastry

Simmer shrimp in water, covered, for 5 minutes. Remove and drain, reserving ¾ cup liquid. Sauté shrimp and onions in butter until tender. Add tomatoes, mushrooms, flour, shrimp stock, salt and pepper. Simmer, covered, for 15 minutes. Fill pastry lined 8-inch pie tin with mixture and sprinkle with chopped eggs and olives. Weave lattice crust and brush with beaten egg. Bake at 450 degrees for 15 to 20 minutes until crust is brown and filling is bubbly.

SHRIMP SUPREME

6 servings

1 bunch green onions,
    minced
6 tablespoons butter
2 pounds raw shrimp,
    shelled and deveined
½ pound fresh mushrooms,
    sliced
1 tablespoon flour
¼ teaspoon salt
½ teaspoon coarsely
    ground pepper
1 16-ounce container sour
    cream

Sauté green onions in 4 tablespoons butter. Add shrimp and cook until pink. In another skillet, sauté mushrooms in 2 tablespoons butter. Add to shrimp mixture. Blend in flour and cook, stirring constantly, for a few minutes. Season with salt and pepper to taste. Just before serving, add sour cream; heat and stir gently. Do not boil. Serve in patty shells, over toast points or with rice.

SHRIMP CREOLE

12 servings

¼ cup flour
¼ cup bacon grease
1½ cups chopped onions
1 cup chopped green onion
1 cup chopped celery with
    leaves
1 cup chopped green
    pepper
2 cloves garlic, minced
1 16-ounce can tomato paste
1 16-ounce can tomatoes,
    chopped, with liquid
1 8-ounce can tomato sauce
1 cup water
5 teaspoons salt
1 teaspoon pepper
½ teaspoon cayenne pepper
    Tabasco, to taste
2 bay leaves
1 teaspoon sugar
1 teaspoon Worcestershire
    sauce
1 tablespoon lemon juice
4 pounds raw shrimp,
    peeled and deveined
½ cup chopped fresh
    parsley
3 cups long-grain rice,
    cooked

In a large heavy Dutch oven, make a dark brown roux (paste) of flour and bacon grease. Add onion, green onion, celery, bell pepper and garlic. Sauté until soft, 20 to 30 minutes. Stir in tomato paste and mix well with vegetables. Add tomatoes, tomato sauce, water, salt, pepper, cayenne pepper, Tabasco, bay leaves, sugar, Worcestershire sauce and lemon juice. Simmer slowly, covered, for one hour, stirring occasionally. Add shrimp and cook until done, 5 to 15 minutes. Add parsley just before serving. Serve with cooked rice. NOTE: This dish should rest awhile before serving. It is much better made the day before. If made the day before, reheat but do not boil. Freezes well.

SHRIMP REMOULADE

8 servings

4 tablespoons horseradish
  mustard
½ cup tarragon vinegar
2 tablespoons catsup
1 tablespoon paprika
½ teaspoon cayenne pepper
1 teaspoon salt
1 whole clove garlic
1 cup salad oil
½ cup finely minced green
  onions, with tops
½ cup finely minced celery
3 pounds cooked shrimp
  Lettuce leaves

Mix all ingredients except shrimp together in a blender or food processor. Pour over cooked shrimp and marinate for 4 or 5 hours. Serve cold on lettuce.

SHRIMP AND SCALLOPS EN BROCHETTE

6 servings

36 shrimp
36 medium scallops or 18
  large, halved
½ cup medium dry sherry
12 slices bacon
  Butter, melted

Shell, devein and butterfly shrimp. Place in a shallow glass dish. Marinate with scallops and sherry, tossing occasionally, for 30 minutes. On a 10-inch metal skewer, thread the end of 1 slice of lean bacon, the narrow end of 1 shrimp, 1 scallop and the wide end of the shrimp; pull the bacon slice around the seafood, threading it onto the skewer. Continue to thread using 6 shrimp, 6 scallops and 2 slices of bacon for each of the 6 skewers. Arrange the brochettes with bacon side up on the rack of a broiler pan, brush with melted butter. Broil under a preheated broiler about 5 inches from heat for 5 minutes, or until the bacon is cooked but not crisp. Turn the brochettes; baste with melted butter and broil for 6 to 8 minutes more until seafood and bacon are cooked. Transfer to heated platter and serve. NOTE: Can also be cooked on a grill.

BAKED SCALLOPS
4 servings

1 lemon, thinly sliced
1½ pounds fresh scallops,
  drained
1 stack pack Ritz
  Crackers, crushed
½ pound butter, melted
  Salt
  Pepper, freshly ground
  Parsley and lemon
  garnish

In a 9x9-inch pan or baking dish layer lemon slices. Top with thoroughly drained scallops. Cover with crushed crackers, salt and pepper. Dribble over all with melted butter. You may wish to cut down on the cracker crumbs and butter, depending on amount needed to cover without drowning scallops. Bake at 350 degrees for 20 minutes. Serve immediately. NOTE: This also makes a good side dish with beef or chicken. Two pounds of scallops serves seven.

SHRIMP AND SCALLOP GRATIN
4 servings

1 pound shrimp, shelled and
  deveined
1 pound small scallops
8 tablespoons medium-dry
  sherry
½ cup packed fresh parsley
  leaves
2 cloves garlic
1 tablespoon chopped scallion
¼ teaspoon dried oregano
¾ cup french bread crumbs,
  lightly toasted
½ teaspoon salt
  Pinch of cayenne pepper
  Pepper to taste
½ cup unsalted butter, melted

Combine shrimp and scallops. Divide among 4 well-buttered 5-inch gratin dishes or baking shells; sprinkle each portion with 2 tablespoons sherry; set aside. Mince together parsley and garlic; add scallion and oregano. Stir in bread crumbs, salt, cayenne and pepper. Sprinkle over seafood and drizzle with melted butter. Bake, in the upper ⅓ of a 400 degree oven for 12 minutes, or until top is browned.

SCALLOPS PARISIENNE

1½ cups fresh or canned
   chicken stock
1½ cups dry white wine
3   shallots or scallions,
   sliced
3   celery tops with leaves,
   cut in 2-inch pieces
4   parsley sprigs
1   bay leaf
10 whole peppercorns
2   pounds bay or sea scallops
   cut into ½-inch slices
¾   pound fresh mushrooms,
   sliced

SAUCE:
4   tablespoons butter
5   tablespoons flour
¾   cup mllk
2   egg yolks
⅓   cup heavy cream
   Lemon juice
1   teaspoon salt
   White pepper
¼   cup grated Swiss cheese

In heavy 4-quart saucepan, bring the stock, wine, shallots, celery, parsley, bay leaf and peppercorns to a boil. Reduce heat and simmer for 20 minutes. Strain through a sieve into a 12-inch enameled or stainless steel skillet. Add scallops and mushrooms; cover and simmer for 5 minutes. Remove from liquid and place in a large bowl. Boil liquid to reduce to 1 cup. Reserve.

Melt butter in a 3-quart saucepan. When foam subsides, remove from heat and stir in flour. Return to heat and cook, stirring constantly, 1 to 2 minutes. Do not brown. Remove from heat and slowly pour in reduced poaching liquid and milk, whisking constantly. Cook over high heat, stirring constantly, until mixture thickens and boils. Reduce heat and simmer for 1 minute. Mix egg yolks and cream together in a small bowl. Stir in 2 tablespoons of hot sauce. Add 2 more tablespoons of sauce; then whisk the mixture back into the sauce In the pan. Bring to a boil, stirring constantly, for 30 seconds. Remove from heat and season with a few drops of lemon juice, salt and pepper. Drain scallops and mushrooms and mix with ⅔ of the sauce. Spoon into 6 buttered scallop shells and place on a baking sheet. Spoon remaining sauce evenly over shells and sprinkle with Swiss cheese. Bake in the top ½ of the oven for 10 to 15 minutes at 350 degrees. When sauce begins to bubble, slide under a hot broiler for about 30 seconds to brown top.

SEAFOOD DELUXE
8 servings

5 slices white bread, cubed
1 6½-ounce can crab
1 4½-ounce can tiny shrimp
1 4-ounce can sliced
   mushrooms
1 cup chopped onion
¾ cup chopped green pepper
1 cup diced celery
½ cup mayonnaise
1 10½-ounce can condensed
   cream of mushroom soup
½ cup shredded Cheddar cheese
4 eggs, beaten
¾ cup milk
   Paprika

Cube 3 slices of bread into a greased 8x10-inch pan. Mix crab, shrimp, onion, green pepper, celery and mayonnaise together. Spread over cubed bread. On top of the seafood layer, add two more slices of cubed bread. Spoon mushroom soup evenly over the bread. Sprinkle with cheese and paprika. Mix the beaten eggs and milk together and pour over the casserole. Refrigerate overnight. Bake at 325 degrees for 1 hour 15 minutes.

CRAB SALAD PIE
6 servings

½ pound frozen crab, thawed
1 10-ounce package frozen,
   chopped broccoli or
   asparagus
1¼ cups flour
2 teaspoons baking powder
½ teaspoon salt
½ cup butter, softened
¼ cup milk
1 tablespoon freeze-dried
   chives
3 hard-boiled eggs, diced
½ cup chopped celery
2 tablespoons minced green
   onions
1 cup grated Cheddar cheese
1 cup mayonnaise

Drain crab and slice. Cook broccoli or asparagus according to package instructions; drain well. Sift together flour, baking powder and salt. Cut in butter. Add milk and chives. Stir until mixture forms a ball. Pat into bottom of 9-inch pie plate. Fold crab, eggs, celery, onion and cheese into mayonnaise. Place broccoli or asparagus in pie shell; spoon crab mixture over vegetables. Bake 30 minutes at 375 degrees or until brown. Serve warm or chilled.

STUFFED FILLET OF SOLE

8 servings

¼ cup chopped onion
¼ cup butter
1 3-ounce can mushrooms,
　　drain and reserve liquid
6 ounces frozen crab, thawed
½ cup cracker crumbs
2 tablespoons snipped parsley
½ teaspoon salt
　　Dash of pepper
2 pounds sole fillets
3 tablespoons butter
3 tablespoons flour
¼ teaspoon salt
　　Milk
⅓ cup dry white wine
½ teaspoon paprika
4 ounces Swiss cheese,
　　shredded

In a skillet, cook onion in ¼ cup butter until tender. Add drained mushrooms, crab, crumbs, parsley, salt and pepper. Spread mixture over fillets. Roll up and place seam-side down in 9x13-inch greased baking dish. In a saucepan melt 3 tablespoons butter; blend in flour and ¼ teaspoon salt. Add enough milk to mushroom liquid to make 1½ cups. Add to pan with wine. Cook and stir until thick and bubbly. Pour over fillets. Bake in 400 degree oven for 25 minutes. Sprinkle with cheese and paprika. Return to oven; bake 10 minutes longer.

SNAPPER SUPREME

4 servings

¼ cup white wine
½ onion, thinly sliced
1 bay leaf
　　Pinch thyme
¼ cup heavy cream
½ cup butter
¼ garlic clove, crushed
1 small slice ginger,
　　peeled and minced
2 sprigs fresh parsley,
　　finely chopped
½ teaspoon soy sauce
2 tablespoons butter
6 red snapper fillets
　　Salt
　　Pepper

Combine wine, onion, bay leaf and thyme; bring to a boil. Cook until liquid is almost evaporated. Add cream and simmer until mixture coats a spoon. Remove bay leaf; press sauce through strainer and return to saucepan. Stir in butter and blend; add garlic, ginger, parsley and soy sauce. Keep warm. Melt 2 tablespoons butter in a heavy skillet. Sprinkle snapper fillets with salt and pepper. Cook on both sides until lightly browned and cooked through. Pour sauce over fillets; heat and serve immediately.

TUNA TEMPTERS

8 crêpes

½ cup chopped onion
½ cup chopped green onion
2 tablespoons butter
⅔ cup mayonnaise
1 tablespoon prepared mustard
¼ cup milk
1 7-ounce can tuna, drained
½ teaspoon salt
¼ teaspoon pepper
1 5-ounce can chow mein
   noodles
8 crêpes
   Sour cream
   Parsley

Sauté onion and green pepper in butter until just tender. Mix together mayonnaise, mustard and milk. Season tuna with salt and pepper. Combine mayonnaise mixture in a saucepan with tuna. Add sautéed vegetables. Stir until smooth and completely warmed. Just before serving, fold in chow mein noodles. Spoon mixture onto 8 crêpes. Roll; garnish with sour cream and parsley.

SEAFOOD THERMIDOR

6 servings

1 pound frozen cod filets,
   thawed
1 small onion, chopped
1 lemon, sliced
1 10-ounce can cream of shrimp
   soup
3 tablespoons flour
¼ cup milk
¼ cup white wine
¼ cup Mozzarella cheese
2 tablespoons chopped parsley
½ cup bread crumbs
2 tablespoons Parmesan cheese
2 teaspoons butter
½ teaspoon paprika

Bring fish, onion and lemon to a boil in a skillet. Simmer 5 to 6 minutes, covered. In another pan, blend together soup and flour. Stir in milk and wine and cook until thick and bubbly. Stir in Mozzarella and parsley. Drain fish; remove lemon and onion. Fold fish into sauce and place in shallow casserole dish. Combine crumbs, Parmesan cheese, butter and paprika. Sprinkle on top and broil 1 to 2 minutes.

DEVILED OYSTERS

4 servings

1 pint oysters
  Milk
¼ cup butter
¼ cup flour
¼ cup dry Sherry
1½ teaspoons lemon juice
1 teaspoon Worcestershire
1 teaspoon grated onion
½ teaspoon beef extract
½ teaspoon Dijon mustard
  Salt
  White pepper
  Parmesan cheese
  Buttered bread crumbs

Drain oysters, reserving liquid. Measure liquid and add milk to make 1 cup. Melt butter and stir in flour. Add liquid; cook, stirring, until it boils and thickens. Add wine, lemon juice, Worcestershire, onion, beef extract and mustard. Season to taste with salt and white pepper. Cool sauce slightly; stir in oysters. Pour into individual greased baking shells; sprinkle with Parmesan and crumbs. Bake at 400 degrees just until hot and browned, about 15 minutes.

SOLE AND OYSTER ROLLS

6 servings

1 10-ounce can frozen condensed oyster stew
1½ pounds sole fillets
12 medium oysters
1½ cups water
1 cup dry white wine or Vermouth
1 slice onion
  Pinch of thyme
4 whole peppercorns
  Salt
⅓ cup butter
⅓ cup flour
¼ cup half-and-half
2 tablespoons dry Sherry
  Salt and pepper
1½ cups cooked or canned crabmeat (or shrimp)
⅓ cup grated Parmesan cheese
  Paprika

Thaw oyster stew. Cut sole in 12 pieces. Wrap each piece around an oyster and fasten with toothpicks. Combine water, wine, onion and seasonings in a large skillet. Heat to simmering. Place fish rolls in liquid; cover and simmer gently 5 to 10 minutes, or until fish is just tender. Carefully remove fish to 6 greased individual casseroles or a shallow 12 x 8-inch baking dish. Remove toothpicks. Strain poaching liquid and boil rapidly until reduced to 1 cup. In a saucepan, melt butter and stir in flour; add reduced fish liquid, oyster stew, and cream. Cook, stirring constantly, until mixture boils and thickens. Add Sherry; season to taste with salt and pepper; add crabmeat. Pour sauce over fish rolls; sprinkle with Parmesan and paprika. Bake at 450 degrees for 10 minutes, or until bubbly and delicately browned.

SORREL SAUCED SALMON FILLETS 4 servings

2	teaspoons minced shallots
3	tablespoons butter
1	cup fish stock
2	cups heavy cream
3	ounces fresh sorrel, chopped
	Salt and white pepper
4	7-ounce salmon fillet slices

Sauté shallots in 1½ tablespoons butter. Add stock and cook until reduced to about 1 tablespoon. Stir in cream; reduce heat to simmer and cook until reduced to half. Stir in sorrel; season to taste with salt and white pepper. Simmer 2 to 3 minutes; keep warm. Sauté fillets in remaining 1½ tablespoons butter; 2 minutes one side, 1 minute after turning. Season to taste. Spoon sauce onto warm plates and top with salmon. NOTE: Chard or spinach can be substituted for the sorrel, but the flavor will be milder.

TROUT ALMONDINE 4 servings

2	pounds trout fillets or 4 individually dressed fish
¼	cup flour
1	teaspoon seasoned salt
1	teaspoon paprika
¼	cup butter, melted
1	cup sliced almonds
2	tablespoons lemon juice
4	drops Tabasco
1	tablespoon chopped parsley

Combine flour, salt and paprika. Roll fish in flour mixture and place in a single layer, skin side down, in a well-greased baking dish. Drizzle with 2 tablespoons melted butter. Broil 4 inches from heat 10 to 15 minutes or until fish flakes easily. While fish is broiling, sauté almonds in remaining butter until golden brown, stirring constantly. Remove almonds from heat and stir in lemon juice, Tabasco and parsley. Pour over fish and serve at once.

STUFFED LAKE TROUT

4 servings

1   3-5 pound trout,
      cleaned
1   small onion, finely
      chopped
5   mushrooms, sliced
3   tablespoons butter
1   teaspoon salt
      Pepper
      Thyme
3   tablespoons chopped
      fresh parsley
1   cup fresh bread crumbs
2   cups shrimp, frozen of
      canned
2   egg yolks
1   cup dry red wine

Sauté onion in butter; add mushrooms, salt, pepper, pinch of thyme and parsley. Combine with crumbs, shrimp and egg yolks. Stuff trout; secure with toothpicks if necessary. Place in well-oiled pan. Sprinkle with salt and pepper. Pour wine over trout and cover with foil. Bake 10 to 15 minutes per pound. Check to see if it needs more wine half way through. NOTE: You can use salmon or sea bass.

TROUT MEUNIERE

4 servings

4   trout, fresh or frozen
      (thawed), ¾-1 pound each
¼   cup flour
1   teaspoon salt
½   teaspoon coarse pepper
6   tablespoons butter or
      margarine
1   cup fresh seedless
      grapes
      Juice of 1 lemon
      Chopped fresh parsley
2   lemons, wedged or sliced
      Radish rosettes

Coat fish with mixture of flour, salt and pepper. Sauté in butter until delicately browned. Remove to heated platter. Sauté grapes with lemon juice in remaining butter until steaming, 2 to 3 minutes. Pour over hot fish. Sprinkle with chopped parsley and garnish platter with lemon slices and radish rosettes. NOTE: Sauce may be doubled depending on taste.

Vegetables

JERUSALEM ARTICHOKES AU GRATIN   4 servings

1 **pound Jerusalem artichokes**
   (also called Sunchokes)
2 **tablespoons butter**
2 **tablespoons flour**
1 **cup milk**
   Salt
   Pepper
   Parmesan cheese
   Bread crumbs

Scrub and peel or scrape artichokes. Cut into bite-size pieces and cook in boiling salted water for 25 minutes or until tender. Drain well and put into shallow ovenproof dish. Make a cream sauce with butter, flour and milk. Add salt and pepper to taste. Pour sauce over chokes, sprinkle on cheese and bread crumbs. Bake for 30 minutes at 375 degrees until bubbly and golden. Serve in place of au gratin potatoes.

ARTICHOKE AND MUSHROOM CASSEROLE   8 servings

3 **cans artichoke hearts**
2 **pounds fresh mushrooms**
¼ **cup butter**
2 **tablespoons olive oil**
2 **tablespoons wine vinegar**
1 **clove garlic, crushed**
1 **teaspoon celery seed**
¼ **teaspoon paprika**
¼ **teaspoon seasoned salt**
⅛ **teaspoon cayenne pepper**
2 **cups cheese sauce**
   Bread crumbs, buttered

Rinse, drain and slice artichoke hearts. Wash mushrooms; sauté in butter. Combine oil, vinegar, garlic, celery seed, paprika, salt and cayenne pepper. Toss with vegetables. Combine the vegetable mixture and cheese sauce and pour into casserole. Top with bread crumbs. Bake at 350 degrees for 40 minutes.

CHEESE SAUCE

2 **tablespoons butter**
2 **tablespoons flour**
¼ **teaspoon salt**
1¼ **cups milk**
1 **cup shredded Cheddar cheese**
1 **cup shredded Swiss cheese**
   Dash of white pepper

Melt butter in saucepan over low heat. Blend in flour, salt and dash of white pepper. Add milk all at once. Cook quickly, stirring constantly, until mixture thickens and bubbles. Remove sauce from heat; add cheeses and stir until melted.

DILLED GREEN BEANS

6 servings

2   16-ounce cans whole
     green beans, drained
1   tablespoon salad oil
1   teaspoon dried minced onion
1   tablespoon vinegar
¼   teaspoon pepper
½   teaspoon salt
¾   teaspoon dill weed
½   teaspoon thyme
1   cup garlic croutons

Mix all ingredients except croutons together and heat thoroughly. Sprinkle croutons on top before serving.

CHEESE BEANS

6 servings

1   pound fresh green beans
1   cup water
½   envelope (¼ cup) onion
     soup mix
3   tablespoons butter or
     margarine
⅓   cup slivered almonds, toasted
3   tablespoons grated Parmesan
     cheese
½   teaspoon paprika

Wash beans; remove ends and cut in 1-inch pieces. In medium saucepan, combine beans, water and onion soup mix. Bring to boil; reduce heat and simmer 15 to 20 minutes or until beans are tender; drain. Turn into serving dish and stir in butter or margarine. Combine almonds, cheese and paprika; sprinkle over beans.

DELICATELY SEASONED GREEN BEANS

4 servings

1   pound fresh green beans or
     1 10-ounce package frozen
     French style beans
½   teaspoon salt
6   slices bacon
¼   cup chopped onion
2   tablespoons chopped green
     pepper
2   tablespoons chopped parsley
⅛   teaspoon dried marjoram
     leaves
     Dash of dried rosemary
¼   teaspoon MSG (optional)
⅛   teaspoon pepper

Cook beans in boiling salted water. Fry bacon, reserving fat. Crumble bacon. In bacon fat, sauté onion and green pepper, until tender. Add beans, crumbled bacon, parsley and seasonings. Mix well. Cook over low heat 5 minutes.

LEMON CREAM FOR ARTICHOKES

4½ cups

2 cups mayonnaise
2 cups sour cream
¼ cup fresh lemon juice
2½ teaspoons finely grated
lemon peel
2 teaspoons white horseradish
2 teaspoons Dijon mustard
1 teaspoon salt
4-6 artichokes, cooked

Combine all ingredients in a bowl and blend. Cover and refrigerate. Serve with hot or cold artichokes.

ASPARAGUS WITH ORANGE BUTTER SAUCE

6 servings

3 10-ounce packages frozen
asparagus
⅓ cup clarified butter
¼ cup orange juice
2 tablespoons grated orange
rind
3 tablespoons chopped mint
Salt and pepper

Cook the asparagus. Drain and rinse under cold water. Place on heated serving platter. In small pan, combine the clarified butter, orange juice and orange rind. Simmer 5 to 6 minutes. Strain; season as desired. Pour sauce over asparagus and garnish with mint. NOTE: To clarify butter, melt 1 stick of butter in heavy sauce pan and pour into a glass jar. Let stand 10 minutes. Pour off the clear fat on top, leaving the milky solids on the bottom. The top is the clarified butter.

ASPARAGUS CHEESE CRÊPES

8 crepes

8 thin slices Swiss cheese
1 16-ounce can asparagus
spears, heated and drained
8 crêpes, warm

SAUCE
3 tablespoons butter, melted
3 cups sliced fresh mushrooms
3 tablespoons flour
¾ cup chicken broth
¼ cup sherry wine
1 tablespoon chopped chives
1 teaspoon horseradish
¼ cup half-and-half

Sauté mushrooms in butter until tender, 3 to 5 minutes. Stir flour into butter and mushrooms. Add broth, wine, chives and horseradish. Boil until thickened. Add half-and-half. Place one cheese slice in each warm crêpe. Add 3 spears of asparagus and roll. Place crêpes in casserole and spoon on sauce. Bake 20 to 30 minutes at 350 degrees.

SWISS CHEESE BEANS

8 servings

¼ cup butter or margarine
2 medium onions, coarsely
   chopped
1 10½-ounce can condensed
   cream of celery soup
1 cup milk
¼ teaspoon seasoned salt
¼ teaspoon pepper
⅛ teaspoon garlic powder
2 1-pound cans cut green
   beans, drained
½ pound sliced Swiss cheese
12 slices French bread, cut ½
   inch thick

Melt butter in a large skillet; add onion and cook until golden. Add soup, milk, salt, pepper and garlic powder; cook stirring until mixture boils. Alternate beans, cheese and sauce, 2 layers each, in shallow 2-quart casserole. Overlap bread slices on top. Bake at 350 degrees for 30 minutes or until bubbly. Crushed crackers may be used in place of bread for topping. No need to serve additional bread with meal. NOTE: Add cubed ham or browned pork chops to make a main dish.

SWEET AND SOUR BEANS

10 servings

10 slices bacon, cut in pieces
4   large onions, cut in rings
1   green pepper, cut in strips
1½ cups brown sugar
1   tablespoon dry mustard
½   teaspoon garlic powder
1   teaspoon salt
½   cup vinegar
2   15-ounce cans butter beans,
    drained
1   16-ounce can green lima
    beans, drained
1   16-ounce can kidney beans,
    drained
1   1½-pound jar B&M baked
    beans, undrained

In very large skillet, fry bacon; remove from skillet reserving grease. Sauté onions and green pepper in bacon grease until transparent. Add brown sugar, mustard, garlic powder, salt and vinegar. Mix well. In a 5-quart casserole, combine all beans, bacon and onion mixture. Cover and bake at 350 degrees for 30 minutes. Uncover and bake 30 minutes or longer. Mixture will be runny.

ITALIAN BROCCOLI

6 servings

2   10-ounce packages frozen
    broccoli spears or pieces
2   eggs, beaten
1   10-ounce can Cheddar cheese
    soup
½   teaspoon oregano
1   8-ounce can stewed tomatoes
3   tablespoons Parmesan cheese

Cook broccoli a few minutes less than stated in package directions; drain thoroughly. Combine broccoli, eggs, soup, oregano and stewed tomatoes. Pour into greased 10x6x2-inch dish. Sprinkle Parmesan cheese over all. Bake uncovered at 350 degrees for 30 minutes.

BROCCOLI WITH HORSERADISH SAUCE

6 servings

1   bunch fresh broccoli
¾   cup sour cream
½   teaspoon horseradish
1½   teaspoons prepared mustard
     Dash of salt
     Paprika

Trim and wash broccoli. Cut lengthwise. Steam on a rack over boiling water for 10 to 15 minutes. Drain. Place in serving dish. Combine sour cream, horseradish, mustard and salt in a saucepan. Stir constantly and heat until warm. Spoon sauce over broccoli. Sprinkle with paprika.

BROCCOLI CASSEROLE

8 servings

2   10-ounce packages frozen
    broccoli pieces or spears
1   cup chopped onion
¼   cup butter
1   10-ounce can condensed
    cream of mushroom soup
1   8-ounce jar pasteurized
    process cheese
¼   teaspoon garlic salt
1   4-ounce can mushrooms,
    stems and pieces
½   cup toasted almonds
½   cup prepared stuffing mix

Cook broccoli about 5 minutes; drain. Cook onion in butter until transparent. Combine cheese, soup, garlic salt, mushrooms and ½ of the almonds. Simmer until cheese melts; add onions. Arrange broccoli in bottom of greased 12x7½x1¾-inch casserole dish. Pour sauce over broccoli and sprinkle stuffing mix and almonds over top. Bake at 325 degrees for 25 minutes until bubbly.

BRUSSEL SPROUTS WITH BACON SAUCE

8 servings

3   10-ounce packages frozen
    brussel sprouts
12 slices bacon
½   cup finely chopped onion
3   tablespoons flour
1½ cups milk
⅓   cup dry white wine
½   teaspoon salt
½   teaspoon oregano
¾   teaspoon dill weed
⅛   teaspoon pepper

Cook sprouts as directed on package; drain and arrange in shallow 2-quart casserole. Fry bacon until crisp; crumble. Drain and discard all but 4 tablespoons of drippings. Add onion; cook until limp. Stir in flour; cook until bubbly. Remove from heat, stir in milk and cook, stirring, until thick. Add wine, salt, oregano, dill, pepper and all but 2 tablespoons bacon. Pour sauce over sprouts. Top with remaining bacon. Bake at 325 degrees for 20 minutes. May be made ahead and refrigerated. Bake 35 minutes if refrigerated.

MICROWAVE CHEDDAR CABBAGE

4 servings

2   tablespoons water
½   teaspoon salt
1   small cabbage, shredded
2   tablespoons butter
2   tablespoons flour
½   teaspoon salt
1   cup milk or half-and-half
¾   cup grated sharp Cheddar
    cheese
¼   teaspoon dry mustard
½   cup whole wheat crumbs

Combine water and salt in 1½-quart glass casserole. Add cabbage and cook, covered, 6 to 7 minutes per pound on high, rotating dish ¼ turn halfway through cooking time. Let stand covered for 5 to 10 minutes. Melt butter in 2-cup glass dish for 30 seconds. Stir in flour and salt and blend to make paste. Add milk gradually, stirring constantly. Cook 1 minute; stir. Cook 1½ to 2½ minutes longer, stirring every 30 seconds until mixture boils. Add cheese and mustard and stir to blend. Cook 1 additional minute; mix well. Drain liquid from cabbage and stir in sauce. Top with bread crumbs and heat 1 minute longer. Great with steak.

MARINATED WHOLE CARROTS

1 pint

1 pound miniature carrots,
    peeled
  Boiling water
2 bay leaves
½ cup white vinegar
¼ cup water
3 tablespoons sugar
½ teaspoon mustard seed
½ teaspoon dill weed
¼ teaspoon crushed red pepper
¼ teaspoon dill seed
1 clove garlic, minced or
    pressed

Arrange whole carrots in a vegetable steamer. Cover and steam over boiling water for 10 to 12 minutes or until just tender when pierced. Carrots may be cooked in a covered baking dish in a microwave oven on full power for 6 to 8 minutes. Plunge into cold water to cool quickly, then drain. Pack carrots in a clean pint jar; tuck in bay leaves. In a measuring cup, stir together the vinegar, water, sugar, salt, mustard seed, dill weed, red pepper, dill seed and garlic until sugar is dissolved. Pour over the carrots; cover. Refrigerate for at least 2 days or as long as 2 to 3 weeks.

BABY CARROTS WITH GRAPES

6 servings

⅓ cup orange juice
½ teaspoon cornstarch
1 teaspoon maple flavoring
⅓ cup lo-cal maple syrup
  Dash of nutmeg (freshly
    grated if possible)
1 medium size jar or can of
    baby or Belgium carrots
    (approx. 2 cups)
1½ cups fresh seedless grapes,
    washed and stemmed

Bring orange juice, syrup, cornstarch, maple flavoring and nutmeg to a boil, stirring constantly. Simmer uncovered for 5 minutes to thicken slightly. Add drained carrots and simmer 5 to 8 minutes or until carrots are glazed. Add grapes; remove from heat and let stand until ready to serve. Reheat and serve immediately. NOTE: 85 calories per serving.

SUNSHINE CARROTS
6 servings

6 medium carrots, scraped
1 tablespoon sugar
¼ teaspoon salt
1 teaspoon cornstarch
¼ teaspoon ginger
¼ cup orange juice
2 tablespoons margarine

Slice carrots about 1 inch thick. Cook, covered, in boiling salted water until tender. Drain. Combine sugar, cornstarch, salt and ginger in small saucepan. Add orange juice and cook, stirring constantly, until mixture thickens. Boil one minute, then add butter. Pour over carrots and toss to coat evenly.

CARROTS, ASPARAGUS AND LEEKS
10 servings

14 medium carrots
2 bunches asparagus
6 medium leeks
8 tablespoons butter
1½ cups chicken broth
   Salt and pepper

Cut carrots into thin strips lengthwise and then into 2 inch pieces. Clean asparagus, cut into 2 inch lengths. Trim green from leeks, slice into ⅛ inch pieces, wash in warm water, drain and blot dry. Sauté leeks, covered, in 4 tablespoons butter; set aside. Cook carrots, covered, in 4 tablespoons butter and ¾ cup chicken broth until just tender but not limp. Set aside; undrained. Cook asparagus, covered, in chicken broth until tender. Drain. Combine, all vegetables and toss gently; heat through. Can be undercooked slightly. Refrigerate until ready to heat and serve.

DELIGHTFULLY DIFFERENT CAULIFLOWER
6 servings

1 head cauliflower
1 cup mayonnaise
4 teaspoons prepared mustard
2 teaspoons Dijon mustard
1 cup shredded Cheddar cheese

Cut off cauliflower leaves; wash the cauliflower; leave whole. Wrap cauliflower head in plastic wrap. Cook in microwave for 9 minutes on high. Let stand wrapped in plastic for 5 to 7 minutes. Combine mayonnaise and mustards. Pour over cauliflower on serving plate. Top with cheese.

CORN BAKE

8 servings

1	small onion, chopped
1	small green pepper, chopped
½	cup margarine
1	15-ounce can cream style corn
1	15-ounce can whole kernel corn
1	8-ounce box corn muffin mix
3	eggs
1	cup sour cream
1	cup grated Cheddar cheese

Sauté the onion and green pepper in margarine in a fry pan; set aside. Combine corn, muffin mix and eggs. Stir well and add sautéed mixture. Pour into greased 2-quart casserole. Combine sour cream and cheese. Spoon mixture on top of corn. Bake at 350 degrees for 45 minutes.

FROZEN CORN

12-15 pints

36	ears sweet corn
1	pound butter
1	pint half-and-half

Husk and clean corn; cut corn off ears. Put into 1 or 2 large roasting pans; add butter and half-and-half. Bake 1 hour at 325 degrees. Stir every 10 minutes. Cool and put into 1 pint containers. Freeze. To serve, thaw and reheat. Season with salt and pepper to taste.

CORN CURRY

4 servings

3	tablespoons butter
2	cups whole kernel corn; fresh, frozen or canned
2	tablespoons chopped green pepper
½	teaspoon curry powder
½	cup sour cream
	Salt and pepper

Sauté vegetables in butter seasoned with curry powder. Stir in sour cream. Heat, stirring constantly, 8 to 10 minutes. Season to taste with salt and pepper. Serve immediately.

STUFFED EGGPLANT

8 servings

1   large eggplant
¾   cup sliced mushrooms
2   tablespoons chopped onion
2   tablespoons chopped green
     pepper
1   clove garlic, minced
2   tablespoons butter
2   tablespoons flour
1   teaspoon salt
⅛   teaspoon pepper
½   cup half-and-half
3   tablespoons pimiento

TOPPING
2   tablespoons buttered bread
     crumbs
     or
1   tablespoon Parmesan cheese
     or
2   slices crisp crumbled bacon

Cut a large lengthwise slice off eggplant; remove pulp. Cut slice of eggplant in cubes. Cook eggplant cubes in a small amount of boiling salted water for 10 minutes; drain. While eggplant is cooking, brown mushrooms, onion, green peppers and garlic in butter. Stir in flour, salt and pepper. Add well-drained, cooked eggplant, cream and pimiento. Fill eggplant shell. Top with desired topping. Bake 40 minutes at 350 degrees.

RATATOUILLE

10 servings

¼   cup olive oil
¾   pound eggplant, peeled and
     cubed (about 4½ cups)
2-3 zucchini, cut in half and sliced
     into ¾-inch cubes
1   large onion, chunked
2   green peppers, cubed
2   tablespoons finely chopped
     garlic
½   teaspoon thyme
1   bay leaf
     Salt to taste
     Pepper to taste
1   pound tomatoes, cored,
     peeled and cut into 2-inch
     cubes (2½ cups)
¼   cup chopped parsley
½   cup black olives

Prepare and cut all vegetables. Heat olive oil over medium-high heat in a large casserole or stove-proof roasting pan. Add the eggplant, cooking and stirring occasionally for about 5 minutes. Add zucchini, onion and green pepper; stir to blend. Stir in garlic, thyme, bay leaf, salt and pepper; cook for about 4 minutes. Add tomatoes and parsley and cook 5 more minutes. Place uncovered casserole in preheated 425 degree oven and bake for 30 minutes. Stir in olives and bake 10 minutes longer. May be served hot, cold or at room temperature.

HEARTS OF PALM BRAZILIAN

6 servings

1   **14-ounce can hearts of palm, drained and cut into chunks**
6   **hard-boiled eggs**
6   **slices of ham, cut in strips**

SAUCE
4   **tablespoons butter**
4   **tablespoons flour**
2   **cups milk**
¾   **cup grated Swiss cheese**
¾   **cup grated, fresh Parmesan cheese**
    Salt and pepper to taste
    Parsley, chopped

Melt butter in heavy saucepan and stir in flour. Cook for a few moments without browning. Add the milk and stir constantly until it comes to a boil. Lower heat and simmer for two minutes. Add the Swiss cheese, Parmesan cheese, salt and pepper. Continue stirring and simmering until the cheeses are melted. Remove from heat. Grease an ovenproof dish with butter and put in the hearts of palm. Cut the hard-boiled eggs into quarters and add them to the dish. Sprinkle the strips of ham over it. Cover with sauce. Put under a preheated broiler until lightly browned and bubbly. Sprinkle with parsley and serve. This can be prepared several hours ahead of time, covered and refrigerated. Heat in a 375 degree oven for about 30 minutes.

MUSHROOMS IN WINE SAUCE

4 servings

¼   **cup cooking oil**
⅓   **cup chopped onion**
1   **clove garlic, minced**
1   **pound mushrooms, sliced**
¾   **cup water**
¼   **cup dry white wine**
1   **chicken boullion cube, crushed**
¼   **teaspoon sweet basil, crushed**
⅛   **teaspoon salt**
⅛   **teaspoon pepper**
1   **tablespoon cornstarch**

Heat oil in large skillet over medium heat. Add onion and garlic; sauté until tender. Mix in mushrooms, ½ cup of water, wine, boullion cube, basil, salt and pepper. Bring to a boil; reduce heat and simmer uncovered, about 10 minutes, stirring occasionally. Blend together cornstarch and remaining ¼ cup of water. Stir into mushroom mixture and cook, stirring until thickened and heated through. NOTE: Good alone or as an accompaniment to steak, scrambled eggs or over buttered, toasted English muffins.

FABULOUS ONION RINGS

30 to 60 rings

1½ cups plus 2 tablespoons
    beer
1   tablespoon baking powder
1   tablespoon seasoned salt
1   egg
1½ cups flour
2   large Spanish onions,
    cut into ¼ to ½ inch slices
    Oil for deep frying

Combine beer, baking powder, salt and egg in a large bowl and blend. Gradually add flour, stirring to form loose paste. Heat oil to 375 degrees. Separate onion slices into rings. Dip rings into batter, coating well. Fry in small batches until golden brown, turning once, about 30 seconds to 1 minute. Remove with a slotted spoon; drain on paper towels. Serve hot. NOTE: Batter can be used with other vegetables and fish.

POTATOES AU GRATIN

6 servings

4   baking potatoes
½   cup grated Parmesan cheese
½   cup grated Gruyere cheese
4   tablespoons butter
    Salt and pepper
¼   cup heavy cream

Peel, thinly slice, wash and pat dry potatoes. Butter a 2-quart baking dish. Starting with potatoes, layer with salt and pepper, dab of butter and a combination of the cheeses. End with cheese. Pour on cream. Cover with foil and bake 1 hour at 350 degrees. Remove foil for last 10 minutes to brown.

SPICY STUFFED POTATOES

4 servings

4   potatoes
    Salt and pepper
4   tablespoons chopped
    black olives
½   cup diced green chili
    peppers
4   tablespoons heavy cream
½   cup grated sharp
    Cheddar cheese
½   cup sour cream
    Chopped black olives

Bake potatoes. Slice off top and carefully remove pulp; reserve skins. Combine pulp with olives and chilies. Add enough cream to make mixture the consistency of mashed potatoes. Season to taste with salt and pepper. Stir in cheese. Stuff mixture into potato skins. Sprinkle with additional cheese if desired. Top with sour cream and black olives. Heat in 350 degree oven until insides are warmed and cheese is melted.

CHEESY POTATOES

8 servings

Mashed potatoes to serve 8
½ teaspoon garlic salt
1 tablespoon snipped parsley
1 cup shredded sharp Cheddar
    cheese
2 teaspoons butter, softened
½ teaspoon dry mustard
½ teaspoon paprika
¼ teaspoon salt
1½ cups crushed seasoned
    croutons

Mix garlic salt and butter with mashed potatoes. Stir in parsley and cheese. Place potatoes in a greased 2-quart casserole. Mix mustard, paprika and salt and sprinkle over potatoes. Top with crushed croutons. Bake at 325 degrees for 20 minutes. NOTE: Crushed potato chips or cornflakes can be used as topping.

POTATO PANCAKES

8 servings

2 cups peeled, grated and
    drained raw potatoes
1 tablespoon flour or matzo
    meal
1 teaspoon salt
⅛ teaspoon baking powder
1 small onion, grated
3 tablespoons oil

In a large bowl, mix potatoes, flour, salt, baking powder and onion. Heat oil in a large heavy skillet over moderately high heat. Drop mixture from tablespoon into the heated skillet. Fry on both sides until browned, adjusting heat and oil as necessary. Serve with sour cream or applesauce.

BAKED FRENCH FRIES

8 servings

6 medium baking potatoes,
    pared and cut into French
    fry slices
3 tablespoons butter
1½ teaspoons salt
    Dash of pepper
½ cup grated sharp American
    or Cheddar cheese
2 tablespoons chopped parsley
½ cup heavy cream

Layer potatoes in heavy duty foil in a shallow baking dish. Mix butter, salt, pepper, cheese, parsley and cream and pour over potatoes. Seal foil. Bake at 450 degrees for 1 hour. If a crispy top is desired, open foil and broil for 5 minutes.

ONION-POTATO BAKE

6 servings

2 medium potatoes, peeled
and thinly sliced
(about 2½ cups)
3 medium onions, thinly
sliced
Salt and pepper
½ cup skim milk
2 tablespoons chopped
pimiento (optional)
2 tablespoons chopped
parsley
½ cup shredded Swiss
cheese

Layer half the potatoes and half the onions in a greased 10x6-inch baking dish. Sprinkle generously with salt and pepper. Combine milk, pimiento and parsley. Pour half the mixture over potato-onion layer. Repeat layers. Cover and bake at 350 degrees until vegetables are tender, about 60 to 65 minutes. Uncover. Sprinkle shredded cheese over top. Return to oven until cheese melts.

STIR-FRY PEA PODS

4 servings

2 cups fresh or 2
packages frozen sugar
pea pods
2 tablespoons soy sauce
1 teaspoon cornstarch
⅓ cup water
2 tablespoons dry sherry
1 teaspoon sugar
1 tablespoon cooking oil
½ cup walnut halves
½ cup water chestnuts, sliced
and drained

Remove strings from fresh peas. Combine soy sauce with cornstarch; stir in water, sherry and sugar. Set aside. Heat a wok or 10-inch skillet (not cast iron) and add oil. Add peas and stir-fry, lifting with an up and over motion, about 2 minutes or until crisp and tender. Add walnuts to pan with a little more oil if necessary. Stir-fry one minute. Stir in soy mixture. Cook a few minutes longer until thick and bubbly. Stir in water chestnuts and cook one minute. Do not overcook. NOTE: Use of a cast iron skillet will turn the sauce a displeasing color.

SPINACH DELIGHT

8 servings

1 **10-ounce package frozen chopped spinach**
3 **eggs, beaten**
4 **tablespoons flour**
¼ **cup melted butter**
 Dash salt
 Pinch nutmeg
1 **16-ounce carton cottage cheese**
¼ **pound American cheese, cubed**
¼ **pound Brick cheese, cubed**

Thaw spinach and drain well. Beat eggs and add flour, melted butter, salt and nutmeg. Add spinach and cheeses and mix well. Pour into 7x11-inch pan. Bake at 350 degrees for 1 hour. Let sit before cutting.

SPAGHETTI SQUASH BAKE

8 servings

1 **spaghetti squash**
½ **cup butter**
½ **pound Velveeta cheese**
1 **8-ounce carton sour cream**
 Salt and pepper to taste
6 **ounces Mozzarella cheese, cubed**

Pierce squash with fork. Microwave 8 minutes (depending on size of squash) on one side, turn and microwave another 8 minutes. It is better a little underdone. Cut squash in half, remove seeds and pull out pulp with a fork. It will string like spaghetti. Melt butter and cheese together; add salt, pepper and sour cream. Pour over squash and mix. Bake at 350 degrees for 30 minutes.

SUMMER SQUASH PARMESAN

6 servings

4 **cups summer squash, unpeeled and sliced**
1 **small onion, sliced**
1 **tablespoon water**
2 **tablespoons butter**
½ **teaspoon salt**
⅛ **teaspoon pepper**
3 **tablespoons Parmesan cheese**

Put all ingredients except cheese in skillet. Cover and cook 1 minute over high heat. Uncover and continue cooking over low heat until barely tender. Sprinkle with cheese and serve.

SPINACH TOPPED TOMATOES
12 servings

2 10-ounce packages frozen
   chopped spinach
2 cups bread crumbs
1 onion, finely chopped
¾ cup melted butter
½ cup grated Romano cheese
1 teaspoon Accent
1 teaspoon thyme
  Dash of salt
  Dash of pepper
4 eggs, beaten
12 tomato slices, thickly cut

Cook spinach according to package directions. Drain well. Combine all ingredients except tomatoes. This can be made ahead and refrigerated. Place tomato slices on greased baking sheet. Mound spinach mixture on each slice. Bake at 350 degrees for 15 minutes.

TOMATO QUICHE
6 servings

1 recipe pie crust
3 large tomatoes, peeled and
   chopped
3 tablespoons butter
1 teaspoon salt
¼ teaspoon thyme
½ pound natural Swiss cheese,
   diced
3 eggs, well beaten
1 cup half-and-half

Bake pie crust in a quiche pan or large pie tin for 10 minutes at 400 degrees. Combine tomatoes, butter, salt and thyme in a saucepan and cook over medium heat until reduced by half. Place cheese on crust. Pour tomato mixture over cheese. Mix eggs and cream and pour over tomato mixture. Bake for 25 minutes at 400 degrees or until set. Let quiche set for 5 minutes before serving.

VEGETABLE SOUFFLÉ
6 servings

1 12-ounce can Niblets corn or
   any cooked vegetable
3 eggs
½ cup mayonnaise
1 cup medium white sauce
5 green onions with tops,
   chopped
  Salt
  Pepper

Put all ingredients in blender and mix. Butter bottom only of 1-quart soufflé dish. Pour in vegetable mixture and bake at 350 degrees for 1 hour. Serve immediately.

VEGETABLE STIR-FRY

6 servings

3   tablespoons peanut oil
2   teaspoons minced garlic
1   tablespoon minced fresh
    ginger
¼   teaspoon crushed dried
    red pepper
3   cups broccoli florets
1   small zucchini, cut lengthwise
    and thinly sliced
2   cups fresh corn kernels (about
    4 ears)
4   green onions with tops, cut
    diagonally in 1-inch pieces
½   cup chicken broth
2   tablespoons soy sauce
2   tablespoons dry sherry
    Salt
2-3 cups hot cooked rice
½   cup cashews or peanuts

Heat oil in wok or large skillet over high heat. Add garlic, ginger and crushed red pepper. Stir-fry 1 minute. Add broccoli and zucchini. Stir-fry 3 minutes. Add corn. Stir-fry 1 minute. Add onions, broth, soy sauce and sherry; cover and reduce heat. Cook until vegetables are crisp-tender, 3 to 4 minutes. Salt to taste. Serve on rice with nuts sprinkled over top. NOTE: Strips of cooked beef, chicken or ham may be added the last 3 to 4 minutes to make this into a main dish.

VEGETABLE MEDLEY

10 servings

1   cup sliced carrots
1   cup sliced fresh green beans
1   cup diced potatoes
½   cup chopped celery
2   medium tomatoes, cored and
    quartered
1   small yellow onion, thinly
    sliced
1   small zucchini, thinly
    sliced
½   bermuda onion, thinly sliced
½   head cauliflower, broken into
    florets
¼   cup julienned red pepper
¼   cup julienned green pepper
½   cup frozen green peas,
    thawed
1   cup beef boullion
⅓   cup olive oil
3   cloves garlic, crushed
2   teaspoons salt
½   bay leaf, crumbled
½   teaspoon savory or thyme
¼   teaspoon tarragon

Wash and prepare all the vegetables, cutting them into sizes and shapes as directed. Mix vegetables and put in ungreased shallow baking dish (13x 9x2). In a small saucepan, mix the boullion, oil, garlic, salt, bay leaf, savory or thyme and tarragon. Heat to boiling. Pour boullion mixture over vegetables. Cover tightly and bake at 350 degrees for 45 minutes until vegetables are tender, stirring once or twice.

ORANGE YAMBOREE

8 servings

8   yams
5   oranges

SAUCE
2   tablespoons cornstarch
⅔   cup brown sugar
⅔   cup sugar
½   teaspoon salt
4   teaspoons grated orange rind
6   tablespoons butter, melted
2   cups orange juice

Bake yams at 350 degrees 40 minutes or until tender. Peel. Slice yams lengthwise. Peel and slice oranges. Layer yams and oranges sideways in alternate rows in a 9x13-inch casserole. Combine all sauce ingredients and cook, stirring constantly, until thickened. Pour sauce over yams and oranges. Bake at 350 degrees for 1 hour.

ITALIAN ZUCCHINI PIE

6 servings

4   cups unpeeled and sliced
      zucchini
1   cup chopped onion
½   cup margarine
½   cup chopped parsley
½   teaspoon salt
½   teaspoon pepper
½   teaspoon garlic powder
½   teaspoon Italian seasonings
2   eggs, beaten
8   ounces Mozzarella cheese,
      shredded
2   teaspoons prepared mustard
1   8-ounce can refrigerated
      crescent dinner rolls

In skillet, cook zucchini and onion in margarine until tender. Stir in parsley and all seasonings. Blend together eggs and cheese; add to vegetables. Separate dough into 8 triangles. Place in ungreased 11-inch quiche pan, 10-inch pie pan or 12x8-inch baking dish; press rolls over bottom and up sides to form crust. Spread crust with mustard. Pour vegetable mixture into the crust. Bake at 375 degrees for 15 to 20 minutes or until knife inserted near center comes out clean. Let stand 10 minutes before serving. Cut into wedges.

MEXICAN ZUCCHINI

8 servings

4 cups peeled and cubed
   zucchini
2 eggs, beaten
1 cup mayonnaise
1 cup Parmesan cheese
1 medium onion, diced
2 tomatoes, chopped
1 4-ounce can green chilies
  Salt
  Pepper
1 cup shredded Cheddar cheese

Boil zucchini in 2 cups water until just tender; drain well. Add mayonnaise, cheese, onion, chilies, tomatoes, salt and pepper to eggs. Mix well. Add zucchini; stir gently. Put in 9x13-inch pan. Bake at 350 degrees for 40 to 45 minutes. Top with cheese during the last 20 minutes.

ZUCCHINI AND TOMATO CASSEROLE

8 servings

2 medium zucchini, sliced
4 tomatoes, sliced and peeled
1 large Bermuda onion, sliced
2 medium green peppers, sliced
1 8-ounce package sliced Swiss
   cheese
  Salt and pepper to taste
½ cup melted butter
2 cups seasoned croutons

Grease a 9x13-inch casserole dish. Layer slices of zucchini, tomatoes, onion, green pepper and cheese in the dish. Repeat with a second layer of the above vegetables. Salt and pepper to taste. Pour melted butter over all and top with seasoned croutons. Cover and bake at 325 degrees 45 minutes to 1 hour.

ZUCCHINI FRIES

4 servings

1 cup flour, sifted
1½ teaspoons baking powder
½ teaspoon salt
  Dash pepper
¼ cup Parmesan cheese
¼ cup minced parsley
1 garlic clove, minced
⅔ cup milk
1 egg
3 small zucchini, unpeeled
  Oil for frying

Sift flour a second time with baking powder, salt and pepper. Add Parmesan cheese, parsley and garlic. Mix milk and egg together and stir into dry ingredients. Cut zucchini into french fry slices. Dip into batter and deep fry in 370 degree oil for 10 minutes or until golden. Drain and hold until serving time in a 200 degree oven, uncovered. Best served as cooked. Serve with extra cheese for sprinkling on fries. NOTE: Cook only a few at a time or they will stick together.

ZUCCHINI CASSEROLE

8 servings

3	large zucchini, sliced
1	can sliced water chestnuts
⅛	cup chopped chives
4	slices crisp bacon, crumbled
1	16-ounce carton sour cream
½	teaspoon salt
⅛	teaspoon pepper
⅛	teaspoon paprika
1	package dry onion soup mix
¼	cup Parmesan cheese
	Parmesan cheese

In a greased baking dish, place a double layer of half of the zucchini. Spread water chestnuts, chives and crumbled bacon over zucchini. Mix the sour cream, salt, pepper, paprika and soup mix; spread half over zucchini. Add grated cheese. Add another layer of zucchini and spread with other half of sour cream-soup mixture. Sprinkle with cheese. Bake 30 minutes at 375 degrees.

Cakes, Cookies
& Candy

NORTON THEATRE CHEESECAKE

20 servings

CRUST

¾ cup coarsely ground walnuts
¾ cup finely crushed graham
    crackers
3 tablespoons butter, melted

Mix walnuts, crackers and butter; press into bottom of 10-inch springform pan.

FILLING

4 8-ounce packages cream
    cheese, softened
4 eggs
1¼ cups sugar
1 tablespoon fresh lemon juice
2 teaspoons vanilla

Beat cream cheese until smooth. Add eggs, sugar, lemon juice and vanilla; beat until well-blended. Pour into crust. Put on cookie sheet and bake at 350 degrees for 50 to 55 minutes.

TOPPING

2 cups sour cream
¼ cup sugar
1 teaspoon vanilla

Mix sour cream, sugar and vanilla; chill. After cake has cooled slightly, spoon on topping. Starting in center of cake, spread to within ½-inch of edge. Bake at 350 degrees for 5 minutes. Chill cake for 24 hours or up to 3 days.

GLAZE

1 12-ounce jar raspberry jelly
1 tablespoon cornstarch
¼ cup Cointreau
¼ cup water
1 quart medium strawberries

Mix jelly and cornstarch over medium heat for 5 minutes until clear. Add Cointreau and water and remove from heat. Place strawberries on cake. Pour glaze over top prior to serving.

BLACK-EYED SUSAN CHEESECAKE

12 servings

1½ 8-ounce packages cream
    cheese, softened
3 sticks butter
3 cups sugar
1½ teaspoons vanilla
    Dash salt
6 eggs
3 cups cake flour
    Fudge sauce

Cream together cream cheese, butter and sugar. Add vanilla and salt. Add the eggs, one at a time; slowly blend in cake flour. Butter an angel food tube pan and pour in batter. Bake at 325 degrees for 1 hour and 20 minutes. Pour fudge sauce into center and serve with ice cream.

AMARETTO CHEESECAKE

12 servings

CRUST
1½ cups graham cracker crumbs
2 tablespoons sugar
1 teaspoon ground cinnamon
6 tablespoons butter, melted

Combine graham cracker crumbs, 2 tablespoons sugar, cinnamon and melted butter. Mix well. Press mixture into bottom and ½-inch up the sides of a 9-inch springform pan.

FILLING
3 8-ounce packages cream cheese, softened
1 cup sugar
4 eggs
⅓ cup Amaretto

Beat cream cheese until light and fluffy. Gradually add 1 cup sugar. Mix well. Add eggs, 1 at a time; beat well after each addition. Stir in ⅓ cup Amaretto. Pour into springform pan. Bake at 375 degrees for 45 to 50 minutes until set.

TOPPING
1 8-ounce carton sour cream
1 tablespoon plus 1 teaspoon sugar
1 tablespoon Amaretto
¼ cup sliced toasted almonds
1 12-ounce chocolate candy bar, grated

Combine sour cream, 1 tablespoon plus 1 teaspoon sugar and Amaretto. Stir well. Spoon over the cheesecake. Bake at 500 degrees for 5 minutes. Garnish with almonds and chocolate. Chill for 48 hours.

GERMAN BROWNIE CHEESECAKE

10 servings

CRUST
1 package German chocolate cake mix
⅓ cup margarine, softened
1 egg

Mix together cake mix, margarine and egg until crumbly. Press into a greased 9x13-inch pan.

FILLING
2 8-ounce packages cream cheese, softened
2 eggs
¾ cup sugar
2 teaspoons vanilla

Beat cream cheese, eggs, ¾ cup sugar and 2 teaspoons vanilla until smooth and fluffy. Spread over cake mixture and bake at 350 degrees for 20 to 25 minutes, until edge of cheese cake is brown.

FROSTING
2 cups sour cream
¼ cup sugar
1 tablespoon vanilla

Mix sour cream, ¼ cup sugar and 1 tablespoon vanilla until smooth. Frost cake while hot. Cool 8 hours.

MOCHA MOUSSE CHEESECAKE

10 servings

CRUST
1   cup chocolate wafer cookie crumbs
¼   cup butter
2   tablespoons sugar

Butter sides of 8-inch springform pan. Combine crumbs, butter and 2 tablespoons sugar. Press into bottom of pan.

FILLING
3   8-ounce packages cream cheese, softened
1   cup sugar
3   eggs
1   8-ounce package semisweet chocolate chips
2   tablespoons cream
1   cup sour cream
1   teaspoon instant espresso coffee (dissolved in 1 teaspoon water and cooled)
¼   cup Kahlua
2   teaspoons vanilla

Beat cream cheese; gradually add sugar and eggs. Beat until smooth. Melt chocolate in double boiler and add to cheese. Stir in sour cream, cream, espresso, Kahlua and vanilla. Beat well. Pour into crust and bake at 350 degrees for 45 minutes. Sides will be puffed and center a little soft until refrigerated. Refrigerate at least 12 hours.

CHOCOLATE POUND CAKE

16 servings

CAKE
2   cups minus 2 teaspoons sugar
1   cup minus 2 teaspoons unsalted butter
4   eggs
1   8-ounce bar Hershey's Special Dark Chocolate, melted
1   16-ounce can Hershey's chocolate syrup
1   cup buttermilk
2   teaspoons baking soda
2   teaspoons vanilla
2½ cups flour
½   teaspoon salt

Using either an electric mixer or food processor, cream sugar and butter. Add eggs, one at a time, mixing well after each addition. Add both chocolates and mix well. Add buttermilk and vanilla; mix. Combine dry ingredients, add to work bowl and pulse on-off to combine. Pour batter into greased and floured 10-inch tube pan. Bake in preheated 375 degree oven for 1½ hours. Remove from oven and let cake cool overnight in pan on rack before removing. Turn out and frost. Cake freezes well.

FROSTING
¼   cup unsalted butter
2   squares unsweetened chocolate
4   tablespoons strong coffee
2   cups confectioners' sugar
1   teaspoon vanilla

Melt butter and chocolate in a double boiler. Place chocolate mixture in work bowl. Add remaining ingredients and process until smooth. Add more coffee if too thick.

PINEAPPLE POUND CAKE

12 servings

CAKE
½ cup vegetable shortening
1 cup butter or margarine
2¾ cups sugar
6 large eggs
3 cups flour
1 teaspoon baking powder
¼ cup milk
1 teaspoon vanilla
¾ cup crushed pineapple
    with juice

GLAZE
¼ cup butter or margarine
1½ cups confectioners' sugar
½ cup crushed pineapple

Cream shortening, margarine or butter and sugar. Add eggs 1 at a time. Sift flour and baking powder together and add to creamed mixture 1 spoonful at a time, alternating with milk. Stir in vanilla and crushed pineapple with juice. Pour cake batter into a well-greased tube pan. Place in a cold oven, heat to 325 degrees and bake for 1¼ hours. Remove from pan to cool. Combine butter or margarine, powdered sugar and pineapple. Pour over warm cake.

RAINBOW CAKE

16 servings

1 large angel food cake
1 3-ounce package each:
    strawberry, lime and orange
    gelatin
2 10-ounce packages frozen
    strawberries
1 10-ounce package frozen
    blueberries, drained
2 11-ounce cans mandarin
    oranges, drained
1 quart vanilla ice cream

Thaw strawberries and blueberries. Slice angel food cake into 3 layers. Tear each layer into bite-size pieces and place in 3 separate bowls. Pour dry strawberry gelatin over 1 bowl of cake pieces, lime over another, and orange over the third. Toss each well until gelatin sticks to cake. To form cake; place the strawberry cake pieces into bottom of an ungreased angel food cake pan. Spoon thawed strawberries on top. Spread with ⅓ of vanilla ice cream. Layer lime cake pieces and another ⅓ of the ice cream, followed with blueberies. Top with orange cake pieces, followed by mandarin oranges and the last ⅓ of ice cream. Cover and freeze. Once cake has frozen, remove from pan, wrap in foil and return to freezer. When ready to serve, slice frozen cake in thin slices. Do not use fresh fruit.

UNICAMERAL CAKE

CAKE

1 cup margarine
3 tablespoons cocoa
1 cup cola drink
2 cups flour
2 cups sugar
½ cup buttermilk
1 teaspoon baking soda
1 teaspoon vanilla
2 eggs, beaten
2 cups miniature marshmallows

Combine margarine, cocoa and cola in a saucepan and bring to a boil. Mix flour and sugar together and add to the hot mixture. Mix buttermilk, baking soda, vanilla, eggs and marshmallows together and add to the other mixture. Pour in a 10x14-inch greased and floured jelly roll pan. Make certain the marshmallows are evenly spaced throughout or mixture will overflow. Bake at 350 degrees for 35 to 40 minutes.

FROSTING

½ cup margarine
3 tablespoons cocoa
6 tablespoons cola drink
1 1-pound box confectioners' sugar, sifted

Combine margarine, cocoa and cola in a saucepan and bring to a boil. Add mixture to confectioners' sugar. Beat until ready to spread. Frost while cake is slightly warm.

MOCHA FUDGE CAKE

10 servings

8 ounces German sweet chocolate
1 cup sugar
1 cup butter
½ cup espresso or strong coffee
4 eggs
¼ cup jelly or preserves, currant or orange marmalade
1 cup heavy cream
¼ cup confectioners' sugar
¼ teaspoon vanilla

Combine chocolate, sugar, butter and espresso in a pan. Place over low heat, stirring, until chocolate and butter are melted. Cool slightly. Beat eggs in a mixer bowl and slowly beat in cooled chocolate mixture. Pour into an 8-inch springform pan. Bake in preheated 350 degree oven about 30 minutes, until cake cracks around sides. Cake will be soft in the center. Cool completely. Cover with foil and refrigerate overnight or up to 1 week. Loosen edge of cake with knife and remove sides of pan. Trim if necessary. Melt preserves or jelly and spread over top of cake. Return to refrigerator to set for 15 minutes. Whip cream until thick; fold in confectioners' sugar and vanilla. Top with whipped cream. NOTE: If 9-inch springform pan is used; increase recipe amounts by ½. Increased cooking time may be necessary.

HAZELNUT MERINGUE TORTE

12 servings

MERINGUE

4   **large egg whites**
    Salt
    Cream of tartar
1   **cup sugar**
1   **cup confectioners' sugar, sifted**
¾   **cup finely ground hazelnuts**
    Sifted confectioners' sugar

In a large bowl, beat 4 egg whites with a pinch each of salt and cream of tartar until they hold soft peaks. Gradually beat in sugar. Continue to beat the meringue until it holds stiff peaks. Fold in sifted confectioners' sugar combined with ground hazelnuts. Spoon meringue into 2 buttered and floured 9-inch cake pans, 1½-inches deep. Make sure each layer is spread evenly. Cover with sifted confectioners' sugar and bake cakes in a preheated 300 degree oven for 1 hour, or until lightly browned. Let cool in pan for 10 minutes, turn onto a rack and let cool completely.

CAKE

4   **large eggs, separated**
⅓   **cup sugar**
    Salt
    Cream of tartar
1   **tablespoon orange juice**
1   **teaspoon grated orange rind**
¼   **cup flour**
2   **tablespoons unsweetened cocoa**

In a bowl, with an electric mixer, beat egg yolks. Add sugar, a little at a time; beat the mixture until it ribbons when the beater is lifted. In another bowl, beat egg whites with a pinch each of salt and cream of tartar until they hold stiff peaks. Beat in orange juice and rind. Stir ¼ of the whites into the yolk mixture, pile the mixture on the remaining whites, and sift over ¼ cup flour and 2 tablespoons unsweetened cocoa. Fold mixtures together gently until there are no traces of white. Line a buttered 9-inch cake pan, 1½-inches deep, with waxed paper. Pour batter into the pan and bake in a preheated 350 degree oven for 15 minutes, or until a cake tester inserted in the center comes out clean. Let the cake cool in the pan, turn out onto a rack and peel off the paper.

COFFEE BUTTERCREAM

6   **large egg yolks**
1   **tablespoon boiling water**
1½   **tablespoons freeze-dried coffee**
1   **cup sugar**
⅓   **cup water**
1   **cup unsalted butter, softened**

In a bowl, with an electric mixer, beat egg yolks at medium speed for 10 minutes, or until they are light and thick. In a cup, combine boiling water and freeze-dried coffee. In a small saucepan, combine sugar and ⅓ cup water. Bring the mixture to a boil over moderate heat, stirring constantly.

Wash down any sugar crystals cling-ing to the sides with a brush dipped in cold water. Cook until it reaches the soft ball stage, or a candy ther-mometer registers 240 degrees. With the mixer running, add the hot syrup to the yolks in a stream. Beat the mixture until it is completely cool. Beat in unsalted butter and 2½ tea-spoons of the coffee extract. Chill the coffee buttercream, covered, un-til it is firm but still soft enough to spread.

CHOCOLATE CREAM

6   **ounces semisweet chocolate**
2   **ounces unsweetened chocolate**
1   **cup heavy cream**
¼   **cup orange flavored liqueur**
¾   **cup finely ground hazelnuts**

In the top of a double boiler set over hot water, melt semisweet and un-sweetened chocolate with heavy cream and orange flavored liqueur. Stir the mixture until it is smooth. Transfer to a metal bowl and cool. Chill for 30 minutes, stirring occasionally. Beat the chocolate cream until it just holds soft peaks; fold in ¾ cup finely ground hazelnuts.

ASSEMBLY
Whole hazelnuts

Slice chocolate cake in half horizon-tally. Spread the bottom layer with ¼ of the chocolate cream. Top the cream with a meringue layer. Spread me-ringue with another ¼ of the choco-late cream and top the cream with the remaining layer of chocolate cake. Spread cake with ¼ chocolate cream and top with the other meringue layer, smooth side up. Cover top and sides of the cake with ½ to ⅔ of the coffee buttercream. Warm the blade of a serrated knife under hot running water, dry it, and run in a zigzag motion over top of the cake. Fill a pastry bag, fitted with a decorative tip, with some of the remaining coffee buttercream. Pipe swirls around the top edge of the cake. Decorate the swirls with the whole hazelnuts. Com-bine leftover chocolate cream and coffee buttercream; frost the sides of the cake. Transfer cake to a platter and chill. Remove cake from refriger-ator 30 minutes before serving.

237

CHOCOHOLIC CAKE

Cocoa
1 18½-ounce package chocolate
cake mix
1 4⅛-ounce package Instant
chocolate pudding mix
¾ cup sour cream
4 eggs
½ cup vegetable oil
½ cup water
¼ cup mayonnaise
1 teaspoon almond extract
3 tablespoons almond liqueur
½ cup almonds, chopped
(optional)
1 cup chocolate chips

GLAZE
1 cup confectioners' sugar
2 tablespoons milk
1 teaspoon almond extract

Grease 10-inch bundt pan and dust with cocoa. Put all ingredients except chocolate chips in bowl and beat 2 minutes with mixer. Mix in chocolate chips. Bake 50 minutes at 350 degrees. When cake is cool, glaze with a mixture of confectioners' sugar, milk and 1 teaspoon almond extract.

ORANGE-NUT CAKE

CAKE
½ cup butter or margarine
¼ cup shortening
1½ cups sugar
3 eggs
2½ cups flour
1½ teaspoons baking soda
¾ teaspoon salt
1½ cups buttermilk
1½ teaspoons vanilla
1 cup finely chopped pecans
2 tablespoons orange rind
Juice from ½ orange

Combine butter, shortening and sugar. Cream until light and fluffy. Add eggs, one at a time and beat well after each addition. Add flour, soda, salt, buttermilk and vanilla. Beat 3 minutes on high. Stir in pecans, rind and juice. Bake at 350 degrees for 30 to 35 minutes in two 8-inch layer cake pans. Cool 5 to 10 minutes in pans; remove and cool completely on a rack. NOTE: This may also be baked in a jelly roll pan and cut into bars.

FROSTING
1½ cups butter
4½ cups confectioners' sugar
2 tablespoons orange juice
3 tablespoons orange rind

Cream together frosting ingredients and frost cake.

MAPLE NUT CAKE

CAKE
¼ cup sugar
¼ cup chopped walnuts
1 teaspoon cinnamon
1 18½-ounce package yellow
    cake mix
1 3¾-ounce package instant
    vanilla pudding mix
¾ cup corn oil
¾ cup water
4 eggs
1 teaspoon maple flavoring
1 teaspoon vanilla

GLAZE
1 cup confectioners' sugar
½ teaspoon maple flavoring
½ teaspoon vanilla
3 tablespoons milk

Mix sugar, nuts and cinnamon in blender. Set aside. Prepare a batter of cake mix, pudding mix, oil, water and eggs. Beat on high for 8 minutes. Add flavorings and mix well. In well-greased bundt or tube pan, layer ½ of nut mixture, ½ of the batter, the rest of the nut mixture and the rest of the batter. Bake at 350 degrees for 1 hour. Remove from oven and cool for 8 minutes. Mix glaze ingredients. Turn cake out on plate and glaze.

COOKIE CRUMB CAKE

4 cups vanilla wafer
    crumbs (12-ounce package)
1 cup butter, softened
2 cups sugar
⅔ cup milk
1 teaspoon baking soda
6 eggs
1 cup flaked coconut
1 cup chopped pecans
1 teaspoon vanilla
    Cream Cheese Frosting
    Chopped pecans

Cream together butter and sugar. Add milk. Beat in eggs, one at a time. Stir in baking soda, crumbs, coconut, nuts and vanilla. Spread batter in greased jelly roll pan. Bake at 350 degrees, 45 to 60 minutes. Frost cooled cake with Cream Cheese Frosting and sprinkle with additional chopped pecans. Cake will keep in refrigerator 1 week to 10 days. Bring to room temperature before serving.

CHOCOLATE FROSTING

¼ **cup margarine or butter**
¼ **cup milk**
1 **6-ounce package semisweet chocolate chips**
1 **egg yolk, beaten**
1 **teaspoon vanilla**
2 **cups confectioners' sugar sifted**

Combine butter and milk in saucepan and bring to a boil. Remove from heat and stir in chocolate until melted. Stir in egg yolk and vanilla. Beat in sugar. Frost cake immediately before frosting sets. Will frost a 2 layer 9-inch cake.

CREAM CHEESE FROSTING

1 **8-ounce package cream cheese, softened**
6 **tablespoons butter, softened**
3 **cups confectioners' sugar**
1 **teaspoon vanilla**
   Juice of ½ lemon (optional)

Cream together cream cheese and butter. Slowly sift in confectioners' sugar and continue beating until mixture is smooth. Stir in vanilla and lemon juice if you use it. Enough frosting for a 2-layer cake.

PROFESSIONAL BAKER'S ICING

1 **1-pound box plus 2 cups confectioners' sugar**
½ **cup milk**
¾ **cup solid shortening**
1 **teaspoon almond extract**

Place all ingredients in bowl and beat for 10 minutes. Don't skimp on beating time. Tint with food coloring. Use with pastry bag to decorate cakes. NOTE: If you want to keep this frosting for several days; substitute water for milk in recipe. Refrigerate until used.

WALNUT COOKIES

2 dozen

2 cups ground walnuts
1 cup butter
⅔ cup sugar
2 teaspoons vanilla
2 cups flour

Cream butter, sugar and vanilla. Gradually add flour; stir in walnuts. Chill for easier rolling. Roll out onto floured board to ¼-inch thickness and cut with floured 2¼-inch cutter. Place on ungreased sheet and bake at 350 degrees for 15 minutes or until edges are slightly browned. Remove to wire racks to cool. When cold, spread 1 cookie with filling and top with another, or frost with glaze and top with a walnut. These are delicious with or without the glaze.

FILLING

1 cup ground walnuts
½ cup raspberry or apricot jam

Mix nuts and jam together. It will be easier to spread if it is slightly warm.

CHOCOLATE GLAZE

2 tablespoons butter, melted
2 tablespoons unsweetened cocoa
2 tablespoons boiling water
3 tablespoons light corn syrup
1½ cups sifted confectioners' sugar
Walnut halves

Stir butter, cocoa and water together; add syrup and mix well. Add sugar and mix until smooth.

NUTTY APPLESAUCE COOKIES

5½ dozen

1 cup flour
¾ cup whole wheat flour
1 teaspoon baking soda
½ teaspoon salt
½ teaspoon cinnamon
½ teaspoon nutmeg
¼ teaspoon ground cloves
1 cup raisins
1 cup chopped nuts
½ cup margarine, softened
¾ cup packed brown sugar
1 egg
1 cup applesauce

Mix flours, soda, salt, spices, raisins and nuts; set aside. Cream margarine and sugar; beat in egg and applesauce. Stir into flour mixture. Drop from teaspoon onto cookie sheet. Bake at 350 degrees for 12 minutes. Cool. These are better the next day.

PECAN COOKIES

4 dozen

1   cup butter, softened
2   cups flour
½   cup sugar
1½ cups finely chopped pecans
    (filberts may be substituted)
½   cup currant jelly
    Confectioners' sugar icing
    Chopped pecans

Combine butter, flour and sugar in large mixing bowl. Blend on low until dough forms. Stir in nuts. Divide dough into 4 equal parts. Shape each part into a roll 6 inches long. Wrap individually and chill at least 3 hours. Heat oven to 350 degrees. Cut rolls into ⅛-inch slices. Place on cookie sheets and bake 10 to 15 minutes. Cool. Put cookies together, sandwich-style, with ½ teaspoon jelly in the center. Frost top with a confectioners' sugar icing and sprinkle with additional nuts.

REAL ORANGE COOKIES

5 dozen

1   cup butter or margarine,
    softened
1½ cups sugar
2   eggs
3   tablespoons grated orange
    rind
½   cup orange juice
3   cups flour
½   teaspoon baking soda
½   teaspoon salt
1   cup pecans or flaked coconut
    (optional)

Cream butter; gradually add sugar. Stir in eggs, rind and juice. Sift together flour, baking soda and salt. Combine with creamed mixture. Add pecans or coconut and drop from teaspoon onto greased cookie sheets. Bake at 350 degrees for 10 to 12 minutes. Excellent with a confectioners' sugar frosting.

SOFT CREAMY JUMBLES

3 dozen

½   cup shortening, softened
    (part butter)
1   cup sugar
1   egg
2   cups flour
½   teaspoon baking soda
½   teaspoon salt
½   cup buttermilk
1   teaspoon vanilla
    Cinnamon-sugar topping
    (optional)

Cream together shortening and sugar; add egg and mix thoroughly. Sift together the flour, soda and salt. Add to the shortening mixture alternately with the buttermilk and vanilla. Drop from teaspoon, about 2 inches apart, onto a lightly greased baking sheet. Bake 12 to 15 minutes at 325 degrees. If a cinnamon-sugar topping is desired, sprinkle cookies generously before baking.

DATE COOKIES

½ cup sour cream
¼ cup butter
½ teaspoon vanilla
¼ teaspoon salt
½ teaspoon baking soda
¾ cup brown sugar
1 egg, beaten
1¼ cups flour
¼ teaspoon baking powder
2 small packages pitted dates
　 Walnut pieces

Mix all ingredients except dates and walnuts into a stiff batter. Stuff dates with walnut pieces and add to the batter. Stir gently but well. Make cookie out of 1 date covered with a small amount of batter. Allow for spreading on cookie sheet. Bake at 350 degrees for 12 minutes. Cool.

FROSTING

½ cup butter, melted
1 cup confectioners' sugar
½ teaspoon vanilla
　 Hot water

Mix butter, sugar and vanilla. Add enough hot water to thin to spreading consistency. If frosting becomes too thick before finishing, add a small amount of hot water. When cookies have cooled, frost them by dipping the top of the cookie into the frosting.

EGGNOG COOKIES

1 cup butter
2 teaspoons vanilla
3 teaspoons rum flavoring
¾ cup sugar
1 egg
3 cups sifted flour
2 teaspoons nutmeg
¼ teaspoon salt

Cream together butter, vanilla and flavoring. Gradually add sugar, beating until fluffy. Blend in egg. Sift flour, nutmeg and salt together. Add to creamed mixture. Shape dough on sugared board into rolls ½-inch in diameter. Cut into 3-inch lengths and place on ungreased cookie sheet. Bake in preheated oven at 350 degrees for 15 minutes. Cool. Mix together frosting ingredients. Frost cookies and sprinkle with nutmeg if desired.

FROSTING

⅓ cup butter, softened
1 teaspoon vanilla
2 teaspoons rum flavoring
2 cups confectioners' sugar,
　 sifted
2 tablespoons cream
　 Nutmeg

SUNFLOWER SEED COOKIES

4 dozen

1 cup butter, softened
1 cup shortening
2 cups sugar
1 teaspoon vanilla
3 cups flour
1 teaspoon baking soda
1 teaspoon baking powder
1 cup sunflower seeds
1 cup flaked coconut

Cream butter, shortening and sugar; stir in remaining ingredients. Shape dough into 2 rolls and refrigerate at least 2 hours. Slice while cold and bake for 10 minutes at 350 degrees. Cool for 10 minutes or more as they break easily while hot. Be careful not to overbake.

POTATO CHIP COOKIES

5 dozen

1 cup margarine, softened
1 cup brown sugar
1 cup sugar
2 eggs, beaten
1 teaspoon baking soda
2 cups flour
2 cups crushed potato chips
1 6-ounce package butterscotch
    chips

Cream margarine and sugars; add eggs. Blend in flour and soda; mix well. Stir in potato chips and butterscotch chips. Shape into balls and place on cookie sheet. Bake 10 minutes in a 325 degree oven.

CEREAL JUMBLES

10 dozen

1 cup butter, softened
1 cup sugar
1 cup brown sugar
1 egg
1 cup oil
1 cup oatmeal
1 cup crushed cornflakes
½ cup flaked coconut
½ cup chopped nuts
3½ cups sifted flour
1 teaspoon baking soda
1 teaspoon salt
1 teaspoon vanilla

Cream together, butter, sugars and egg. Add remaining ingredients in order given. Form 1-inch balls and place on an ungreased cookie sheet. Bake for 8 to 10 minutes at 350 degrees until golden brown.

CREAM WAFERS

2 dozen

1 cup butter, softened
⅓ cup heavy cream
2 cups flour

Mix butter, cream and flour thoroughly. Chill well, about 2 hours. Roll dough into small balls in palm of hand; about the size of a nickle. Place on cookie sheet and flatten with a small glass dipped in sugar. Prick with a fork 4 times. Bake in 375 degree oven for 7 to 9 minutes, until slightly brown.

FILLING

¼ cup butter, softened
¾ cup confectioners' sugar, sifted
1 egg yolk
1 teaspoon lemon juice
Yellow food coloring (optional)

Blend butter, sugar, egg yolk and lemon juice together. Add a few drops of yellow food coloring. Match up cooled wafers similar in size and put together with filling.

SUGAR COOKIES

6 dozen

1 cup margarine
2 cups sugar
2 eggs
1 cup salad oil
⅛ teaspoon salt
1 teaspoon vanilla
5 cups flour
2 teaspoons baking soda
2 teaspoons cream of tartar
Sugar

Mix together margarine, sugar, eggs, oil, salt and vanilla. Add flour, soda and cream of tartar and mix well. Roll dough into balls. Roll in sugar and place on ungreased cookie sheet. Flatten balls with bottom of a glass. Bake 10 to 15 minutes in 350 degree oven.

CHOCOLATE TIPPED WALNUT COOKIES

5 dozen

1 cup heavy cream
6 tablespoons sugar
½ cup unbleached flour
1 tablespoon grated orange peel
⅔ cup chopped walnuts
5 1-ounce squares semisweet chocolate
3 1-ounce squares unsweetened chocolate

Mix cream and sugar in a large bowl. Blend in flour and orange peel. Stir in walnuts. Drop batter from teaspoon onto buttered and floured baking sheet. Space cookies 1 inch apart. Bake at 350 degrees until golden, about 10 to 15 minutes. Cool on wire rack. Melt chocolates in a double boiler. Dip cookies into chocolate to cover ½ of the cookie. Dry on waxed paper.

HOLIDAY FRUITCAKE COOKIES 4 dozen

1 pound candied pineapple
½ pound candied cherries
1 quart pecans, chopped
¼ cup butter, softened
⅔ cup brown sugar
1½ tablespoons milk
1½ tablespoons baking soda
1½ cups flour
1 egg
1 ounce bourbon
1 teaspoon cinnamon
1 teaspoon nutmeg
½ teaspoon allspice
½ teaspoon cloves
  Cream cheese frosting

Chop fruit. Use a food processor if available. Mix fruit with a small amount of the flour to separate the pieces. Cream together butter and sugar. Combine milk and baking soda. Add flour, egg, bourbon and spices. Stir in fruit pieces and chopped pecans. Drop from teaspoon onto cookie sheet. Bake at 250 degrees for 20 to 25 minutes. Frost with cream cheese frosting.

CRUNCHY CHOCOLATE CHIPS 2 dozen

1 cup brown sugar
1 cup sugar
1 cup margarine, softened
1 cup oil
1 egg
2 teaspoons vanilla
1 teaspoon salt
1 teaspoon baking soda
1 teaspoon cream of tartar
3½ cups flour
1 cup flaked coconut
1 cup rolled oats
1 cup crispy rice cereal
1 6-ounce package chocolate
  chips

Thoroughly mix ingredients in order given. Chill dough for 10 minutes. Drop by teaspoon onto cookie sheet. Bake at 350 degrees for 12 to 15 minutes.

CHOCOLATE-COVERED MACAROONS

2 dozen

24 almond macaroon cookies
7 tablespoons sugar
7 tablespoons water
4 egg yolks
⅔ cup butter
4 teaspoons cocoa
5 1-ounce squares semisweet
   chocolate
1 tablespoon plus 2 teaspoons
   solid shortening

In a small pan, stir together sugar and water. Bring to a boil and continue boiling until syrup reaches 230 to 234 degrees on a candy thermometer, or until syrup spins a 2-inch thread when dropped from a fork or spoon. With an electric mixer, beat the egg yolks until blended. Continue beating, slowly adding hot syrup in a thin steady stream. Beat in butter, a tablespoon at a time, just until blended. Stir in 4 teaspoons cocoa. If mixture gets dark and runny from overbeating, chill it and then rebeat. Spread a tablespoon of the chocolate buttercream over the bottom of each cookie. Place cookies, buttercream-side up, in a single layer in a pan and chill until buttercream mixture is firm, at least 15 minutes. Combine chocolate and shortening in the top of a double boiler and stir over simmering water just until melted. Transfer chocolate to a small shallow bowl for easier handling and let cool, stirring occasionally until chocolate feels lukewarm (80-85 degrees). Dip buttercream-side of cookies, one at a time, in the chocolate to coat buttercream. Place cookies on a pan or plate, chocolate-side up, and chill until chocolate coating is set, at least 10 minutes. Cover lightly and store in refrigerator or freeze. If frozen, thaw 3 hours before serving.

CHRISTMAS MERINGUE COOKIES
3 dozen

2   egg whites, room temperature
⅛   teaspoon salt
⅛   teaspoon cream of tartar
¾   cup sugar
½   teaspoon vanilla
1   cup semisweet chocolate
    pieces
1   cup chopped walnuts or
    pecans
3   tablespoons crushed
    peppermint candy

Place egg whites in small bowl and beat at high speed until foamy. Add salt and cream of tartar and continue beating until soft peaks form. Add sugar, 1 tablespoon at a time, beating well after each addition. When meringue is stiff and white, fold in vanilla, chocolate pieces, nuts and crushed candy. Drop by teaspoonsful, about 1½ inches apart, onto lightly greased cookie sheets. Bake 40 minutes at 250 degrees. Remove to wire rack to cool. Store in airtight container. Do not double recipe.

BROWNIE CONFECTIONS
4 dozen

1   23 ounce package brownie
    mix
½   cup butter
4   cups sifted confectioners'
    sugar
4   tablespoons heavy cream
2   teaspoons vanilla
2   1-ounce squares unsweetened
    chocolate
2   tablespoons butter

Follow directions on mix and bake brownies in a 9x13-inch pan. Brown ½ cup butter to a delicate brown; blend in sugar. Stir in cream and vanilla until smooth. Spread on cooled brownies. Melt together the unsweetened chocolate and butter; cool. Spread over sugar mixture. When topping is set, cut into 1-inch squares.

EASY BROWNIES
1 dozen

¼   cup butter
2   squares unsweetened
    chocolate
1   cup sugar
½   cup flour
2   eggs
    Confectioners' sugar

Melt butter and chocolate in large skillet. Add sugar, flour and eggs, mixing well with wooden spoon after each addition. Pour into greased and floured 8x8-inch pan. Bake at 350 degrees for 25 to 30 minutes. Test with toothpick before removing. Cool and sprinkle with confectioners' sugar. Easily doubled; bake in a 9x13-inch pan.

THREE-LAYER MINT BROWNIES

3 dozen

FIRST LAYER

½ cup butter or margarine,
    melted
¼ cup sugar
5 tablespoons cocoa
1 teaspoon vanilla
1 egg, beaten
2 cups graham cracker crumbs
1 cup flaked coconut

Blend sugar, cocoa, vanilla and egg. Add to melted butter. Add graham cracker crumbs and coconut and press firmly into ungreased 9x13-inch pan. Chill while preparing second layer.

SECOND LAYER

½ cup butter or margarine,
    melted
2 tablespoons instant vanilla
    pudding
3 tablespoons milk
2 cups confectioners' sugar

Blend butter, pudding, milk and sugar. Spread on the first layer. Refrigerate for 15 minutes.

THIRD LAYER

6 ounces mint chocolate (chips
    or candies)
3 tablespoons butter

Melt butter and chocolate in top of double boiler. Spread on top of second layer and refrigerate. Cut into 1½ or 2-inch squares.

MOIST AND CHEWY BROWNIES

2 dozen

1 cup sugar
1 cup brown sugar
⅔ cup vegetable oil
4 eggs
½ cup cocoa
1 teaspoon vanilla
1½ cups flour
1 teaspoon baking powder
1 teaspoon salt
1 cup chopped nuts
    (optional)
    Confectioners' sugar

Mix together sugars, oil and eggs. Add cocoa and vanilla. Sift flour, baking powder and salt together and add. Add nuts. Bake in 9x13-inch pan at 325 degrees for 40 to 60 minutes. Do not overbake. Can be dusted with confectioners' sugar while warm.

APPLE PIE SLICES

24 bars

CRUST
3 cups flour
1 cup shortening
1 egg, beaten
1 tablespoon vinegar
4 tablespoons water
1 teaspoon salt

FILLING
⅔ cup crushed corn flakes
5 cups pared and sliced apples
1½ cups sugar
1 teaspoon cinnamon

TOPPING
1 egg white
1 cup confectioners' sugar
2 tablespoons lemon juice

Cut shortening into flour. Mix egg, vinegar, water and salt together and add to flour mixture. Roll half of dough into a 11x15-inch rectangle. Transfer to a baking sheet. Cover with corn flakes, then apple slices. Mix sugar and cinnamon and sprinkle over apples. Roll out other half of dough for top crust and place over apples. Pinch edges together. Score top crust to allow steam to escape. Beat egg white until frothy. Spread on top crust. Bake in 400 degree oven 40 minutes. Mix confectioners' sugar and lemon juice and drizzle over pie while still hot. Cool and cut into bars.

RASPBERRY SNOW BARS

2 dozen

¾ cup shortening
¼ cup sugar
¼ teaspoon salt
¼ teaspoon almond extract
2 eggs, separated
1½ cups sifted flour
1 cup red raspberry preserves
1 cup flaked coconut
½ cup sugar

Cream shortening, salt and ¼ cup sugar until fluffy; blend in almond extract and egg yolks. Mix in flour. Pat dough into ungreased 9x13-inch pan. Bake 15 minutes at 350 degrees. Spread hot crust with preserves and top with coconut. Beat egg whites until foamy; gradually beat in ½ cup sugar until stiff peaks form. Spread over coconut; bake 25 minutes. Cool on a rack. Cut into 2 dozen bars. NOTE: If higher meringue is desired, add 2 more egg whites.

APRICOT BARS

⅔   **cup dried apricots**
½   **cup butter, softened**
½   **cup sugar**
1   **cup flour**

TOPPING
½   **teaspoon baking powder**
¼   **teaspoon salt**
⅓   **cup flour**
1   **cup brown sugar**
2   **eggs**
½   **teaspoon vanilla**
½   **cup chopped pecans**
    Confectioners' sugar

Rinse apricots; cover with water and simmer for 10 minutes. Drain, cool and chop. Set aside. Mix butter, sugar and flour until crumbly. Pack into a greased 9-inch square pan. Bake 25 minutes at 300 degrees.

Sift flour, baking powder and salt. In a separate bowl beat eggs well, gradually adding brown sugar. Add flour mixture and vanilla. Stir in nuts and apricots. Spread over baked layer and bake 30 minutes at 300 degrees. Cool in pan before cutting and roll each bar in confectioners' sugar.

DATE-WALNUT DOUBLE DECKER

20 bars

1¼ **cups flour**
⅓   **cup sugar**
½   **cup butter or margarine,**
    softened

TOPPING
⅓   **cup brown sugar**
⅓   **cup sugar**
2   **eggs**
1   **teaspoon vanilla**
2   **tablespoons flour**
1   **teaspoon baking powder**
½   **teaspoon salt**
8   **ounces snipped dates**
1   **cup chopped walnuts**
    Confectioners' sugar

Cream together flour, sugar and butter; pack into 9-inch square pan and bake 20 minutes at 350 degrees.

Beat together sugars, eggs and vanilla. Sift together and add the flour, baking powder and salt. Stir in walnuts and dates. Pour over pastry layer and continue baking 12 to 15 minutes longer. Sprinkle with confectioners' sugar and cut into bars when completely cooled.

ICED OATMEAL BARS

3 dozen

1   cup quick-cooking oats
1½ cups hot water
½   cup margarine
1   cup sugar
1   cup brown sugar
2   eggs
1   teaspoon burnt sugar flavoring
1   teaspoon vanilla
½   teaspoon almond flavoring
1½ cups flour
½   teaspoon salt
1   teaspoon baking soda
1   teaspoon cinnamon
½   cup raisins

Pour hot water over oatmeal, stir and mix in margarine. Beat together sugars, flavorings and eggs; add to oatmeal mixture. Add flour, salt, baking soda, cinnamon and raisins and mix well. Bake in greased and floured 10x15-inch pan at 350 degrees for 30 to 40 minutes. Cool. Cream together frosting ingredients and spread over bars.

FROSTING
1   3-ounce package creamed
     cheese, softened
2   tablespoons margarine
1   teaspoon vanilla
1   teaspoon milk
1   cup confectioners' sugar

WALNUT SQUARES

2 dozen

2   cups brown sugar
3   eggs
1   cup flour
½   teaspoon salt
½   teaspoon vanilla
2   cups chopped English walnuts

Beat together sugar and eggs with an electric mixer for three minutes. Add flour, salt, vanilla and walnuts and pour into buttered 9x13-inch pan. Bake at 350 degrees for 20 to 25 minutes. Cool before cutting.

BANANA BARS

4 dozen

½ cup margarine, softened
1½ cups sugar
2 eggs
¾ cup sour milk
1 cup whole wheat flour
1 cup flour
½ teaspoon salt
1 teaspoon baking soda
1 teaspoon vanilla
3 bananas, mashed

FROSTING
1 8-ounce package cream
     cheese, softened
2 cups confectioners' sugar
1 teaspoon vanilla
½ cup margarine, softened

Cream margarine, sugar and eggs. Add milk, alternately, with flours, soda and salt. Add vanilla and bananas. Mix well. Bake in greased jelly-roll pan at 350 degrees for 30 minutes. Cool. Cream together ingredients for frosting and frost bars.

PUMPKIN BARS

3 dozen

2 cups sugar
1 cup vegetable oil
4 eggs
2 cups flour
2 teaspoons baking soda
    Pinch of salt
1½ teaspoons cinnamon
2 cups canned pumpkin

FROSTING
3 cups confectioners' sugar
1 3-ounce package cream
     cheese, softened
6 tablespoons margarine
1 teaspoon vanilla
    Pinch of salt

Mix sugar, oil and eggs. Sift together flour, soda and salt; add to egg mixture. Mix and add cinnamon and pumpkin. Spread in ungreased jelly-roll pan. Bake at 350 degrees for 20 minutes; cool bars. Mix frosting ingredients and frost cooled bars. These freeze well.

CARAMEL MERINGUE SQUARES

1½ dozen

1¼ cups sifted cake flour
1½ cups light brown sugar
2 eggs, separated
⅛ teaspoon salt
¼ cup butter
½ cup chopped walnuts
1 cup cut up caramels

Combine flour and ½ cup sugar, unbeaten egg yolks and salt. Cut in butter and mix until consistency of cornmeal. Press firmly into an ungreased 9x13-inch pan. Sprinkle ¾ of the nuts on top and press into crust. Beat egg whites until stiff; gradually add rest of sugar. Fold in caramels and spread over crust. Sprinkle with remaining nuts. Bake at 300 degrees, 30 to 35 minutes.

CARAMEL PECAN DREAM BARS

3 dozen

BASE
1 package yellow cake mix
⅓ cup butter, softened
1 egg

Grease a 9x13-inch pan. In large bowl, combine cake mix, butter and egg. Mix at high speed until crumbly. Press into greased pan.

FILLING
1 14-ounce can sweetened
   condensed milk
1 egg
1 teaspoon vanilla
1 cup chopped pecans
½ cup Bits 'O Brickle Baking
   Chips

In small bowl, beat together milk, egg and vanilla. Stir in pecans and chips. Pour over base in pan. Spread to cover. Bake at 350 degrees 25 to 30 minutes or until golden brown. Center may appear loose, but will set when cool. Allow to cool completely before cutting.

SALTED NUT CHEWS

3 dozen

1 package yellow cake mix
with pudding
⅓ cup butter, softened
1 egg
3 cups miniature marshmallows

In large bowl, combine cake mix, butter and egg. Beat at low speed until crumbly. Press in ungreased 9x13-inch pan. Bake for 12 to 18 minutes at 350 degrees until golden brown. Remove from oven and immediately sprinkle with marshmallows. Return to oven 1 to 2 minutes until marshmallows begin to puff. Cool.

TOPPING

⅔ cup light corn syrup
¼ cup butter
2 teaspoons vanilla
1 12-ounce package peanut
butter chips
2 cups crisp rice cereal
2 cups salted peanuts

In large saucepan, heat corn syrup, butter, vanilla and chips, stirring constantly until chips are melted and mixture is smooth. Remove from heat and stir in cereal and nuts. Immediately spoon warm topping over marshmallows; spread to cover. Chill; cut into bars. Store covered.

TURTLE BARS

3 dozen

2 cups flour
1 cup brown sugar
½ cup butter
1½ cups pecan halves
¾ cup brown sugar
⅔ cup plus 3 tablespoons butter
1½ cups chocolate chips

Mix flour, 1 cup brown sugar, and ½ cup butter; pat firmly into 9x13-inch pan. Sprinkle with nuts. Combine ¾ cup brown sugar and remaining butter in heavy saucepan and heat to boiling for 60 seconds, stirring constantly. Pour evenly over crust. Bake for 20 minutes at 350 degrees until bubbly and light brown. Remove from oven and sprinkle with chocolate chips; spreading when melted. Cool and cut into bars.

TASSIES

2 dozen

6 tablespoons butter or
    margarine, softened
½ cup confectioners' sugar
1 egg yolk
½ teaspoon vanilla
1⅓ cups flour
    Preserves or marmalade
4 ounces German sweet
    chocolate
¼ cup sugar
¼ cup heavy cream
2 tablespoons butter or
    margarine
½ teaspoon vanilla

Cream butter and sugar until light and fluffy. Beat in egg yolk and vanilla until well-blended. Add flour, ⅓ cup at a time. Form dough into smooth ball and press rounded teaspoonsful into small greased muffin tins; covering bottom and halfway up the sides. Bake at 350 degrees for 12 to 15 minutes. Let cool for 5 minutes. Use 2 knives to gently remove shells from muffin tins. Transfer to rack to cool completely. Spoon ½ teaspoon preserves into each shell. Melt chocolate and sugar in double boiler. Stir in cream, butter and vanilla. Cook, stirring, until sugar is melted and mixture is hot. Let cool to room temperature. Spoon 1 teaspoon over preserves to cover. Store in cool dry place.

CHOCOLATE PEANUT BARS

3 dozen

1 12-ounce package chocolate
    chips
1 12-ounce package
    butterscotch chips
1 square unsweetened chocolate
2 cups peanut butter
1 cup margarine
½ teaspoon vanilla
⅓ cup evaporated milk
2 pounds confectioners' sugar
1 pound peanuts

Melt chips, chocolate square and peanut butter in saucepan. Spread ½ the mixture in a greased jelly-roll pan. Boil together margarine, evaporated milk and vanilla; add sugar. Spread over chocolate mixture. Add peanuts to other ½ of chocolate mixture; spread over sugar layer. Refrigerate or freeze. Cut into squares when bars are at room temperature.

CANDIED ORANGE PEEL

1½ cups

2 large oranges
1½ cups water
1 cup sugar
½ cup water
2 ounces semisweet chocolate

Grate oranges slightly. With sharp knife score peel of oranges into quarters. Gently remove peel from oranges with fingers. Cut peel into thin strips and remove white membrane. Place in heavy pan; cover with water. Slowly bring to a boil and simmer for 10 minutes. Drain. Repeat process 4 more times, draining well each time. For each finished cup of peel, make a syrup of ¼ cup water and ½ cup sugar. Add peel and simmer until syrup is absorbed and peel is transparent. Roll each peel in sugar and dry thoroughly on a rack. Slowly melt chocolate over water in a double boiler. Dip half of peel in chocolate and dry on rack covered with waxed paper. Store in cool place in airtight container for several weeks. NOTE: Lemon, grapefruit or lime peel is also good. This candy is nice for a garnish, to grate into recipes or serve on the side with espresso and rum-soaked raisins.

SALTED PEANUT CANDIES

20 candies

1½ cups flour
½ cup butter or margarine
¾ cup brown sugar
⅛ teaspoon salt
1 12-ounce package butterscotch chips
1½ tablespoons butter or margarine
1½ tablespoons water
¼ cup white corn syrup
1½ cups salted peanuts

Mix together flour, ½ cup butter, brown sugar and salt, cutting together as for pie crust. Pat into a 9x13-inch pan. Bake 10 minutes at 375 degrees. Combine butterscotch chips, 1½ tablespoons butter, water and corn syrup in the top of a double boiler. Heat over simmering water until melted. Add peanuts. Spread mixture over baked crust as soon as it is taken from the oven. Return to oven and bake 8 minutes at 375 degrees. Loosen edges from sides of pan while warm. Allow to cool before cutting into 1 inch squares.

MICROWAVE FUDGE

1 to 1½ pounds

1   pound confectioners' sugar
½   cup cocoa
¼   cup milk
¼   pound butter or margarine
1   tablespoon vanilla
½   cup chopped nuts

Sift confectioners' sugar and cocoa into glass mixing bowl. Add milk and butter cut into 4 to 5 pieces. Place in microwave and cook 2 minutes. Do not mix these ingredients before placing in oven; simply place them in the bowl. Remove bowl from oven and stir just to mix. Add vanilla and nuts, stirring until blended. Pour into 8-inch square pan. Place in freezer for 20 minutes or in refrigerator for 1 hour. Cut into 1-inch squares. NOTE: This is a fun recipe for children to make. It takes 10 minutes from start to finish.

OLD TIME PEANUT BRITTLE

1½ pounds

1   cup white corn syrup
2   cups sugar
½   cup water
1   pound raw spanish peanuts
2   tablespoons butter
2   teaspoons vanilla
2   teaspoons baking soda
½   teaspoon salt

Combine syrup, sugar and water in saucepan. Heat slowly to 230 degrees or until syrup spins a thread. Add peanuts and continue to cook to 300 degrees. Remove from heat. Add butter, vanilla, soda and salt; stir until blended. Pour into well buttered jelly roll pan, 15½x10½-inches. When cool, break into pieces.

PEANUT BARK CANDY SQUARES

5 pounds

2   pounds white almond bark
1   cup peanut butter
2   cups miniature marshmallows
2   cups dry-roasted peanuts
3   cups Rice Krispies cereai

Place bark and peanut butter in large mixing bowl. Preheat oven to 325 degrees. Turn oven off. Place bowl in oven 12 to 15 minutes. Remove and stir until smooth. Add the other ingredients. Spread into buttered jelly roll pan 11x17-inches, or drop from teaspoon onto waxed paper. Place in refrigerator until hard. Cut into squares. Store in covered tin.

PEANUT CRUNCH CLUSTERS

40 pieces

½ cup peanut butter,
    smooth or crunchy
2 cups chocolate chips
2 cups dry roasted peanuts

Melt together chocolate chips and peanut butter in top of a double boiler over hot water. Stir in peanuts. Drop from teaspoon onto foil or waxed paper.

ENGLISH TOFFEE

1 cup butter
1 cup sugar
    Dash of salt
1 teaspoon vanilla
1 12-ounce package pecans,
    broken
1 12-ounce package
    semisweet chocolate
    chips

Place sheet of foil or waxed paper on cookie sheet. Sprinkle about 1½ cups pecans on top of foil, saving some for topping. Melt butter over low heat, just enough to mix in the sugar. Add salt and vanilla. Be sure sugar is dissolved and there is no "gritty" sound. Turn up heat and boil to 290 to 295 degrees, stirring constantly and moving candy thermometer around occasionally. Pour mixture over pecans; before spreading, wait a few seconds. Sprinkle with chocolate chips. Wait 15 seconds, then spread chocolate with a knife. Crush remaining pecans and sprinkle over mixture. Let set overnight. Crack off in small pieces. NOTE: Do not use margarine in this recipe.

EASY ENGLISH TOFFEE

16 graham crackers
⅔ cup brown sugar
1½ cups butter
⅔ cup chopped pecans
1 12-ounce package chocolate
    chips
1 6-ounce package Bits 'O
    Brickle chips

Lay whole graham crackers in a greased jelly roll pan. In a saucepan, heat brown sugar, butter and pecans to a boil; boil for 3 minutes. Pour syrup evenly over graham crackers. Bake at 350 degrees for 10 minutes; remove from oven. Sprinkle with chocolate chips; spreading as they melt. Sprinkle Bits' O Brickle chips over chocolate and press in lightly. Chill until firm. Break into pieces. Store in refrigerator or freeze.

CHOCOLATE FONDANT ROLL

4 rolls

⅔ cup evaporated milk
1⅓ cups sugar
¼ cup butter
2 cups miniature marshmallows
¼ teaspoon salt
1½ cups semisweet chocolate
    chips
1 teaspoon vanilla

FONDANT
¼ cup butter
1¾ cups confectioners' sugar
1 tablespoon evaporated milk
1 teaspoon vanilla
1 cup chopped pecans

Combine in a saucepan; milk, sugar, butter, salt and marshmallows. Bring to a boil over medium heat, stirring constantly. Cook at low boil for exactly 5 minutes. Remove from heat and add chocolate chips, stirring until melted. Stir in vanilla. Spread in a buttered 8x8-inch pan and cool. Cream together butter, confectioners' sugar, evaporated milk and vanilla. Fondant must be thick enough to handle without sticking to fingers. If necessary, add more sugar. Shape into four rolls, 5 inches long. Wrap each in Saran Wrap and freeze. To assemble, cut fudge into fourths and work each around one of the frozen fondants until it is covered. Roll in chopped pecans. Repeat with others. Slice into round candies. Freezes well.

CHOCOLATE-COVERED CHERRIES

60 cherries

60 maraschino cherries with
    stems
3 tablespoons butter
3 tablespoons light corn
    syrup
¼ teaspoon salt
2 cups confectioners' sugar,
    sifted
1½ pounds semisweet
    chocolate

Drain cherries; blot on paper towels. Combine butter, corn syrup and salt. Stir in confectioners' sugar. Knead until smooth. Cover and chill 1 hour. Shape fondant into balls; flatten and wrap around cherries. Place on waxed paper; chill 1 hour. Slowly melt chocolate. Hold cherries by the stem and dip into chocolate. Spoon extra sauce' on the top, leaving stem uncovered. Be sure all of fondant is covered. Return to waxed paper and chill until hardened. Store tightly covered in a cool place; not in the refrigerator. Wait 2 weeks before eating.

TURTLES

36 pieces

14 ounces caramels
2 tablespoons evaporated
   milk
1 tablespoon butter
1 8-ounce package pecan
   halves
1 12-ounce package chocolate
   chips
1 square inch parafin

In the top of a double boiler, melt caramels with evaporated milk and butter. Keep warm over hot water until ready to use. On greased cookie sheets arrange 3 to 4 pecans in clusters to form turtles. Spoon about 1 tablespoon of melted caramel on each cluster. Refrigerate candy for 30 minutes. In the top of a double boiler, melt together chocolate chips and parafin. Keep warm over hot water. Spoon chocolate over caramel. Refrigerate candy until firm.

FORES

150 caramels

1   cup dark Karo syrup
1   cup white sugar
1   cup brown sugar
½   pound butter
2   cups heavy cream
1   tablespoon vanilla
1   pound whole pecans
1½ pounds semisweet
    chocolate

Mix syrup, sugars, butter and cream in a dutch oven over medium heat. Boil until it is caramel consistency when dipped in cold water (soft ball stage). Remove from heat and add vanilla and pecans. Butter the bottom and sides of a 9x13-inch pan. Pour candy into pan and freeze. Cut into small squares when partially frozen. Melt chocolate over double boiler and dip each square. Candy dips best when chocolate is very warm and caramels are very cold. You may use any kind of chocolate you wish; chocolate chips, candy bars, etc.

STRAWBERRIES

3½ dozen

1 egg, slightly beaten
1 cup sugar
2 tablespoons butter
1½ cups chopped dates
1 cup chopped nuts
2½ cups Rice Krispies
1 teaspoon vanilla
 Red decorating sugar
 Green tinted frosting

Combine and cook eggs, sugar and butter in the top of a double boiler, stirring until thick; cool. When mixture is cool, add dates, nuts and cereal, mixing well. Butter hands. Roll mixture to size of small walnuts, shaping one end down to look like a strawberry. Drop into bowl of red decorating sugar. Place on waxed paper to dry. When dry, make "stem" outlines with green decorating frosting.

KID'S FAVORITE KRUNCHIES

5 dozen

½ cup white corn syrup
⅔ cup brown sugar
1 cup crunchy peanut butter
4½ cups "Special K" cereal
1 teaspoon vanilla
1 12-ounce package chocolate
 chips

In medium pan, bring syrup to a rolling boil. Dissolve sugar in syrup; stir in peanut butter until smooth. Remove from stove and stir in cereal and vanilla. Pack into greased 9x13-inch pan. Pour chips on top and place in 350 degree oven for 1 minute to melt chocolate. Remove from oven and swirl chocolate over cereal mixture. Refrigerate for ½ hour and cut into small squares; return to refrigerator until chocolate hardens. Store in covered container.

ALMOND NUT CRUNCH

2 pounds almond bark
2 cups Captain Crunch cereal
2 cups Rice Crispies cereal
2 cups miniature marshmallows
1 cup mixed nuts
1 cup cashews

Melt almond bark in a large saucepan over low heat or in microwave. In a large mixing bowl, combine all ingredients and drop from teaspoon onto waxed paper. Let cool. Store in tightly covered container. May be frozen for several months.

Pies &
Desserts

STRAWBERRY RHUBARB PIE
8 servings

1 double crust unbaked pie
   shell
1⅓ cups sugar
⅓ cup flour
½ teaspoon grated orange peel
2 cups cubed fresh rhubarb
2 tablespoons butter
2 cups sliced strawberries
   Milk
   Sugar

Coat strawberries and rhubarb with sugar and flour. Add grated orange peel. Pour into pie crust; dot with butter. Cover with top crust. Drizzle milk over top crust and sprinkle liberally with sugar. Bake at 425 degrees for 40 to 50 minutes on bottom rack of oven.

PEACHES AND CREAM
8 servings

1 cup sugar
4 tablespoons flour or 5
   tablespoons cornstarch
½ cup water
6 ripe peaches
1 pint heavy cream, whipped
1 9-inch baked pie shell

Mix sugar, flour or cornstarch and water in top of double boiler. Cook mixture, stirring constantly, until clear. If mixture does not become clear, discontinue cooking after 15 minutes. Peel and mash 3 peaches. Add to clear mixture and heat until thickened. Set aside to cool. Peel and slice remaining peaches into pie shell. Pour cooled peach mixture over sliced peaches and refrigerate. Before serving, spread whipped cream over top.

CRACKER PEACH PIE
8 servings

CRUST
3 egg whites
1 cup sugar
14 squares soda crackers
¼ teaspoon baking powder
½ cup chopped pecans
1 teaspoon vanilla

Beat egg whites until very stiff. Gradually beat in sugar. Roll crackers to fine crumbs. Fold into egg whites. Add baking powder, pecans and vanilla. Spread in buttered 9-inch pie plate. Bake at 325 degrees for 30 minutes. Cool.

FILLING
5 peaches, peeled and sliced
1 cup heavy cream, whipped
1 tablespoon sugar

Place fruit in crust and cover with whipped cream sweetened with sugar. Store in refrigerator overnight or for several hours. Can be served immediately.

PEACH STREUSEL PIE

6 servings

STREUSEL
½   **cup brown sugar**
½   **cup flour**
½   **cup butter**

Combine brown sugar and flour; mix well. With pastry blender, cut in butter to make coarse crumbs. Sprinkle ½ crumb mixture in bottom of pie shell.

FILLING
1   **9-inch unbaked pie shell**
2   **pounds ripe peaches, peeled and quartered**
½   **cup sugar**
¼   **teaspoon nutmeg**
1   **egg**
2   **tablespoons half-and-half**
1   **teaspoon vanilla**

Measure 4 cups peaches; place in pie shell. Sprinkle with sugar and nutmeg. Beat together egg, cream and vanilla. Pour over peaches and cover with remaining crumb mixture. Bake 40 to 45 minutes in 400 degree oven until top is golden brown. Cool.

GINGER-PEAR PIE

2 9-inch pies

1   **cup sugar**
½   **cup light brown sugar**
6   **tablespoons flour**
1   **teaspoon cinnamon**
½   **teaspoon ground ginger**
6   **tablespoons orange juice**
12 **pears, pared, cored and sliced (12 cups)**
4   **tablespoons butter**
    Pastry for 9-inch double-crust pie

Mix sugar, brown sugar, flour, cinnamon and ginger in small bowl. Sprinkle orange juice over pears. Toss to coat. Fill a 9-inch pie shell with ½ of mixture. Add 2 tablespoons butter. Cover with pastry and make holes for steam to escape. Bake in 425 degree oven for 15 minutes. Lower oven temperature to 350 degrees and bake for 40 minutes or until pastry is golden brown and pie juices bubble. Cool at least 1 hour on a wire rack. Line a second 9-inch pie pan with a double thickness of heavy duty aluminum foil, using 2 18-inch square pieces. Spoon second ½ of pear mixture into foil-lined pan. Add butter. Freeze. When firm, wrap snugly and remove from pan. When ready to use, remove foil wrapping and place frozen pie mixture in pastry-lined pie plate. Bake according to instructions for unfrozen pie. Cover crust edges with foil if they get too brown before filling is done.

CHOCOLATE PECAN PIE

10 servings

½   cup butter or margarine
1   cup chocolate chips
½   cup flour
½   cup sugar
½   cup brown sugar
1   cup chopped pecans
1   teaspoon vanilla
2   eggs, lightly beaten
1   9-inch unbaked pie shell

Melt butter. Mix chips, flour, sugars and pecans together. Add butter, vanilla and eggs. Pour into shell and bake for 35 to 40 minutes at 375 degrees.

NEBRASKA BAKED ALASKA

8 servings

SAUCE
¼   cup butter or margarine
1   cup sugar
2   tablespoons cornstarch
¼   teaspoon salt
1   tablespoon grated lemon peel
⅓   cup lemon juice
3   egg yolks

Melt butter in top of double broiler; stir in sugar, cornstarch and salt. Blend thoroughly. Add lemon peel and juice. Add egg yolks and stir until smooth. Cook over simmering water, stirring constantly, 8 to 10 minutes or until mixture is thick. Cool.

FILLING
1   quart vanilla ice cream
1   9-inch baked pastry crust

Soften ½ of the ice cream at room temperature; smooth into pastry shell; freeze until firm. Spread half the lemon sauce over frozen ice cream. Return to freezer until firm. Repeat with remaining ice cream and sauce. Freeze until firm.

MERINGUE
3   egg whites
¼   teaspoon cream of tartar
⅓   cup sugar

Beat egg whites and cream of tartar until soft peaks form. Gradually add sugar; continue beating until sugar is dissolved and meringue is stiff and glossy. Cover top of pie with meringue, sealing well to edge of pie. Place pie on a board. Bake at 475 degrees for 3 minutes or until meringue is lightly browned. Return to freezer. Before serving, alow pie to stand at room temperature several minutes to soften slightly.

FROSTY PUMPKIN PIE

9-inch pie

1½ quarts butter pecan ice cream
1 cup sugar
1 cup canned pumpkin
1 teaspoon cinnamon
¼ teaspoon nutmeg
¼ teaspoon ginger
¼ teaspoon salt
1 cup heavy cream
¼ cup brown sugar
2 tablespoons butter
1 tablespoon water
½ cup chopped pecans

Put a 9-inch pie pan in freezer for 30 minutes. Make crust in the pan by molding ice cream on bottom and ½ inch up the sides. Freeze at least 2 hours. Combine sugar, pumpkin and spices in saucepan and cook on low 3 minutes. Cool. Whip 1 cup cream. Reserve ¼ cup; fold remaining cream into pumpkin mixture. Spoon into crust and return to freezer for 2 hours. In saucepan, bring brown sugar, butter and water to a low boil; cook for 1 minute. Remove from heat and add chopped pecans. Spoon on top of pie and top with reserved dollop of whipped cream in center. Freeze. Let stand at room temperature 10 minutes before cutting.

PEPPERMINT PATTY PIE

10 servings

CRUST
1½ cups crushed chocolate
    wafers
⅓ cup butter or margarine,
    melted

In 9-inch pie plate, combine crushed wafers and butter. Press against bottom and sides to form a crust. Bake 6 to 8 minutes at 350 degrees. Let cool completely on wire rack. Place in freezer for at least 30 minutes.

FILLING
1½ quarts peppermint stick ice
    cream, softened
8 egg whites
¼ teaspoon cream of tartar
½ cup sugar

Fill chilled crust with ice cream, mounding it slightly in the center. Return to freezer while preparing meringue. In small bowl, at high speed, beat egg whites and cream of tartar until foamy. Gradually add sugar, 1 tablespoon at a time, beating well after each addition. Beat until sugar is completely dissolved and whites are stiff but not dry. Spread meringue over ice cream, sealing it well to the crust. Place in freezer 8 hours to 3 days.

SAUCE
1 6-ounce package semisweet
    chocolate pieces

In top of double boiler over hot, not boiling water, melt chocolate pieces

½ cup butter or margarine, cut into pieces

with butter. Stir until blended. Keep warm. Remove pie from freezer and bake in preheated 475 degree oven about 2 minutes, or until meringue turns golden. Drizzle 3 tablespoons of chocolate sauce over pie. Serve immediately. Pass remaining sauce.

KEY LIME PIE

9-inch pie

1 envelope unflavored gelatin
½ cup sugar
¼ teaspoon salt
4 eggs, separated
½ cup fresh lime juice
¼ cup water
1 teaspoon grated lime peel
½ teaspoon green food coloring
½ cup sugar
1 cup heavy cream
1 9-inch baked pie shell
    Thin lime slices or shelled
    Pistachio nuts

Combine and mix gelatin, ½ cup sugar and salt in a saucepan. Set aside. Beat together egg yolks, lime juice and water. Stir into gelatin mixture. Bring to a boil, stirring constantly. Remove from heat as soon as mixture boils. Add lime peel and food coloring. Chill until syrupy; watch closely. Beat egg whites until they form stiff peaks; slowly add ½ cup sugar. Set aside. Whip heavy cream, combine with egg whites and fold into cooled pie filling. Pour into crust and refrigerate until ready to serve. Top with sliced limes or Pistachio nuts.

CHOCOLATE SILK PIE

8-inch pie

CRUST
1½ cups crushed vanilla wafers
¼ cup finely crushed almonds
1½ tablespoons sugar
6 tablespoons butter, melted

Combine wafers, crushed almonds, sugar and melted butter. Press into an 8-inch pie pan. Bake 7 to 10 minutes at 350 degrees. Cool.

FILLING
12 tablespoons butter, softened
1¼ cups sugar
1½ 1-ounce squares unsweetened chocolate, melted
1½ teaspoons vanilla
3 eggs

Beat butter until creamy. Gradually add sugar and continue beating until fluffy. Stir in chocolate and vanilla. Add 2 eggs and beat for 3 minutes; add remaining egg and beat for 3 minutes. Pour into cooled crust and chill.

TOPPING
½ pint heavy cream
1 tablespoon confectioners' sugar
⅓ cup slivered almonds, toasted

Whip cream sweetened with confectioners' sugar. Sprinkle almonds on top.

CALYPSO PIE

8 servings

CRUST

2 cups crushed cream-filled chocolate cookies
¼ cup butter or margarine, melted

Combine crushed cookies and butter. Press into bottom and sides of a 10-inch pie pan. Chill

SAUCE

3 1-ounce squares unsweetened chocolate
¼ cup butter or margarine
⅔ cup sugar
1 6-ounce can evaporated milk
1 teaspoon vanilla
2 drops almond extract

Melt chocolate and butter in top of double boiler. Remove from heat. Stir in sugar and milk; blend well. Return to heat and cook 4 minutes, stirring constantly. Add vanilla and almond extract; cool.

FILLING

2 pints coffee ice cream
1 cup heavy cream, whipped
¾ cup chopped walnuts or pecans

Set out ice cream to soften slightly. Press into pie shell and freeze. When ice cream is thoroughly hardened, cover with chocolate sauce. Freeze again until sauce is hard. Just before serving, beat whipping cream. Spread on pie and sprinkle with nuts. Let stand at room temperature about 5 minutes before serving.

RASPBERRY RIBBON PIE

9-inch pie

RED LAYER

1 3-ounce package raspberry gelatin
¼ cup sugar
1¼ cups boiling water
1 10-ounce package frozen raspberries
1 tablespoon lemon juice

Dissolve raspberry gelatin and sugar in boiling water. Add frozen berries and lemon juice. Stir until berries thaw; chill until partially set.

WHITE LAYER

1 3-ounce package cream cheese, softened
⅓ cup confectioners' sugar
1 teaspoon vanilla
  Dash of salt
1 cup heavy cream, whipped
1 9-inch baked pastry shell

Blend cream cheese, confectioners' sugar, vanilla and salt. Fold in a small amount of whipped cream; fold in the remaining cream. Spread ½ of white layer over bottom of cooled pastry shell. Cover with ½ of red layer. Repeat layers. Chill until firm.

IT'S THE BERRIES

8 servings

1 8-ounce package cream
   cheese, softened
1 14-ounce can sweetened
   condensed milk
⅓ cup fresh lime juice
1 pint fresh strawberries, sliced
   and sugared; or
1 10-ounce package frozen
   strawberries, thawed and
   drained
½ teaspoon vanilla
   Whole strawberries
   Sliced almonds
1 9-inch baked graham-cracker
   crust

Beat cheese and milk until smooth; add lime juice. Stir in strawberries and vanilla. Pour into crust and chill. Garnish with whole strawberries and sliced almonds.

DAIQUIRI PIE

12 servings

CRUST
1¼ cups graham cracker crumbs
¼   cup sugar
6   tablespoons butter or
    margarine, melted

Combine graham cracker crumbs, ¼ cup sugar and butter. Remove 2 tablespoons crumbs; set aside. Press remaining crumbs in bottom and 1¾-inches up sides of a 9-inch spring-form pan. Chill 45 minutes.

FILLING
1   envelope unflavored gelatin
½   cup sugar
½   cup rum
2   teaspoons grated lime peel
1   teaspoon grated lemon peel
½   cup lime juice
4   egg yolks, beaten
2   8-ounce packages cream
    cheese, cubed and softened
4   egg whites
½   cup sugar
1   cup heavy cream
    Kiwi fruit or lime slices

Combine gelatin and ½ cup sugar in a medium saucepan. Stir in rum, citrus peels, lime juice and egg yolks. Cook over medium heat, stirring constantly until slightly thickened, 8 to 10 minutes. Remove from heat. Beat in cream cheese until smooth. Beat egg whites at medium speed to soft peak stage. Gradually add remaining sugar; beat to stiff peaks. Whip cream. Fold egg whites and whipped cream into gelatin mixture. Turn into pan. Sprinkle reserved crumbs around edge. Cover and chill until firm, several hours or overnight. Garnish with slices of kiwi fruit or lime.

PEANUT BUTTER PIES

3 8-inch pies

3 8-inch baked graham-cracker
   crusts
2 8-ounce packages cream
   cheese, softened
1 1-pound package
   confectioners' sugar, sifted
1⅓ cups peanut butter
1 16-ounce carton non-dairy
   whipped topping
   Milk chocolate bar

Beat cream cheese until light and fluffy. Add sugar slowly; beat well. Add peanut butter; beat well. Slowly beat in whipped topping. Pour into chilled shells. Top with grated chocolate bar shavings. Wrap in foil and freeze.

COFFEE-TOFFEE PIE

9-inch pie

PASTRY

1 stick pie crust mix
¼ cup light brown sugar
¾ cup finely chopped walnuts
1 1-ounce square unsweetened
   chocolate, grated
1 teaspoon vanilla
1 tablespoon water

Combine crust mix with brown sugar. Blend well. Add walnuts and chocolate. Add water and vanilla; blend with a fork. Turn into well-greased 9-inch pie plate. Press to cover. Bake 15 minutes at 375 degrees. Cool. If crust seems too thick, do not use all of crust mixture. Otherwise, it will be hard to cut.

FILLING

½ cup butter, softened
¾ cup sugar
1 1-ounce square unsweetened
   chocolate, melted and
   cooled
2 teaspoons instant coffee
2 eggs

Beat butter until creamy. Add sugar; beat until light and fluffy. Blend in chocolate and instant coffee. Add 1 egg; beat 5 minutes. Add second egg and beat additional 5 minutes. Turn filling into pie shell. Refrigerate several hours, covered.

TOPPING

2 cups heavy cream
2 tablespoons instant coffee
½ cup confectioners' sugar
   Semisweet chocolate curls

Several hours before serving, cover pie with topping. Combine cream, sugar and coffee. Refrigerate for 30 minutes. Beat until stiff. Spread over pie. Garnish with chocolate curls. Refrigerate 2 additional hours before serving.

TILLIE'S BLACK BOTTOM PIE

8 servings

CRUST

1⅓ cups rolled graham crackers
5 tablespoons butter, melted
1 tablespoon sugar

Combine crackers, butter and sugar. Mix well and press into bottom and sides of deep 9-inch pie plate. Bake 10 minutes at 300 degrees.

CHOCOLATE LAYER

1½ 1-ounce squares unsweetened chocolate
1 tablespoon gelatin
4 tablespoons cold water
2 cups heavy cream
4 eggs, separated
1¼ tablespoons cornstarch
½ cup sugar

Slowly melt chocolate; set aside. Soften gelatin in water; set aside. Scald cream. In top of double boiler, beat egg yolks over simmering water; slowly add cream. Combine cornstarch and sugar; add to eggs. Cook, stirring constantly, for 20 minutes or until custard generously coats a spoon. Remove from heat. Add 1 cup custard to melted chocolate. When cool, pour into pie shell and chill.

MERINGUE LAYER

1 teaspoon rum flavoring
½ cup sugar
¼ teaspoon cream of tartar

While remaining custard is still hot; blend in softened gelatin. Cool, but do not allow to stiffen. Make a stiff meringue by beating egg whites until frothy. Add cream of tartar. Beat until stiff peaks form. Gradually add sugar; beat until glossy. Fold meringue into custard mixture; blend in rum flavoring. When chocolate layer is set, cover with meringue layer and chill until set.

TOPPING

1 cup heavy cream
Confectioners' sugar
½ ounce square unsweetened chocolate, shaved

Whip cream; sweeten with a little confectioners' sugar. Spread over top of pie. Garnish with shaved chocolate.

LEMON SURPRISE

6 servings

SHELL

4	**egg whites**
¼	**teaspoon cream of tartar**
¾	**cup sugar**

Beat egg whites with cream of tartar until stiff. Gradually beat in ¾ cup sugar until smooth and glossy. Empty into 9-inch pie plate, making a nest 1-inch deep with a 2-inch rim. Bake 1½ hours at 225 degrees. Cool.

FILLING

4	**egg yolks**
½	**cup sugar**
1	**teaspoon lemon rind**
6	**tablespoons fresh lemon juice**
1	**cup heavy cream**

Beat egg yolks; add ½ cup sugar. Stir in lemon rind and lemon juice. Cook until thick. Cool. Beat 1 cup heavy cream until stiff and fold into lemon custard mixture. Pour into meringue and chill overnight.

TOPPING

½	**cup cream, whipped**
2	**tablespoons sugar**
6	**fresh strawberries**

Beat ½ cup whipping cream with 2 tablespoons sugar. Spread on pie and garnish with large strawberries.

CHOCOLATE ANGEL PIE

8 servings

CRUST

3	**egg whites**
⅛	**teaspoon salt**
⅛	**teaspoon cream of tartar**
½	**cup sugar**
½	**cup pecans, chopped**
½	**teaspoon vanilla**

Beat egg whites until foamy. Add salt and cream of tartar. Beat until mixture stands in soft peaks. Add sugar gradually; beat until stiff. Fold in nuts and vanilla. Turn into a lightly greased 9-inch pie plate. Make a nest-like shell, building the sides up above the edge. Bake at 300 degrees for 55 minutes. Cool.

FILLING

1	**4-ounce package Bakers German sweet chocolate**
3	**tablespoons hot water**
1	**teaspoon vanilla**
1½	**cups heavy cream, whipped**
	Grated chocolate

Melt chocolate in top of double boiler. Blend in hot water. Cool. Add vanilla. Fold chocolate mixture into whipped cream; turn mixture into cooled meringue crust. Sprinkle with grated chocolate. Chill.

TARTE A LA ORANGE

1 **12-ounce package frozen patty shells**
6 **medium oranges**
4 **egg yolks**
⅓ **cup sugar**
¼ **cup flour**
1 **teaspoon grated lemon rind**
6 **ladyfingers**
½ **cup apricot preserves**
1 **tablespoon sugar**
5 **tablespoons Grand Marnier**

Arrange patty shells in a circle on floured pastry sheet. Roll out to a 12-inch circle. Fit into a 9-inch springform pan. Turn top edge under and crimp. Place piece of foil in bottom of pan. Place beans or rice on foil. Put in 450 degree oven; turn oven down to 400 degrees. Bake 15 minutes. Remove beans and foil. Sprinkle bottom with sugar and prick lightly with fork. Bake 20 minutes until golden brown. Cool. Grate 1 orange; reserve rind. Squeeze oranges to yield 1½ cups juice. Beat yolks slightly in top of double boiler. Beat in sugar and flour. Stir in orange juice. Cook over hot water until very thick. Cool. Add orange and lemon rind; set aside. Simmer apricot preserves, 1 tablespoon sugar and 1 tablespoon Grand Marnier for 2 minutes. Rub through sieve. Cool and reserve. Slice 2 oranges very thin. Remove seeds. Sprinkle with 4 tablespoons Grand Marnier. Let stand 10 minutes. Drain oranges, saving juice; set aside. Spoon orange cream into shell. Split ladyfingers in half, then in half again. Arrange over cream. Sprinkle drained Grand Marnier and juice from oranges onto ladyfingers. Arrange oranges over ladyfingers in a circle. Brush with preserves. Refrigerate.

CREME BRULÉ

2 **cups heavy cream**
2 **egg yolks**
2½ **tablespoons sugar**
1 **teaspoon vanilla**
¼ **cup sifted light brown sugar**

Heat cream in top of double boiler. Beat egg yolks; add sugar gradually. Remove cream from heat and pour slowly over egg mixture while stirring. Add vanilla. Pour into 6 ramekins. Set in a pan of water and bake at 325 degrees for 45 minutes. When custard is set, sprinkle with sifted brown sugar. Place under broiler for a few minutes, until sugar melts. Watch carefully. Do not burn. Chill and serve.

BRANDIED CARAMEL FLAN

8 servings

¾ **cup sugar**
2 **cups whole milk**
2 **cups half-and-half**
6 **eggs**
½ **cup sugar**
½ **teaspoon salt**
2 **teaspoons vanilla**
⅓ **cup brandy**
   Boiling water
1 **tablespoon brandy**

Place ¾ cup sugar in heavy skillet. Cook until sugar melts and forms a light brown syrup. Stir to blend. Immediately pour syrup into a heated 10-inch pie plate. Holding the plate with pot holders, quickly rotate to cover bottom and sides; set aside. In medium saucepan, heat milk and cream just until bubbles form around edge of pan. In a large bowl, beat eggs slightly; add sugar, salt and vanilla. Gradually stir in hot milk mixture and ⅓ cup brandy. Pour into prepared pie plate. Set plate in a baking pan and pour ½-inch boiling water around dish. Bake at 325 degrees for 35 to 40 minutes, or until knife inserted in center comes out clean. Let cool; refrigerate overnight. Run a knife around edge of dish to loosen. Invert on serving dish, shake gently to release. Warm 1 tablespoon brandy; ignite and pour over flan at serving time. Cut into wedges.

BREAD PUDDING WITH BRANDY CREAM

8 servings

PUDDING
15 **slices day-old bread,**
    broken into pieces
4 **cups whole milk, scalded**
1 **cup half-and-half**
4 **eggs**
1 **cup sugar**
1 **teaspoon vanilla**
1 **teaspoon cinnamon**
½ **teaspoon nutmeg**
¼ **cup butter, melted**
⅔ **cup seedless raisins**

BRANDY CREAM
3 **egg yolks, slightly beaten**
1 **cup sugar**
1 **teaspoon vanilla**
1½ **cups whole milk**
¼ **cup water**
1 **tablespoon cornstarch**
1½ **ounces brandy**

Butter a 2-quart baking dish or 2 loaf pans. Combine bread, milk and cream. Beat together eggs and sugar. Stir in bread mixture; add vanilla, cinnamon and nutmeg. Stir in butter and raisins; pour into prepared dish. Set dish in a pan of warm water, about 1 inch deep. Bake at 350 degrees for 1 hour or until knife comes out clean.

In a saucepan, combine egg yolks, sugar, vanilla and milk; blend well. Cook over low heat until mixture comes to a boil. Blend cornstarch with water, stir into sauce and cook until mixture thickens. Remove from heat and add brandy. Cool to room temperature and serve on top of bread pudding.

RUM PUDDING

12 servings

PUDDING

4　egg yolks
¾　cup sugar
¾　cup milk
1　tablespoon unflavored gelatin
¼　cup water
4　egg whites, beaten
2　cups heavy cream, whipped
4　tablespoons light rum

Beat egg yolks well; add sugar. Scald milk and add to egg mixture. Dissolve gelatin in water and stir into egg mixture. Cook in top of double boiler until mixture coats a spoon. Do not overcook. Cool. Fold egg whites and whipped cream into cooled mixture. Add rum; pour into sherbet glasses. Chill.

SAUCE

2　egg yolks, beaten
1　cup confectioners' sugar
1　cup heavy cream, whipped
3　tablespoons light rum

Combine egg yolks with confectioners' sugar and whipped cream. Stir in rum. Float on top of pudding in sherbet glasses. May be garnished with additional unsweetened whipped cream.

PEKING ALMOND DESSERT

4 servings

1　envelope unflavored gelatin
1½　cups cold water
¼　cup sugar
1　5-ounce can evaporated milk
2　teaspoons almond extract

Dissolve gelatin in ¼ cup cold water. Set aside for 10 minutes. In a saucepan, heat remaining 1¼ cups water; add sugar. Bring to a boil; remove from heat and add milk, stirring well. Add gelatin and almond extract. Stir well. Pour into an 8x8-inch pan and refrigerate. While gelatin mixture is setting up, make the syrup.

SYRUP

1½　cups cold water
½　cup sugar
1　teaspoon almond extract
1　11-ounce can mandarin
　　orange segments
1　20-ounce can Lychee nuts

Bring cold water and sugar to a boil. Remove from heat and allow to cool. Add almond extract. Chill syrup in a jar in refrigerator. To serve, cut gelatin mixture into diamond shapes and place in individual bowls. Top with fruit and nuts; pour syrup over top. Can be prepared in advance and kept in refrigerator to be assembled just before serving.

SWEDISH CREME

10 servings

2 cups heavy cream, whipped
1 cup sugar
1 envelope unflavored gelatin
¼ cup water
2 cups sour cream
1½ teaspoons vanilla
1 10-ounce package frozen
   raspberries or strawberries

Whip cream with sugar. Dissolve gelatin in water. Add gelatin to cream and heat, stirring, to just below boiling. Cool. Add sour cream and vanilla. Refrigerate 6 hours or overnight. Serve in sherbet glasses topped with raspberries or strawberries.

MARASCHINO MOUSSE

4 servings

1 chocolate bar with almonds
1 pint ice cream, softened
4 maraschino cherries, minced
8 tablespoons Crème de Cacao
   Cocoa powder
4 cherries

Chop chocolate bar and combine with minced cherries and 4 tablespoons of liqueur. Add softened ice cream and stir gently to marble. Spoon into 4 sherbet dishes. Place in freezer to harden. To serve, sift cocoa over each top. Press with spoon to make a depression. Fill depression with 1 tablespoon liqueur and a cherry. Let soften a few minutes before serving.

COCONUT-PISTACHIO MOUSSE

4 servings

2 cups half-and-half
1 cup coconut cream
3 egg yolks, lightly beaten
1½ tablespoons unflavored
   gelatin
   Pinch of salt
3 egg whites
1 tablespoon sugar
6 tablespoons pistachio nuts
   or toasted almonds
4 ½-inch slices pound cake
   Whipped cream
   Toasted, shredded coconut

Combine half-and-half, coconut cream, egg yolks, gelatin and salt in saucepan. Heat over medium heat until gelatin is dissolved. Pour into bowl placed in a larger bowl of ice. Chill until it starts to thicken, about 20 to 30 minutes, stirring often. Do not let it get too thick, or it will not blend. Beat egg whites until thick peaks form. Add sugar and beat until stiff and glossy. Fold into gelatin mixture; add nuts. Pour into individual molds and place a slice of cake, trimmed to fit, on top of each. Chill at least 2 hours. Unmold and top with whipped cream sweetened with some of the leftover coconut cream. Top with coconut. If desired, do not unmold. Push the cake slightly into the pudding and top with coconut. NOTE: Coconut cream can be found in liquor stores.

RHUBARB-RASPBERRY SOUFFLÉ
10 servings

4 cups frozen unsweetened cut
   rhubarb or 1 pound fresh
¾ cup sugar
1 cup water
2 tablespoons cornstarch
   Dash salt
⅓ cup orange liqueur or juice
1 tablespoon lemon juice
2 envelopes unflavored gelatin
½ cup cold water
1 10-ounce package frozen
   raspberries
4 large egg whites, room
   temperature
½ cup sugar
1 cup heavy cream

Mix rhubarb, ¾ cup sugar, cornstarch and salt in large saucepan; stir in 1 cup water. Cook mixture until rhubarb is tender, stirring often. Stir in orange liqueur and lemon juice; cook 1 minute more. Reserve 2 cups of mixture for sauce. Refrigerate until needed. Sprinkle gelatin over ½ cup water; let stand a minute to soften. Stir into rhubarb remaining in pan; add raspberries. Cook mixture over low heat just until raspberries are thawed. Pour mixture into container of electric blender. Cover and blend until smooth. Strain to remove seeds. Cool slightly. In large bowl, with electric mixer, beat egg whites until foamy. Beat in ½ cup sugar, 1 tablespoon at a time, until soft peaks form. Fold rhubarb mixture gently into whites. Wash and dry beaters. Whip cream in a small bowl until stiff. Fold into rhubarb mixture. Pour into a glass bowl or 8-cup soufflé dish with a 2-inch foil collar. Chill until firm. Spoon rhubarb sauce on top or serve in bowl with the soufflé.

GRASSHOPPER TORTE
12 servings

1 cup finely crushed
   chocolate wafer crumbs
2 tablespoons butter, melted
1¼ cups half-and-half
2½ cups mini-marshmallows
½ cup green Crème de Menthe
⅓ cup Crème de Cacao
2 egg whites
3 tablespoons sugar
1½ cups heavy cream
   Semisweet chocolate curls

Mix chocolate crumbs with melted butter and spread onto bottom of 8 or 9-inch springform pan. Set aside. Pour half-and-half into large pan; add marshmallows and cook over low heat, stirring until completely melted. Set pan in cold water and stir until cooled. Blend in liqueurs. Place in refrigerator to cool. Beat cream until stiff; set aside. Beat egg whites until stiff; add sugar. Continue beating until peaks are glossy. In large bowl, combine marshmallow mixture, whipped cream and meringue. Stir until smooth. Pour into chocolate crust and freeze 8 hours or more. When ready to serve, unmold and garnish with chocolate curls. Allow to soften 5 minutes before serving.

CHERRY-BERRY CLOUD

15 servings

MERINGUE
6   egg whites
½   teaspoon cream of tartar
½   teaspoon salt
1¾ cups sugar

Heat oven to 275 degrees. Grease 9x13-inch pan. Beat egg whites, cream of tartar and salt until frothy. Gradually beat in 1¾ cups sugar. Beat until stiff and glossy, about 15 minutes. Put in pan. Turn off oven; place meringue in oven. Leave meringue in oven 12 hours or overnight.

FILLING
2   3-ounce packages cream
       cheese, softened
1   cup sugar
1   teaspoon vanilla
2   cups heavy cream, whipped
2   cups miniature marshmallows

Mix cream cheese with sugar and vanilla. Gently fold in whipped cream and marshmallows. Spread over meringue and refrigerate 12 hours or more. Cut in serving pieces and top with Berry Topping.

BERRY TOPPING
1   cup cherry pie filling
1   teaspoon lemon juice
2   10½-ounce packages frozen
       strawberries, thawed

Stir pie filling and lemon juice into strawberries. Prepare topping 2 nights before serving and refrigerate until used.

CHOCOLATE TERRONE LOAF

10 servings

1   pound semisweet chocolate
8   tablespoons dark rum or
       brandy
1   pound butter
4   tablespoons superfine sugar
4   eggs, separated
3   cups ground almonds
24 Pepperidge Farm Bordeaux
       cookies, crumbled
2   teaspoons oil
       Confectioners' sugar
2   cups heavy cream, whipped

Combine pieces of chocolate with rum in saucepan; heat slowly until melted. Remove from heat and set aside to cool. Cream butter and sugar; add egg yolks, nuts and cooled chocolate. Beat egg whites until stiff; fold into chocolate mixture. Fold in crumbled cookies. Lightly oil 1-quart loaf pan or mold; spoon in mixture. Tap to remove bubbles; cover with foil and refrigerate overnight. Unmold by dipping quickly into warm water. Sprinkle with confectioners' sugar. Cut in thin slices and serve with whipped cream.

CHOCOLATE-FILLED PECAN ROLL

8 servings

4   large eggs, separated
1   cup sifted confectioners' sugar
2   cups ground pecans, almonds
    or walnuts

Beat egg yolks and confectioners' sugar until thick and lemon colored. Fold in nuts. Beat egg whites until stiff but not dry. Fold ¼ of the whites into yolk mixture to loosen; fold in remaining whites. Spread evenly on buttered jelly roll pan lined with buttered waxed paper. Bake at 400 degrees for 15 to 20 minutes until lightly browned. Remove from oven and turn onto a sheet of waxed paper. Lift pan from cake. Do not remove waxed paper. Roll cake lengthwise; allow to cool completely.

FILLING

1   cup heavy cream
3   tablespoons sugar
2   teaspoons cocoa
½   teaspoon vanilla
    Confectioners' sugar

Combine cream, sugar, cocoa and vanilla. Chill for 30 minutes. Beat cream mixture until it forms firm, not stiff peaks. Unroll cake very gently and peel off waxed paper. Spread with filling and roll up again. Sprinkle with confectioners' sugar.

MOCHA CHOCOLATE ROLL

8 servings

CAKE

1   cup confectioners' sugar
3   tablespoons cocoa
1   tablespoon cake flour
¼   teaspoon baking powder
6   eggs, separated

Sift together sugar, cocoa, flour and baking powder. Beat egg yolks until light. Add dry ingredients. Beat egg whites until they stand in peaks, fold gently into rest of mixture. Bake in long, buttered jelly roll pan for 12 minutes at 375 degrees. Loosen cake while hot; invert onto a towel and roll. When cake is cool; unroll and fill.

FILLING

1   cup heavy cream, whipped
1   tablespoon sugar
½   tablespoon vanilla

Whip cream flavored with sugar and vanilla; spread on unrolled cake. Roll up tightly.

ICING

1   cup confectioners' sugar
3   tablespoons cocoa
2   tablespoons butter, melted
2   tablespoons cold coffee
    Vanilla flavoring (optional)

Mix together sugar, cocoa, butter and coffee. Beat until smooth. Flavor with vanilla if desired. Frost top and all sides of cake. Decorate as desired with chocolate sprinkles, whipped cream, holly leaves or cinnamon candies.

BOCCONE DOLCE

10 servings

MERINGUE

4   **egg whites**
     Pinch of salt
¼   **teaspoon cream of tartar**
1   **cup sugar**

Beat egg whites until stiff; add salt and cream of tartar. Gradually beat in sugar and continue to beat until meringue is stiff and glossy. Line baking sheets with waxed paper. On the paper, trace 3 8-inch circles. Spread meringue evenly over circles, about ¼ inch thick. Bake in 250 degree oven for 20 to 30 minutes, or until pale gold but still pliable. Remove from oven and carefully pull waxed paper from bottom. Put on cake racks to dry.

FILLING

1   **6-ounce package semisweet**
     chocolate bits
3   **tablespoons water**
3   **cups heavy cream**
⅓   **cup sugar**
1   **pint fresh strawberries**

Melt chocolate and water in top of double boiler or in microwave. Whip cream until stiff. Gradually add sugar and beat until very stiff. Slice strawberries. Leave 5 or 6 berries whole for topping. Place 1 meringue layer on a serving plate and spread with a thin coating of melted chocolate. Cover with a ¾-inch layer of whipped cream; top with half the sliced strawberries. Repeat layers and top with third meringue. Frost with remaining whipped cream. Drizzle remaining chocolate over top and garnish with whole berries. Refrigerate for 2 hours.

BANANA SPLIT CREAM PUFFS

10 servings

CREAM PUFFS

½   **cup butter**
1   **cup boiling water**
1   **cup sifted flour**
¼   **teaspoon salt**
4   **eggs**

Melt butter in boiling water; add flour and salt all at once. Stir and cook until mixture forms a ball. Remove from heat; cool slightly. Add eggs, one at a time, beating after each addition until smooth. Drop by heaping tablespoons, 3 inches apart, on greased cookie sheet. Bake at 450 degrees for 15 minutes. Lower heat to 325 degrees and bake for 25 minutes. Remove from oven and split. Turn oven off; return cream puffs to oven to dry, about 20 minutes.

FILLING

1	**cup milk**
1	**cup heavy cream**
½	**cup sugar**
2	**tablespoons cornstarch**
2	**tablespoons flour**
½	**teaspoon salt**
2	**egg yolks, slightly beaten**
1	**teaspoon vanilla**
2-3	**fresh bananas, sliced**
1	**pint fresh strawberries, sliced**
1	**fresh pineapple, sliced**
	Chocolate sauce

Scald milk and cream in heavy saucepan. Combine sugar, cornstarch, flour and salt. Gradually add milk mixture to dry ingredients. Stir until smooth. Cook until thickened. Add a little hot mixture to egg yolks. Quickly stir into remaining mixture in pan. Cook 2 minutes over low heat, stirring constantly. Remove from heat and add vanilla. Cool. Fill bottom half of cream puff with filling; add layers of bananas, strawberries and pineapple. Cover with filling and replace top half of cream puff. Drizzle with chocolate sauce and serve.

AUSTRIAN TART

8 servings

1	**3¾-ounce box instant vanilla pudding**
1	**egg yolk**
1	**cup milk**
¼	**teaspoon almond extract**
2	**cups flour**
2	**tablespoons sugar**
2	**egg yolks**
2	**teaspoons lemon peel**
1	**cup margarine**
1	**pint small strawberries, sliced**
1	**banana, sliced**
1	**kiwi, sliced**
1	**10-ounce jar currant or apple jelly, melted**

Combine pudding mix and milk. Beat at low speed until well blended. Add 1 egg yolk and almond extract. Whisk constantly until thickened. Remove and chill. Mix flour, sugar, 2 egg yolks, lemon peel and margarine to form a soft ball for the crust. Press into a 12-inch fluted tart pan with removable bottom. Prick entire bottom and bake at 375 degrees for 15 to 20 minutes. The pudding and crust can be done a day ahead. About 4 hours before serving, spread cooled cream filling on baked shell. Arrange fruit on custard in concentric circles. Strawberries should be hulled and placed upside down. The top of this tart may be decorated with any combination of fruits or with one variety. Make sure fruit covers the custard. Pour melted jelly over all fruit. Refrigerate until ready to serve.

ALMOND CREAM CRÊPES

5 servings

CRÊPES
⅓ cup sifted flour
1 tablespoon sugar
　 Dash of salt
1 egg
1 egg yolk
¾ cup milk
1 tablespoon butter, melted

Blend crêpe ingredients together and chill several hours until thick. Heat heavy 6-inch skillet; grease lightly and pour in 2 tablespoons batter. Lift off heat and tilt from side to side until batter covers bottom evenly. Return to heat and brown underside for about 1½ minutes. To remove, invert skillet over paper towels. Repeat.

FILLING
1 cup sugar
¼ cup flour
1 cup milk
2 eggs
2 egg yolks
3 tablespoons butter
2 teaspoons vanilla
½ teaspoon almond extract
½ cup ground, roasted blanched
　 almonds
　 Melted butter
　 Grated unsweetened
　 chocolate
　 Confectioners' sugar
　 Whipped cream

Cook sugar, flour and milk together until thick. Cook 1 or 2 minutes longer stirring constantly. Beat eggs and egg yolks slightly. Stir some of hot mixture into eggs, then add warmed eggs to hot mixture. Bring to boil; continue to stir. Remove from heat. Add butter, vanilla, extract and almonds to mixture. Cool to room temperature. Refrigerate if not promptly used. Spread 2 tablespoons almond filling on unbrowned side of each crepe. Roll up and place folded side down in buttered 9x13-inch baking dish. Brush crêpes with melted butter and heat at 350 degrees for 20 to 25 minutes. Sprinkle with grated unsweetened chocolate; sift confectioners' sugar over top. Serve with whipped cream.

SUNSHINE CRÊPES

8 servings

⅓ cup butter
½ cup orange marmalade
2 tablespoons sugar
1 tablespoon cornstarch
3 large bananas, sliced
8 crêpes, hot
　 Confectioners' sugar
　 Sour cream
　 Nutmeg

Melt together butter and marmalade. Stir in sugar and cornstarch. Fold in bananas. Divide filling among crêpes. Roll each crêpe around filling. Top with confectioners' sugar, sour cream and nutmeg.

CRÊPES FITZGERALD

4 servings

2 cups strawberries, hulled and halved
½ cup sugar
6 tablespoons sour cream
6 tablespoons cream cheese, softened
8 dessert crêpes
3 tablespoons butter
1 ounce apricot liqueur or Amaretto
1½ ounces Kirsh

Toss strawberries with sugar; set aside. Combine sour cream and cream cheese; spread on crêpes. Roll each crêpe and set aside. Combine in saucepan and heat; strawberries, butter and liqueurs. Pour sauce over crêpes. Serve immediately.

CHOCOLATE CRÊPES

12 servings

12 to 14 cooked dessert crêpes

FILLING
½ cup butter or margarine, softened
⅔ cup sugar
2 eggs
2 1-ounce squares unsweetened chocolate, melted

Beat butter in large bowl of electric mixer until creamy. Add sugar gradually; beat until pale-colored and fluffy. Add eggs, one at a time, beating well. Stir in melted chocolate and blend well. Spread 1½ tablespoons of chocolate mixture on one edge of each crêpe. Roll into tight rolls. Spread tops of crêpes with Caramel Sugar Topping, sweetened whipped cream or confectioners' sugar. Store in refrigerator until ready to serve.

TOPPING
⅔ cup sugar
⅓ cup water

Place sugar in heavy 8-inch skillet or 2-quart saucepan, over medium high heat. Sugar will first turn liquid and then gradually turn a caramel color. Scrape bottom of pan with a wooden spatula, stirring constantly. If mixture begins to smoke, remove from burner. Sugar will burn easily. Keep stirring, removing from heat if necessary. Do not leave on burner unattended. When all sugar is liquid, remove from heat. Add water a little at a time. Be careful not to burn your hand in steam. Stir until all water is combined with sugar. Mixture will be a sticky, caramel consistency.

APRICOT DESSERT CRÊPES
8 servings

CRÊPES
1   cup cold water
1   cup milk
4   eggs
½   teaspoon salt
2   cups sifted flour
4   tablespoons butter, melted

FILLING
1   8-ounce package cream
      cheese, softened
2   tablespoons butter
¼   cup sugar
1   teaspoon grated lemon rind
1   teaspoon vanilla

SAUCE
1   jar apricot preserves
      Cointreau
      Whipped cream
      Slivered almonds

Put crêpe ingredients in a blender at high speed for 1 minute. Scrape sides; blend for 5 seconds more. Refrigerate at least 2 hours. Pour ¼ cup batter into crêpe pan or electric crêpe maker. Bake until lightly browned. Mix together ingredients for filling. Lightly frost each crêpe and stack together. Warm crêpes slightly before serving. Pour over crêpes a sauce made of apricot preserves thinned with Cointreau. Top with a dollop of whipped cream and slivered almonds

CHOCOLATE FONDUE
8 servings

2   cups semisweet chocolate
      chips
1½   cups light corn syrup
2   teaspoons vanilla
      Pinch of salt
1   tablespoon butter
1   tablespoon rum or coffee
      liqueur (optional)
      Pound or sponge cake cubes
      Pineapple chunks
      Whole strawberries
      Walnut or pecan halves
      Orange wedges, peel removed

Combine all ingredients in the top of a double boiler. Heat, stirring, over hot water until melted and smooth. Serve immediately or hold and reheat just before serving. Keep warm while serving in a fondue pot or chaffing dish. Each person spears a piece of fruit or cake and dips it into the warm sauce. Any assortment of fruits can be served.

STRAWBERRIES SABAYON

12 servings

4   **pints strawberries, sliced and hulled**
4   **large egg yolks**
½   **cup sugar**
¾   **cup Amaretto liqueur**
1½ **cups heavy cream, whipped**
1½ **teaspoons grated lemon or orange rind**

Sprinkle strawberries with sugar; place in large bowl or individual dessert dishes and chill. In top of double boiler, combine egg yolks, sugar and Amaretto; whisk while cooking over hot water until it coats a spoon or until you see traces of the whisk. Chill until almost set; whisk in whipped cream and rind of lemon or orange. Just before serving, spoon over strawberries. NOTE: Sabayon may be frozen and served alone as a mousse.

FRESH FRUIT SORBET

2   **pounds fresh fruit, peeled and cored if necessary, cut into pieces**
½   **cup sugar**
    Lemon juice

Purée all ingredients in a blender or with steel blade in food precessor. Sieve if necessary to remove seeds. Spread in an 8-inch cake pan and freeze until not quite firm. Process again until fluffy. Transfer to airtight container and freeze. Before serving, let soften in refrigerator for 30 minutes. Fruit: blueberries, use 2 tablespoons lemon juice; kiwi, omit lemon juice; pineapple, use 1 large pineapple and 2 teaspoons lemon juice; raspberry, omit lemon juice; strawberry, use 1 tablespoon lemon juice; peach, use 2 tablespoons lemon juice and add ¼ teaspoon ascorbic acid; banana, use 1 tablespoon lemon juice and ¼ teaspoon ascorbic acid; apples, use 1 tablespoon lemon juice and ¼ teaspoon ascorbic acid. For a lighter sorbet, any of these may be mixed in equal parts with apple.

PINK CHAMPAGNE SORBET

6 servings

1 quart lemon sherbet
½ pint raspberry sherbet
1 cup pink champagne

In a large bowl, soften lemon and raspberry sherbets. Beat together; blend well. Stir in ½ cup pink champagne. Freeze until very firm, at least 2 hours or longer if possible. To serve, scoop into 6 6-ounce parfait glasses. Serve immediately with some of the reserved champagne poured over each glass. NOTE: You can freeze in parfait glasses; pour champagne over just before serving.

PEACH MELBA RIPPLE ICE CREAM

3½ quarts

1 cup sugar
3 tablespoons flour
   Dash of salt
1½ cups milk
3 eggs, slightly beaten
3 cups heavy cream
½ teaspoon almond extract
2 10-ounce packages frozen peaches, thawed and drained
1 10-ounce package frozen raspberries, thawed
2 tablespoons sugar
1 teaspoon cornstarch
1 tablespoon water

Combine sugar, flour and salt in medium saucepan. Add milk gradually. Cook over medium heat, stirring constantly until mixture thickens and bubbles. Remove from heat. Stir small amount of hot mixture into eggs. Return egg mixture to saucepan and cook, stirring constantly, for 1 minute. Remove from heat and cool to room temperature. Stir in heavy cream and almond extract. Chill. Crush drained peaches with a potato masher or fork; reserve. Press raspberries through sieve into a saucepan. Add 2 tablespoons sugar. Mix cornstarch with 1 tablespoon water in a cup. Add to raspberries. Cook over medium heat, just until thickened and bubbly. Cool completely; reserve. Pour cream mixture into ice cream freezer. Add peaches and freeze according to directions. Working very fast, spoon about ⅕ of the ice cream into a large bowl and drizzle with part of the raspberry sauce. Repeat layers of ice cream and sauce. Freeze until firm.

LEMON VELVET ICE CREAM

1 gallon

1 pint heavy cream
3 cups sugar
1½ quarts milk
1 cup fresh lemon juice

Whip cream until stiff. Put into chilled ice cream freezer can. Dissolve sugar in milk. Stir into whipped cream. Freeze according to freezer directions, until ice cream is at mush stage. Add lemon juice. Continue to freeze until done. Pack to ripen for several hours before serving.

CHOCOLATE MINT ICE CREAM

1 quart

2 eggs, beaten
3 cups heavy cream
1 cup milk
½ cup sugar
¼ cup light corn syrup
1 teaspoon vanilla
¼ teaspoon salt
⅓ cup Crème de Menthe
Green food coloring
⅓ cup shaved semisweet
chocolate

Beat eggs until light. Add cream, milk, sugar, corn syrup, vanilla and salt. Beat until sugar is dissolved. Add Crème de Menthe and food coloring. Put in ice cream freezer and process according to directions. When frozen, stir in shaved chocolate. Freeze.

STRAWBERRY ICE CREAM

1 gallon

1 3-ounce package strawberry
gelatin
2½ cups sugar
1½ cups boiling water
1 quart fresh strawberries,
mashed
2 tablespoons vanilla
1 quart heavy cream

Dissolve sugar and gelatin in boiling water. Cool to room temperature. Add mashed strawberries and vanilla. Chill until cold. Stir in cream. Pour into ice cream freezer and process according to directions. NOTE: Strawberries will not turn hard if you let them sit in sugar mixture until cold.

RASPBERRY WATERMELON SURPRISE

16 servings

1 small watermelon
6½ cups water
2 cups sugar
3 16-ounce packages frozen
strawberries, thawed
1 10 or 12-ounce
package frozen raspberries,
thawed
Chocolate chips

Cut watermelon in half lengthwise; scoop out all fruit pulp. Save pulp for another use. Cover shell with foil and freeze. Boil water with sugar for 5 minutes until it forms a syrup. Chill. Whirl berries in a blender for a few seconds. Push through a fine strainer to remove seeds and coarse pulp. Combine berries with chilled syrup. Pour mixture into ice cream freezer and freeze according to instructions. When frozen, spoon into watermelon shell. Smooth the top to look like a split watermelon. Press chocolate chips into top to resemble seeds of melon. Cover with plastic wrap and freeze until ready to serve.

BANANA SPLIT SUPREME

15 servings

1 package graham crackers,
crushed
¼ cup sugar
¾ cup butter, melted
3 bananas
½ gallon Neopolitan ice cream
1 cup chopped nuts
1 6-ounce package chocolate
chips
½ cup butter, melted
2 cups confectioners' sugar
½ cup evaporated milk
1 teaspoon vanilla
1 pint non-diary whipped
topping

Combine graham cracker crumbs (reserve 2 tablespoons), ¾ cup butter and sugar. Press into a 9x13-inch pan. Slice bananas over crust. Slice ice cream in ½-inch slices and place over bananas. Sprinkle nuts over ice cream. Freeze. Combine chocolate chips, ½ cup butter, confectioners' sugar and evaporated milk. Cook until thick, stirring constantly. Remove from heat; add vanilla. Cool. Pour over frozen ice cream. Freeze. Frost with whipped topping. Sprinkle with reserved crumbs. Let stand at room temperature 30 minutes before serving.

TORTONI SQUARES

½ cup slivered almonds
6 tablespoons butter, melted
2 cups finely ground vanilla
     wafers
2 teaspoons almond extract
1 quart softened French vanilla
     ice cream
1 12-ounce jar apricot or peach
     preserves
     Whipped cream
     Maraschino cherries

Combine almonds, butter, wafers and extract. Line a 9-inch square pan with foil and sprinkle ⅓ of almond mixture on bottom. Spoon on top ½ of the ice cream, spread evenly. Spread with ½ of preserves. Repeat layers ending with almond mixture. Freeze, cut into squares. Garnish with whipped cream and cherries.

BUSTER BAR DESSERT

1 15-ounce package cream-
     filled chocolate cookies
4 tablespoons butter, melted
1 cup margarine
3 cups confectioners' sugar
3 1-ounce squares semisweet
     chocolate
4 eggs
½ gallon vanilla ice cream
1 cup Spanish peanuts

Crumble cookies until fine, reserving ⅓ cup crumbs for top. Mix with butter and put in a 9x13-inch pan. Set aside. Cook together margarine, sugar, chocolate and eggs until boiling; let cool. Spread vanilla ice cream over crumbs in pan. Sprinkle peanuts over ice cream and pour cooled sauce over peanuts. Sprinkle reserved crumbs on top. Place in freezer until ready to serve.

BOURBON CHOCOLATE PARFAIT

½ cup cocoa powder
⅔ cup hot water
1 tablespoon butter
½ cup honey
⅓ cup light corn syrup
¼ teaspoon vanilla
¼ cup bourbon
1 quart vanilla ice cream
½ cup heavy cream, whipped

Blend cocoa, water, butter, honey and corn syrup. Heat and bring to a boil. Stir in vanilla and bourbon. Cool. Place alternate layers of ice cream and sauce in parfait glasses. Freeze. Top with whipped cream.

BUTTERSCOTCH BOMBE

12 servings

1 cup crushed gingersnaps
3 tablespoons butter, melted
2 quarts vanilla ice cream
1 bag Heath Bits
1 cup chocolate chips, crushed

SAUCE
½ cup brown sugar
½ cup half-and-half
4 tablespoons butter
1 teaspoon vanilla
¼ cup slivered almonds

Mix gingersnaps and butter together; press into bundt or pie pan and freeze. Soften ice cream. Blend in crushed bits and chips. Spoon into crust. Cover and freeze firm. Bring sugar, cream and butter to a boil, stirring constantly. Remove from heat, stir in almonds and vanilla. Spoon over sliced pie pieces.

SUGAR-BROILED FRUITS

6 servings

2 large bananas, sliced
1 tablespoon lemon juice
1 cup quartered strawberries
2 oranges, peeled and cut in bite-size pieces
1 cup brown sugar
6 tablespoons butter, melted
¾ cup slivered almonds
   Vanilla ice cream

Gently toss bananas with lemon juice. Place in 11x7-inch pan. Cover with layer of strawberries and oranges. Combine sugar, butter and almonds. Sprinkle over fruit. Broil 6 inches from heat until sugar is melted and almonds are toasted. Cool a few moments, then tap crust to break. Spoon fruit and juice into dishes. Top with ice cream.

EASY GRAPE DESSERT

6 servings

4 cups green seedless grapes
1 cup brown sugar
1 cup sour cream
¼ cup rum

Mix sour cream, sugar and rum together. Pour over grapes. Let stand overnight. Serve in glass dessert dishes.

GERMAN PLUM PUDDING

2 puddings

4   cups flour
2   cups minced beef kidney suet
4   ounces candied citron
2   cups raisins
½   cup chopped dates
4   ounces candied pineapple
4   ounces candied cherries
1   teaspoon salt
1   teaspoon baking soda
1   teaspoon ground cloves
2   teaspoons cinnamon
½   cup chopped nuts
1   cup buttermilk
1½ cups sugar
½   cup sorghum
2   eggs

Mix suet with 2 cups of flour. Mix and add fruit, spices, nuts and remaining flour. Combine buttermilk, sugar, sorghum and eggs; add to mixture. Pour into 2 greased pudding molds. Do not fill to top, pudding will expand. Steam for 4 hours, covered tightly. Serve warm with hard sauce or lemon sauce. NOTE: This may be made several weeks ahead and kept in refrigerator or freezer. To heat, wrap tightly in foil and heat in low oven until hot. Serve on Christmas, decorated with holly.

STEAMED PRUNE PUDDING

1 pudding

PUDDING
2   eggs
½   cup butter, melted
1   cup brown sugar
2   cups cooked prunes, drained
        and chopped
1   cup sifted flour
1   tablespoon buttermilk
1   teaspoon baking soda

Beat eggs. Dissolve soda in buttermilk. Mix together butter and sugar. Add eggs, prunes, and soda in buttermilk and flour. Mix. Put in greased 2-pound coffee can or 2-quart baking dish. Cover with aluminum foil; secure tightly with string or rubber band. Steam 1 hour. Serve warm with sauce.

SAUCE
5   tablespoons butter, melted
1   egg, beaten
1½ cups sifted confectioners'
        sugar
2   teaspoons vanilla
    Dash of salt
1   cup heavy cream

Work butter slowly into beaten egg. Add confectioners' sugar, vanilla and salt. Whip heavy cream; fold into above mixture. Serve over warm pudding.

CRANBERRY PUDDING

12 servings

PUDDING
½   **cup water**
⅓   **cup molasses**
2   **teaspoons soda**
½   **teaspoon salt**
2   **cups cranberries, cut in half**
1½ **cups flour**

SAUCE
½   **cup butter**
½   **cup heavy cream**
1   **cup sugar**

Mix together pudding ingredients. Pour into greased 1-quart mold. Cover tightly with foil. Steam in pan of boiling water on top of stove for 2 hours. Combine sauce ingredients and bring to a boil. Serve hot over pudding.

PLUM PUDDING SAUCE

½   **cup butter**
1   **cup sugar**
1   **egg**
3   **tablespoons water**
1   **teaspoon vanilla extract**

Cream butter and sugar. Add egg, vanilla and water. Cook 15 minutes in top of double boiler. Serve warm over pudding.

NANA'S RUM SAUCE

2 cups

½   **cup dark brown sugar,**
       loosely packed
½   **cup sugar**
⅛   **teaspoon salt**
¼   **cup butter**
½   **cup heavy cream**
½   **cup light corn syrup**
½   **teaspoon vanilla**
3   **tablespoons dark rum**

Combine sugars, salt, butter, cream and corn syrup in saucepan. Heat, stirring, until mixture comes to a boil. Cool to lukewarm and add vanilla and rum. Keeps indefinitely in refrigerator. Serve on fruitcake, pound cake or ice cream.

MICROWAVE CUSTARD SAUCE

2 cups

3 tablespoons butter
1 cup sugar
1 cup heavy cream
2 large eggs, beaten
¼ teaspoon mace
¼ teaspoon lemon extract

Melt butter in 4-cup glass measuring cup. Add remaining ingredients and blend well. Cook 2 minutes. Stir. Cook 1½ minutes more. Mix until smooth. Serve warm over pound cake or fruit.

MICROWAVE CHOCOLATE RUM SAUCE

1½ cups

2 1-ounce squares unsweetened chocolate
1 cup sugar
⅛ teaspoon cream of tartar
6 tablespoons evaporated milk
6 tablespoons dark rum
1 teaspoon vanilla
  Pinch of salt

Place chocolate in 4-cup glass measuring cup and heat 2 to 2½ minutes or until chocolate is melted. Remove and stir until smooth and creamy. Blend in sugar and cream of tartar. Gradually stir in milk and rum, blending well. Heat 1½ minutes. Stir. Heat 30 to 45 seconds more. Add vanilla and salt. Mix until smooth and thick.

MICROWAVE CARAMEL SAUCE

1 cup

½ pound vanilla caramels
½ cup heavy cream

Place caramels and cream in 4-cup glass measuring cup. Heat in microwave for 1½ to 2 minutes. Stir. Heat 1½ to 2 minutes more and mix until smooth. Serve warm. This can also be done in a double boiler on the stove.

GOOD-WITH-ANYTHING CHOCOLATE SAUCE

20 servings

1 8-ounce package cream cheese
⅓ cup milk
2 1-ounce squares unsweetened chocolate
2 cups confectioners' sugar
1 teaspoon vanilla

Heat cream cheese, milk and chocolate together in saucepan over low heat. Stir until smooth. Add confectioners' sugar and vanilla. Stir until completely blended. Refrigerate until serving time. Serve warm over ice cream or heat in fondue pot and use as dip for fruit and cake pieces.

SAUCE LICOR DE CAFÉ
2 cups

1 cup sugar
1 teaspoon instant coffee
⅛ teaspoon cinnamon
⅛ teaspoon ground cloves
⅛ teaspoon ground nutmeg
1 cup water
¼ cup Licor de Café (Kahlua, Tia Maria or other coffee liqueur)

Combine all ingredients except liqueur. Stir until dissolved. Slowly bring to a boil and cook for 5 minutes. Skim off any foam that rises to the surface. Cool. When cold, stir in liqueur. Serve over coffee ice cream, garnished with slivered almonds.

FLAMING DATE-WALNUT SAUCE
2 cups

1 cup water
2 cups brown sugar
½ cup brandy
1 8-ounce package pitted dates
1 cup walnut halves

Cook water and brown sugar over medium heat for 20 minutes. Stir occasionally. Add ¼ cup brandy, dates and walnuts. Let cool. Store tightly covered in a glass jar in refrigerator. Before serving, heat sauce over low heat. Pour into serving dish. Heat remaining ¼ cup brandy in small saucepan until vapor starts to rise. Ignite. At the table, pour flaming brandy into sauce. While sauce is still flaming, serve over ice cream.

TOFFEE CRUNCH SAUCE

1 cup brown sugar
½ cup sugar
2 tablespoons butter
¼ cup water
1 6-ounce can evaporated milk
3 ¾-ounce English Toffee bars, crushed

Combine sugars, butter and water. Cook and stir until sauce boils. Boil 3 minutes. Remove from heat and cool slightly. Stir in milk. Add toffee bars.

NO-WILT WHIPPED CREAM

½ teaspoon unflavored gelatin
1 tablespoon cold water
1 cup heavy cream
2 teaspoons sugar (optional)
½ teaspoon vanilla (optional)

Place gelatin in small saucepan and pour cold water over it. Let stand 1 minute to soften. Dissolve gelatin over medium heat. Place cream, sugar and vanilla in a chilled bowl and beat with electric mixer. Gradually add gelatin mixture; continue to beat until cream holds shape.

Melting Pot

SIMPLE SIMON PICKLES
1 quart

5 cups cucumbers, unpeeled
    and sliced
1 large onion, thinly sliced
⅓ teaspoon turmeric
⅓ teaspoon celery seed
⅓ teaspoon mustard seed
1⅓ cups sugar
1⅓ cups vinegar
2 teaspoons non-iodized salt

Place cucumbers and onion in a large glass jar or bowl with cover. Mix spices with sugar and vinegar until sugar is nearly dissolved. Pour over cucumbers and onion; cover and refrigerate. Stir occasionally. Keep indefinitely in the refrigerator.

EASY REFRIGERATOR PICKLES
7 cups

6 cups thinly sliced cucumbers
2 cups thinly sliced onions
1½ cups sugar
1½ cups vinegar
½ teaspoon salt
½ teaspoon mustard seed
½ teaspoon celery seed
½ teaspoon ground turmeric

In glass or crockery bowl, alternately layer the sliced cucumbers and onions. In medium saucepan, combine sugar, vinegar, salt, mustard seed, celery seed and ground turmeric. Bring to a boil, stirring constantly, until sugar is dissolved. Pour vinegar mixture over cucumbers and onions. Cool slightly. Cover tightly and refrigerate pickles at least 24 hours before serving. Store up to 1 month in refrigerator.

FROZEN BREAD AND BUTTER PICKLES
8 cups

7 cups thinly sliced cucumbers
1 cup thinly sliced onions
2 tablespoons pickling salt
2 cups sugar
1 cup white vinegar
1 teaspoon celery seed

Mix cucumbers, onions and salt. Let stand overnight (or 4 to 5 hours) at room temperature. Drain in colander. Do not rinse. In another bowl, mix sugar, vinegar and celery seed. Stir until sugar is dissolved. Pour over cucumbers and leave overnight again at room temperature. Put in jars or plastic boxes and freeze. Just thaw and eat. Should be eaten very cold.

RED HOT PICKLES

10 quarts

2 gallons large cucumbers, peeled, seeded, sliced
2 cups pickling lime
8½ quarts water
1 cup vinegar
1 tablespoon alum
1 bottle red food coloring
  Water to cover
3 cups vinegar
11 cups sugar
1 package red hot candies
3 cups water
10 cinnamon sticks

Combine sliced cucumbers, pickling lime and 8½ quarts of water. Let soak 24 hours. Drain, rinse and wash thoroughly to remove lime. Soak in cold water for 3 hours. Drain. Combine 1 cup vinegar, alum, red food coloring, drained cucumbers and water to cover. Simmer 2 hours; drain. Combine 3 cups vinegar, sugar, red hots, 3 cups water and cinnamon sticks. Bring to a boil. Pour over cucumbers. Let stand 24 hours. Drain liquid into another pan and reheat. Pour same liquid over the cucumbers, soak another 24 hours. Do this a total of 3 times, allowing the cucumbers to stand 24 hours between each draining. The last time, place 1 of the cinnamon sticks and cucumbers in hot sterilized jars. Pour hot juice over them and put on the lids. Process in boiling water bath for 5 minutes.

PICKLED BEETS

6 pints

8 medium beets
3 medium onions, sliced
2 cups sugar
1 tablespoon whole allspice
1½ teaspoons pickling salt
1½ cups water
2 sticks cinnamon
3½ cups cider vinegar

Cook beets in boiling water until done, 30 to 45 minutes. Cool and slice. Place beets and onion rings in 6 sterilized, pint jars. Cook sugar, allspice, salt, vinegar, water and cinnamon sticks together until mixture boils and sugar is dissolved. Pour hot liquid over beets and onions. Seal with lids and process for 30 minutes as you would other canned vegetables. May be eaten after 1 week.

CUCUMBER RELISH

4½ quarts

4 quarts cucumbers, ground (20 medium or 12 large)
4 tablespoons salt
2 quarts white onions, ground (12 medium)
1 tablespoon salt
6 cups vinegar
2 teaspoons turmeric
1½ teaspoons celery seed
¾ teaspoon mustard seed
6 cups sugar

Use large, firm, green cucumbers. Scrape out seeds and soft centers. Cut up into small pieces. Using the coarse blade of a food processor, grind the cucumbers, skin and all. Add 4 tablespoons salt; mix and let sit 2 hours. In another bowl, grind onions. Add 1 tablespoon salt and let stand 2 hours. Place cucumbers and onions in a colander to drain. In a large kettle or roaster combine sugar, vinegar and spices. Bring to a boil, stirring well. Add cucumbers and onions, stirring constantly so mixture will be evenly cooked. Sterilize caning jars, disks and lids. Fill hot jars with relish. Seal tightly and turn upside down to cool. The heat of the relish against the disk heats the rubber around the rim. As it cools, it will have a tighter seal.

RUBY CHUTNEY

1 quart

2 16-ounce cans whole cranberry sauce
1 cup sugar
½ cup vinegar
2 teaspoons salt
⅓ teaspoon ginger
1 cup white raisins
1 tablespoon curry powder
1 tablespoon Worcestershire
2 tablespoons molasses
½ teaspoon Tabasco

Mix all ingredients in a saucepan. Bring to a boil and simmer for 15 minutes. Pour into sterilized jars. Seal with paraffin or keep in refrigerator for several months. Serve with ham or pork, or use as appetizer over cream cheese.

CHILI SAUCE

7 pints

1	gallon (6¼-pounds) ripe tomatoes, peeled and quartered
⅔	cup chopped white onion
1	green pepper, chopped
1½	cups sugar
1	teaspoon grated nutmeg
¾	teaspoon Tabasco
½	teaspoon curry powder
2	cups vinegar
5	teaspoons salt
2	teaspoons ginger
1	teaspoon cinnamon
1	teaspoon dry mustard

In a large, heavy kettle (3 to 5-quart size), mix together all ingredients. Bring to a boil. Reduce heat and simmer for 1½ to 2 hours; stir frequently to prevent burning. Skim off foam as it forms. Reduce most of the liquid and pour into sterilized, self-sealing pint jars. Will keep unsealed in refrigerator for a month.

TOMATO GRAVY

7 cups

4	cups chopped onions
4	garlic cloves, minced
½	cup olive oil
14	tomatoes, peeled and seeded, reserve strained juice
4	teaspoons salt
1	12-ounce can tomato paste
2	teaspoons oregano
1	tablespoon sugar
½	cup minced fresh parsley

In a large Dutch oven, sauté onions and garlic in olive oil until soft and golden. Add tomatoes and salt. Simmer uncovered until tomatoes are soft, about 30 minutes. Purée. Return to Dutch oven and add remaining ingredients. Simmer uncovered to a purée consistency, about 1 hour. If mixture is too thick before simmering, add desired amount of the reserved juice from the tomatoes. This can be served as a gravy or tomato sauce over pasta, hamburgers or meat loaf. Freeze in pint containers.

RED PEPPER PRESERVE

1 quart

1	dozen large or 15 small sweet red peppers
1	tablespoon salt
3	cups sugar
2	cups vinegar

Clean and grind peppers. Soak for 3 hours with salt. Put into a colander and drain. Add sugar and vinegar. Cook over medium heat until thick about ¾ hour. Pour into 4 8-ounce jelly glasses. Seal with airtight lids or cover with paraffin.

PEACH CHUTNEY

4 ½-pint jars

½   **lemon, chopped and seeded**
½   **teaspoon garlic salt**
1⅛ **cups brown sugar**
4   **ounces seeded raisins**
2½ **ounces Spice Island**
     crystallized ginger, chopped
½   **teaspoon salt**
⅛   **teaspoon cayenne**
1   **cup cider vinegar**
2   **tablespoons Worcestershire**
2   **ounces mustard seed**
½   **cup slivered almonds**
1   **teaspoon horseradish**
½   **teaspoon curry powder**
½   **teaspoon dry mustard**
     Dash of Tabasco
4   **cups peaches, peeled and**
     sliced

Combine all ingredients except peaches. Cook until raisins are plump. Add peaches and cook slowly until tender, stirring frequently, about 2 hours. Fill hot, sterilized ½-pint jars and seal. Process in a hot water bath for 5 minutes.

THANKSGIVING RELISH

7 cups

1   **16-ounce package cranberries**
2   **cups sugar**
1   **cup water**
1   **cup orange juice**
1   **cup golden or dark raisins**
1   **cup chopped walnuts**
1   **cup chopped celery**
1   **tablespoon grated orange peel**
1   **teaspoon ground ginger**

In a 3-quart saucepan, over medium heat, heat the cranberries, sugar and 1 cup water to boiling; stir frequently. Reduce the heat to low; simmer 15 minutes. Remove from heat and stir in remaining ingredients. Cover and refrigerate. NOTE: This may be made 2 hours before serving or up to 1 week ahead.

PEACH JAM
7 cups

24 peaches, peeled and
    quartered
6 oranges
16 cups sugar
1 cup Maraschino cherries

Mash quartered peaches in large heavy pot. Remove peel from 3 oranges; discard peel. Chop the 6 oranges into small pieces. Add to peaches. Add sugar and cherries. Stir and bring to a hard boil for 20 minutes. Skim off foam and ladle into sterilized containers. Seal.

SUNSET MARMALADE
7 cups

2 pounds fresh rhubarb,
    skinned and diced
2 pounds sugar
2 oranges, ground or chopped
    fine in food processor

Combine rhubarb and sugar; let stand overnight. Add ground oranges and bring to a boil in saucepan. Simmer until thick. Seal in jars. May be frozen. NOTE: 2 packages frozen rhubarb may be substituted; use 2½ cups sugar. The flavor is better with fresh rhubarb.

CHRISTMAS PEPPER JELLY
2 pints

3 large green peppers, chopped
½ cup vinegar
1 tablespoon cayenne pepper
6½ cups sugar
1 cup vinegar
1 6-ounce bottle Certo
    Green food coloring (optional)
    Melted paraffin

Clean and cut up green peppers, removing seeds. Purée in blender with ½ cup vinegar. Add cayenne pepper, sugar and additional vinegar. Place mixture in saucepan and boil 5 minutes. Cook 2 to 3 minutes; add Certo and food coloring. Pour into small sterilized jars and cover with melted paraffin. Serve as an appetizer over cream cheese. Spread on crackers. Very good served with pork. Decorated jars of this jelly make easy Christmas gifts.

BRANDIED CRANBERRIES

6 servings

4 cups fresh cranberries
2 cups sugar
⅓ cup brandy

Place cranberries in a 13x9-inch baking pan. Sprinkle evenly with sugar. Cover and bake in 300 degree oven for 1 hour and 15 minutes. Stir in brandy. Store in refrigerator in covered container. Serve in hollowed-out orange shells.

BERRY SYRUP

1 quart

1 cup maple-flavored syrup
¼ cup margarine
2 cups strawberries, fresh or frozen
1 cup blueberries, fresh or frozen

Heat margarine and syrup together until margarine melts. Add berries and heat through.

SANGRIA JELLY

5 cups

2 cups Sangria wine
3 cups sugar
6 tablespoons liquid fruit pectin
Paraffin to seal

Combine Sangria and sugar in saucepan; bring to boil. Boil until sugar is dissolved, 3 to 5 minutes. Add pectin; boil for 1 minute longer. Pour into sterilized glass containers. Seal with hot paraffin. Pretty and unusual gift jelly.

CHERRY-RHUBARB JAM

4½ cups

5½ cups fresh rhubarb, finely chopped
3 cups sugar
1 3-ounce package cherry gelatin

Combine rhubarb and sugar; let stand until syrupy. Cook over medium-low heat until tender, 30 to 45 minutes. Stir in cherry gelatin and cool. Seal in jars. May be kept in freezer.

CUMBERLAND SAUCE
1½ cups

6   **ounces frozen orange juice concentrate**
¾   **cup currant jelly**
1   **teaspoon dry mustard**
¼   **teaspoon ginger**
    Dash Tabasco

Mix all ingredients together in saucepan. Stir over low heat until well blended. Serve with pork, game or duck.

HENHOUSE BARBECUE SAUCE
¾ cup

2   **tablespoons lemon juice**
1   **teaspoon Worcestershire**
    Dash paprika
1   **stick butter**
¼   **cup water**
    Dash salt
    Dash pepper
    Dash garlic salt

Melt butter in small saucepan. Add remaining ingredients. Baste skinned or unskinned chicken with a brush. Continue basting while baking or grilling chicken.

BACK RIB BARBECUE SAUCE
4 cups

2   **medium onions, chopped**
1   **10¾-ounce can condensed tomato soup**
¾   **cup water**
3   **tablespoons white vinegar**
2   **tablespoons Worcestershire**
1   **teaspoon salt**
¼   **teaspoon cinnamon**
1   **teaspoon chili powder**
¼   **teaspoon pepper**
1   **cup brown sugar**
1½   **tablespoons cornstarch mixed with 2 tablespoons water**

Mix together onions, soup, water, vinegar, Worcestershire, salt, cinnamon, chili powder and pepper; cook until onions are soft. Add brown sugar and cook a few minutes more. Stir in cornstarch and water mixture and heat to a boil. Can be doubled and stored in refrigerator for a few weeks. Serve over browned back ribs. Enough sauce for 8 pounds of ribs.

TERIYAKI RIB SAUCE

6 servings

1   15-ounce can tomato sauce
1   6-ounce can tomato paste
¾   cup brown sugar
½   cup soy sauce
¼   cup cider vinegar
½   cup minced onion
1   teaspoon chili powder
1   teaspoon black pepper
1   teaspoon garlic salt
1   teaspoon sweet basil leaves
1   tablespoon ginger
1   tablespoon mustard seed
1   tablespoon Kitchen Bouquet

Combine all ingredients for basting sauce and heat, stirring, for 5 minutes. Baste ribs as they cook. Enough sauce for 6 pounds of ribs. Reheat remaining sauce and serve with the ribs.

HORSERADISH SAUCE FOR MEAT

2 cups

½   cup sugar
2   eggs, beaten
1   teaspoon prepared mustard
5   tablespoons vinegar
1   tablespoon water
    Salt and pepper
¼   bottle of prepared horseradish
1   cup heavy cream, whipped

Combine sugar, eggs, mustard, vinegar, water, salt and pepper. Bring to a boil and cook, stirring, until thick. Cool and refrigerate until needed. Just before serving, combine whipped cream and horseradish. Fold into chilled mustard sauce. Serve with ham or beef.

WINE SAUCE FOR BEEF

3½ cups

1½ cups sliced fresh
       mushrooms
1   bunch green onions, chopped
½   cup butter
1   cup red wine
2   cups beef broth
    Pepper
    Flour

Sauté mushrooms in ¼ cup butter. Sauté onions separately in the remaining butter until tender. Add pepper and enough flour to thicken. Stir in wine and beef broth. Add mushrooms and heat until thickened. Serve over sliced meat.

EPICUREAN SAUCE

1	tablespoon tarragon vinegar
2	tablespoons grated horseradish
1	teaspoon dry mustard
½	teaspoon salt
	Dash pepper
3	tablespoons mayonnaise
½	cup heavy cream

In small bowl, combine vinegar, horseradish, mustard, salt and pepper. Stir in mayonnaise. Whip the heavy cream and fold into vinegar mixture. Can be prepared several hours ahead and refrigerated until serving. Serve with beef or ham.

MALIBU MUSTARD

1 cup

½	cup Coleman's Dry Mustard
½	cup white vinegar
1	egg, slightly beaten
½	cup sugar
2	tablespoons horseradish
1	tablespoon grated onion
¼	teaspoon salt
⅛	teaspoon cloves
⅛	teaspoon cayenne

Combine mustard and vinegar. Refrigerate overnight. In pan, whisk egg with sugar. Add remaining ingredients and cook over low heat, stirring 2 to 3 minutes or until thick. Do not boil. Cool and refrigerate. Keeps well. Perfect for egg rolls.

MUSTARD SAUCE

2½ cups

4	ounces Coleman's Dry Mustard
1	cup cider vinegar
2	eggs, beaten
1	cup sugar
1	cup mayonnaise

Soak mustard and vinegar several hours or overnight. Add beaten eggs and sugar. Cook slowly in a double boiler, stirring constantly. Dilute with mayonnaise to taste. Serve "hot" with oriental foods, mild with vegetables or meat.

FAIL-SAFE HOLLANDAISE

1 cup

2   **egg yolks**
    Scant teaspoon salt
    Dash of cayenne pepper
    Juice of 1 small lemon
½   **cup butter, melted**

Put the yolks in a blender and beat. Add the salt and pepper. Alternately, add the juice and butter, beating constantly. Sides of blender should be scraped when finished. The consistency should be fairly thick. Sauce may be kept warm or reheated by placing in a sink or pan of hot water. It will not curdle.

Alternate Method: Combine butter and egg yolks in a saucepan. Refrigerate for 30 minutes. When ready to make sauce, stir butter and yolks constantly over medium heat until butter melts. Add lemon juice. Continue to cook, stirring, until sauce is of desired consistency.

HERB MAYONNAISE

1½ cups

1   **cup mayonnaise**
½   **tablespoon lemon juice**
½   **teaspoon salt**
¼   **teaspoon paprika**
1   **teaspoon Italian minced herbs**
      (or 1 teaspoon chopped
      parsley)
1   **tablespoon grated onion**
1   **tablespoon chopped chives**
⅛   **teaspoon curry powder**
½   **teaspoon Worcestershire**
1   **clove garlic, crushed**
1   **tablespoon capers**
½   **cup sour cream**

Combine and blend all ingredients. Serve as dipping sauce for artichokes or a fondue meal.

305

TURKEY BASTING SAUCE
2 cups

¼ cup vegetable oil
½ cup white wine
¼ cup water
¾ cup butter, melted
½ teaspoon savory salt
½ teaspoon onion salt
½ teaspoon celery salt
½ teaspoon garlic salt
2 tablespoons Worcestershire
2 tablespoons soy sauce

Combine all ingredients. Baste turkey with sauce every 30 minutes until done. Remove turkey from pan. Drippings make a fantastic gravy base.

MARINADE FOR ROAST
2 cups

1 teaspoon dry mustard
1 teaspoon prepared mustard
1 teaspoon onion salt
1 teaspoon garlic salt
1 16-ounce bottle catsup
¼ cup red wine
6 ounces chili sauce
1 teaspoon Worcestershire
½ teaspoon salt
½ teaspoon pepper
¼ teaspoon Tabasco
3 tablespoons lemon juice
½ cup white vinegar
1 5-ounce bottle soy sauce

Mix all ingredients. Pour over roast or steaks. Refrigerate overnight. Turn 3 to 4 times. Baste with sauce while cooking.

CARAWAY BEEF MARINADE
1½ cups

1 8-ounce can tomato sauce
2 tablespoons brown sugar
1 teaspoon salt
1 teaspoon caraway seeds
3 tablespoons Worcestershire
2 tablespoons cider vinegar

Mix all ingredients together until brown sugar is dissolved. Pour over family steak or similar cut. Marinate all day, turning meat several times to assure even flavor. Best if meat is barbecued. Drained marinade may be passed with meat. Serve thin slices of meat.

BOURBON STEAK MARINADE

2 cups

1   5-ounce bottle soy sauce
¼   cup brown sugar
1   teaspoon lemon juice
¼   cup bourbon
1   tablespoon Worcestershire
1½ cups water

Combine all ingredients. Pour over meat and marinate 4 hours in refrigerator, turning twice. Grill, basting twice with marinade.

STEAK KABOB MARINADE

1¾ cups

¼   cup catsup
¼   cup Worcestershire
¼   cup cider vinegar
¼   cup oil
½   cup water
¼   cup Heinz Savory Sauce
1   tablespoon sugar
2   teaspoons salt

Combine all ingredients and bring to a boil; remove from heat and cool. Cut up steak in chunks and marinate meat for up to 2 days. Put meat on skewers with raw vegetables and grill. Will marinate 5 pounds of meat. NOTE: In doubling or tripling recipe, do not increase sugar and salt amounts. Just add sugar and salt to taste.

Contributors

Our thanks to the many friends and members who contributed to **Amber Waves.**

Sally Symmes Abbott
Barbara Wenstrand Abernathy
Susan Ogborn Adams
Jane O'Keefe Addy
Ginny Calame Aita
Kathy Bowman Allen
Robyn Jacobsen Amis
Cheryl West Andersen
Linda Matson Andersen
Donna Anderson
Kathryn Ann Anderson
Marcia Wetzler Andrew
Joan Angotti
Kay McDevitt Armstrong
Janet Moran Baeder
Lynn Ballard Railey
Susan Reinhardt Bailey
Emily Reynolds Baker
Barbara Burdic Barchus
Carol Bunz Beam
Ardis Johnson Beeler
Madeleine Ortman Begley
Cynthia Jane Bekins
Sally Grainger Bekins
Joanne Nilson Belitz
Barbara Loucks Berger
Dodie Devitt Billig
Patricia Cockle Billotte
Debbie Diesing Blank
Judy Church Blazek
Pat James Bleick
Carol Gelontor Bloch
Barbara Johnson Bock
Janice Pehrson Bock
Pat Kehoe Bock
Ann Waldie Boelens
Kandie Rasmussen Borchman
Patricia Hanrahan Bowen
Lynne Durham Boyer
Ann Gooch Bradford
Kathleen Bradley
Barbara Allen Brady
Barbara Bos Brantigan
Kathleen Dillon Brennan
Jean Dahl Bressman
Sally Sveska Bridges
Barbara Christiansen Briggs
Debbie Coe Brower

Natalie Gunlock Brown
Nonie Neary Brown
Geil Mitchell Browning
Elizabeth Thurmond Brownrigg
Sandi Ericzon Bruns
Sandra Schuele Buchanan
Rose Schomer Bucholz
Mary Erickson Burbridge
Jennifer Arp Buresh
Karen Thompson Burkley
Karen Stacke Burmood
Marilyn Edwards Busch
Patricia Melby Bush
Martha DeLong Cady
Barbara Blanich Call
Jancy Carman Campbell
Katherine Baxter Campbell
Merrilee Anne Carlson
Fredericka Nash Carpenter
Martha Shaffer Chamberlain
Phyllis Nyberg Chapin
Christine Cook Chilian
Phyllis Donaldson Choat
Cheryl Goyette Christensen
Jacqueline Evans Christianson
Bonnie Naughtin Clark
Janie Baker Clinton
Kathryn Keith Cobb
Merry Ann Whinery Coe
Sue Coffee
Jane McGeehan Conley
Janice Blazek Connor
Cheryl Milder Cooper
Elaine Finn Cotton
Sandy McBeath Cotton
Nancy Lenmark Covolo
Mary Whittaker Cramer
Catherine Corp Crawford
Jane Madden Crosby
Catherine VanStory Crossman
Jean Horstman Crouchley
Elliott Downs Crummer
Carol Daws Dale
Rosemary Gaughan Daly
Janet Larsen Darst
Nancy Miller Darst
Joan Fulton Demgen
Phyllis Griess Devereux

Alice Henry DiBiase
Mary Lauterbach Diers
Terri Moore Diesing
Marjorie Herrill Dietrich
Susan Morse Dietz
Dorothy Hume Dinsmore
Marilou Pantano DiPrima
Karen Ann Scott Dixon
Linda Long Donaldson
Ami Cotton Douglas
Ann McDaniel Duff
Anne Trowbridge Durrie
Carol Cockson Dvorak
Lou Kemp Dye
Shirley Moore Ebert
Dorothy Lane Eckstrom
Gertrude Porter Edwards
Barbara Robbie Elliott
Jane Porteous Ellsworth
Kathy Carney Encell
Trillion Anderson Engdahl
Julie Ann Denton Erickson
Kathryn Runcie Esping
Nancy Ruth Ethington
Karla Strahan Ewert
Katherine Shearer Falk
Toni Donohue Fangman
Mary Laura Young Farnham
Helen Pennewill Fauntleroy
Susan Vash Feagler
Anne Shontz Fenner
Jodeen Mueller Fletcher
Paula Ide Floth
Mary Shonsey Focht
Nancy Riley Ford
Annette Flanagan Fraser
Lynn McWhorter Fraser
Gail Pratt Frasier
Catherine Tucker Freimuth
Amy Cassman Friedman
Pamela Newberry Fuchs
Caye Sosalla Fulcher
Agneta Anderhagen Gaines
Joanne Swerre Gilmore
Marcia Stransky Gilmore
Ann Kennedy Goldstein
Betty Hatteroth Gordon
Mary Gay Westering Gordon
Wanda Brammer Gottschalk

Katherine Fitzgerald Grandsaert
Margaret Meyer Grennan
Mary Shannon Grier
Betty Lu Joos Groth
Linda Goth Grubb
Nancy Lewis Guild
Cynthia L. Hadsell
Judith Adams Haecker
Wendy Engman Hahn
Linda Harman Hall
Vicki Packard Hallett
Christine Johnson Hammans
Diane Young Hamsa
Ann Chandler Hancock
Ibby Black Hancock
Becky Boyer Hansen
Elinor Frye Hansen
Mary Rosborough Hansen
Jean Smith Hanson
Janet Bailey Harley
Nancy Rose Harling
Mimi Whitehead Harm
Maryanne Hough Harry
Nathalie Faris Hart
Cyndi Artman Hartman
Katherine Hasselbalch
Judy Motte Haugsland
Mary Anne Timmons Hauser
Karen Harkert Hawkins
Marianne Graham Hawkins
Patricia Gardiner Hawkins
Paula Jackson Hazelrigg
Willow Shoemaker Head
Juliana Nicholsen Hefflinger
Constance Dorman Heiden
Anne Leigh Hellbusch
Diane Housel Henry
Donna Ratner Hersch
Julie Sivers Hertzler
Jane Wolter Hicks
Naomi Carpenter Hoagland
Holly Jepsen Hoberman
Judy Vincent Hoenshell
Margaret Olwine Hoffmaster
Nancy Odum Holloran
Susan Collie Holmes
Sally Payne Holmquist
Maren Roth Hood
Marjorie Clark Horgan

Marietta Alexander Horning
Nancy Venger Hornstein
Ann Strauss Hosford
Patsy Miller Hosman
Angela How
Jeanne How
Mary Jane Huerter
Annette Edwards Huff
Trisha Hughes
Julie Hasselbalch Jacobsen
Paula Mastin Jacobsen
Nancy Brickson Jacobson
Eva M. Jay
Kathleen Turner Jeffries
Marilyn Heck Jensen
Jennifer Jochim Jetter
Rickey Zeidler Jiranek
Mary Jochim
Sheryn Cohn Joffe
Dede Meyer Johnson
Sally Jacobsen Johnson
Sue Holthusen Johnson
Eileen Delaney Jones
Fanny Shaw Jones
Marcia Lewis Jones
Marjorie Holmquist Jones
Virginia Slaughter Jones
Ellanore Baxter Judd
Sandy Munger Kadavy
Sally Willsie Kampfe
Elizabeth Lueder Karnes
Randi Turkel Katelman
Deborah Jean Keating
Ruth Haley Keene
Theresa Stuhlsatz Kehm
Penny Dudley Keim
Anne Morton Kelley
Shari Foster Kellstrom
Jane Walrath Kennedy
Judy Wenger Keyser
Bridget Kinerk
Alice Plochi King
Patricia Sheehy Kinney
Mary Ellen Ostrand Knowles
Linda Fitzpatrick Knox
Susan Baird Knox
Gail Young Koch
Connie Cassel Kollasch
Karen Koontz

Vicki Elliott Krecek
Elizabeth Allen Kress
Willetta A. Krohn
Alicia Chavez Kroupa
Sandy Singer Kutler
Barbara Moore Lage
Mary Shirley Landen
Carole Grube Langan
Susan McGee Lantz
Kathryn Nicoll Larimer
Mary Sumerall Larsen
DeDe Collins Laughlin
Susan Denis Laughlin
Elizabeth Davis Lauritzen
Kim Bowles Lauritzen
Rosemarie Bucchino Lee
Mary Kay Leicht
Barbara Lucas Lewis
Debra Erpelding L'Heureux
Liz Barrett Liakos
Anne Lundholm Lieben
Susan Coder Lipsey
Nano Naughtin Little
Marjorie Benson Loring
Shirley Martens Loring
Linda Hoeppner Lovgren
Phyllis Faasse Ludwig
Mary Shelledy Lueder
Sunny Durham Lundgren
Sandra Johnson Lundholm
Lynda Krohn Madden
Carol Varnes Maginn
Judy Haag Manuel
Patricia Heelan Marcuzzo
Janet Schenken Mardis
Sally Johnston Marshall
Marilyn Lippold Martin
Sharon Gidley Marvin
Kathleen Hussey Marx
Nancy Hawkins Mason
Joan Ann Rohver Masterson
Elizabeth Karnes Max
Elsa Weiffenbach Mazanec
Patricia McCormack McClellan
Barbara Barnum McCollister
Shirlee Rushton McCollister
Sonja Hovland McCollister
Dede Stewart McFayden
Virginia Townsend McFayden

Ruth Dunbar McLeay
Susan Thurmond McMannama
Susan Hime McWhorter
Carol Vingers Meier
Merrilee Moshier Miller
Nancy Rumbolz Mitchell
Mary Ellen Cummings Monen
Maureen Keenan Monen
Marian Kelly Monnig
Tamara Zabel Monson
Dian Jones Moore
Harriet Rogers Moore
Margaret Bugbee Moore
Elizabeth Swanson Moran
Christina Mills Morgan
Kay Dillon Morgan
Elizabeth Hooven Morsman
Janice Shrader Mossman
Ruth Mummert Muchemore
Bernice Kellner Muller
Cindy Cook Mullins
Barbara Tanner Musselman
Nancee Peterson Neely
Diane Morin Nelson
Jo Nelson
Kathleen Rierden Nelson
Kathy Lillie Nelson
Lyndall Fisher Newens
Kathy Behrens Nielsen
Nancy White Nielsen
Sandy Racines Nogg
Sharon Sales O'Brien
Roxanne Wiebe O'Gara
Linda Losch O'Hare
Andrea Betts Olson
Elizabeth Iverson Olson
Kitty Kiddo O'Neil
Virginia Johnson Ostrand
Dorothy Dose Otis
Rita Faimon Otis
Dee Carlson Owen
Kay Fuchs Owen
Jennifer Inman Pansing
Arlene James Pantano
Ann Lauritzen Pape
Caroly A. Pape
Gail Shearer Parsonage
Arlis Swanson Patterson
Lou Ann Ross Patterson

Mary Rosman Patterson
Sandra Moredick Pavel
Tish Low Pemberton
Marilyn Newman Pendleton
Linda Quigley Perrin
Kathy Kovarik Petersen
Debra Anne Peterson
Pipi Campbell Peterson
Ginger Kelley Pettegrew
Sue Slagle Pfeifer
Katherine Larson Quinlan
Sara Coffee Radil
Christie Reed Rasmussen
Connie Rasmussen
Barbara Handschuh Reed
Gretchen Shellberg Reeder
Patricia Hall Reeder
Mary Lynn Durrie Reiser
Lois Hall Renner
Mary C. Richardson
Mary Monen Ries
Norma Mason Riley
Sandra Lichtenberg Robinson
Marilyn Hamer Roe
Jean Stuekerjuergen Rogers
Martha Ann Rogers
Wendy Burden Rogers
Susan Kareer Rohrig
Marie Paulus Roth
Carolyn Anne Rothery
Kathy Murphy Rowen
Karen Kranz Rozmarin
Martha Christensen Rozmarin
Carol Madson Russell
Laurie Forst Russell
Jeanne Garner Salerno
Marian Johnson Sample
Deborah Barger Sandstedt
Wendy Louis Schneiderwind
Helen Dinsmore Schorr
Pam Matt Scott
Linda Smith Shearer
Patricia Unthank Shefte
Jane Quisenberry Shepard
Julianne How Sherrets
Clo Ann Kaul Shirley
Kathleen Clark Sibbernsen
Shirley Johnson Siebler
Barbara Curtis Slabaugh

Thelma Haggerty Slattery
Connie Greenblatt Slutzky
Stacie Schmid Smith
Susan Lastovica Smith
Evelyn Kirchner Solonynka
Sara Spear
Connie Hoy Spellman
Denese Handschuh Stalnaker
Julia Bixby Stanek
Susan Mack Stemm
Marie Swoboda Stitt
Mary Ann Sieman Strasheim
Jane McGrath Strattan
Sandra Hodges Sueper
Suzette Bradford Sutton
Juliana Criley Swartzbaugh
Nessie Miller Swedlund
Sherry Foster Taxman
Linda Reid Telfeyan
Sybil Gibson Thailing
Vickey Thayer
Lynda Wiand Thomas
Sara Miessler Thomas
Barbara Koll Thompson
Karen Rasmussen Thompson
Paulette Behrens Thomsen
Nancy Lueder Tiedeman
Mary Kay Fangman Tighe
Becky Seim Timmons
Christine Felix Tracey
Martha Mullen Tritsch
Dina Mastarone Tuft
Lynne Steele Ullerich
Jean Maginn Ullrich
Gail Schwartz Veitzer
Karen Alger Venteicher
Sonja Ruckl Vicker

Karen Holm Vierk
Mary Helen Davis Vogel
Colleen Curran Wachter
Madeline Baumer Waechter
Francie Hielen Wagner
Mary Grube Wahl
Barbara Waldron Waldie
Cynthia Reeke Waltz
Charlott Johnson Ware
Sarah Watson
Sharon English Watson
Anne Weaver
Roxy Lash Weaver
Barbara Spear Webster
Babs Hansen Weinberg
Jean Mari Berger Welch
Wini Foxley Wells
Rita Carlson Welsh
Kristin Marie Westin
Nancy O'Connor Whitted
Patricia Greco Wiederholt
Roxanne Herman Williams
Susan Darst Williams
Sharon Bauer Wilson
Jane Condon Winnail
Sydney Marshall Winstrom
Eileen Wirth
Joan Knutson Wolfgram
Deborah Estell Wood
Judy Watson Woodbury
Lillian Richards Wunsch
Wilberta Heinly Yager
Gail Walling Yanney
Gertrude Kinsler Young
Muriel Kennedy Young
Terri Milder Zacharia
Hermene Davis Zweiback

328

NOTES

332

NOTES

NOTES

AMBER WAVES COOKBOOK
Junior League of Omaha
808 South 74th Plaza
Omaha, Nebraska 68114
Telephone: 402-391-8986

Please send _____ copies of AMBER WAVES at $11.95 each $_____

Plus postage and handling per shipment ___2.00___

Nebraska residents add sales tax _____

Please gift wrap .50 each _____

Enclosed is my check or money order Total _____

Make checks payable to **AMBER WAVES COOKBOOK**

Name _____

Address _____

City _____ State _____ Zip _____

All profits from cookbook sales are returned to the community through the projects of the Junior League of Omaha, Inc.

- -

AMBER WAVES COOKBOOK
Junior League of Omaha
808 South 74th Plaza
Omaha, Nebraska 68114
Telephone: 402-391-8986

Please send _____ copies of AMBER WAVES at $11.95 each $_____

Plus postage and handling per shipment ___2.00___

Nebraska residents add sales tax _____

Please gift wrap .50 each _____

Enclosed is my check or money order Total _____

Make checks payable to **AMBER WAVES COOKBOOK**

Name _____

Address _____

City _____ State _____ Zip _____

All profits from cookbook sales are returned to the community through the projects of the Junior League of Omaha, Inc.

- -

AMBER WAVES COOKBOOK
Junior League of Omaha
808 South 74th Plaza
Omaha, Nebraska 68114
Telephone: 402-391-8986

Please send _____ copies of AMBER WAVES at $11.95 each $_____

Plus postage and handling per shipment ___2.00___

Nebraska residents add sales tax _____

Please gift wrap .50 each _____

Enclosed is my check or money order Total _____

Make checks payable to **AMBER WAVES COOKBOOK**

Name _____

Address _____

City _____ State _____ Zip _____

All profits from cookbook sales are returned to the community through the projects of the Junior League of Omaha, Inc.

All copies will be sent to the same address unless otherwise specified. If you wish books sent as gifts, please include a list of names and addresses of recipients. If you wish to enclose your own gift card with each book, please write name of recipient on outside of envelope, enclose with order, and we will include it with your gift.

All copies will be sent to the same address unless otherwise specified. If you wish books sent as gifts, please include a list of names and addresses of recipients. If you wish to enclose your own gift card with each book, please write name of recipient on outside of envelope, enclose with order, and we will include it with your gift.

All copies will be sent to the same address unless otherwise specified. If you wish books sent as gifts, please include a list of names and addresses of recipients. If you wish to enclose your own gift card with each book, please write name of recipient on outside of envelope, enclose with order, and we will include it with your gift.